Building the Executive Team

A GUIDE TO MANAGEMENT DEVELOPMENT

PRENTICE-HALL INDUSTRIAL RELATIONS AND PERSONNEL SERIES

Dale Yoder, Editor

BELCHER *Wage and Salary Administration*
BELLOWS *Creative Leadership*
BELLOWS *Psychology of Personnel in Business and Industry,* 3rd ed.
CARPENTER *Case Studies in Collective Bargaining*
DANKERT *Contemporary Unionism in the United States*
DANKERT *An Introduction to Labor*
DAVEY *Contemporary Collective Bargaining,* 2nd ed.
DUBIN *Human Relations in Administration: The Sociology of Organization*
DUBIN *Working Union-Management Relations*
GALENSON *Comparative Labor Movements*
GOMBERG *A Trade Union Analysis of Time Study,* 2nd ed.
HABER AND COHEN *Readings in Social Security*
HARDMAN AND NEUFELD *The House of Labor: Internal Operations of American Unions*
HENEMAN AND TURNBULL *Personnel Administration and Labor Relations: A Book of Readings*
LINDBERG *Cases in Personnel Administration*
MAHONEY *Building the Executive Team: A Guide to Management Development*
MILLER *American Labor and the Government*
OTIS AND LEUKART *Job Evaluation,* 2nd ed.
PFIFFNER *Supervision of Personnel: Human Relations in the Management of Men,* 2nd ed.
SHARTLE *Executive Performance and Leadership*
SHARTLE *Occupational Information: Its Development and Application,* 3rd ed.
SMITH *Collective Bargaining*
STONE AND KENDALL *Effective Personnel Selection Procedures*
TAYLOR *Government Regulation of Industrial Relations*
THOMPSON *Personnel Management for Supervisors*
YODER *Personnel Management and Industrial Relations,* 4th ed.
YODER *Personnel Principles and Policies,* 2nd ed.

THOMAS A. MAHONEY, *Ph.D.*

Industrial Relations Center
University of Minnesota

Building the Executive Team

A GUIDE TO MANAGEMENT DEVELOPMENT

Prentice-Hall, Inc., *Englewood Cliffs, N. J.*
1961

LIBRARY OF CONGRESS CATALOG CARD NO: 61-7269

PRINTED IN THE UNITED STATES OF AMERICA
08752

Preface

Today, the need for competent management and leadership is probably greater than it has ever been. Rising levels of skill and education in the labor force, an abundant and rising standard of living, and an increasing population with the consequent organization of social activity have made it clear that the quality of managerial leadership can be expected to be an even more critical factor in the future.

A growing awareness of the importance of management and leadership throughout all social activity in recent years has prompted corporations, trade unions, governmental agencies, the armed forces, and various schools and universities to institute programs aimed at the development and utilization of leadership talents and abilities.

Effective management or leadership is a complex phenomenon involving the organization and coordination of the skills and abilities of groups of individual managers who must later form functioning teams of executives and managers. Development of effective executive or management teams is management development in its broadest sense. The concern for management development has forced a necessary evaluation of management practice and has focused attention upon the need for study and research into problems basic to management development. But we cannot wait until this study and evaluation have been completed. We must initiate action now and revise this action as further knowledge is acquired in the future.

It is in this spirit that this book has been written. It is intended, first, as a framework for the consideration of problems in developing an effective management team. It discusses the nature and role of management and the need and pressure for management development. The book is intended as a guide to the development of the management team. It points up areas that call for increased understanding, reviews current approaches to the study of present problems, and suggests approaches for the evaluation of management development practices.

The audience for whom the book is intended is as broad and diverse as the range of interests in management and leadership development. One portion of this audience is composed of all executives and managers who have responsibilities for the development of subordinate teams of managers. Those managers who administer specific management development programs should also be interested in this book. Another intended audience is composed of students in executive development programs, as well as students engaged in regular academic programs. The book can be used as the framework for a course in management development or as a supplement in courses concerning managerial administration, industrial psychology, industrial relations, and public administration.

Recognition of the need for a book such as this grew out of experiences in the management development laboratory of the Industrial Relations Center at the University of Minnesota. Here a group of progressive companies have joined with university staff members in the examination of problems of management development. Many of the ideas and concepts discussed here have evolved out of discussions with participating company officials and research staff members, as well as from research and evaluative studies conducted within the laboratory. Though it is impossible to identify everyone who contributed to the development of these ideas, those present and former associates at the University of Minnesota who are due special credit for their support, encouragement, and participation in the program of the management development laboratory include Professors Dale Yoder, Herbert G. Heneman, Jr., Donald G. Paterson, George England, and Thomas Jerdee. Typing and preparation of the manuscript was accomplished by Marjorie Peltier. As usual, the author is responsible for any shortcomings.

THOMAS A. MAHONEY

Contents

Building the Executive Team

A GUIDE TO MANAGEMENT DEVELOPMENT

Chapter ONE

The Changing Role of Management

INTRODUCTION

We speak or read every day about "management's prerogatives," "management's position," "management development," and the "problems of management." But what is management? The concept of management has been defined in various ways, all of them referring generally to leadership, coordination, and direction of people in the performance of organized group activity. It is the unifying and coordinating activity which combines the actions of individuals into meaningful and purposeful group endeavor. This management activity is necessary for successful group action, whether the group be political, economic, or social in orientation.

The critical importance of the role of management in business and industrial undertakings has been recognized for some time. The importance of leadership and management in other group activities has been less apparent, and we have become generally aware of this importance only in recent years. Furthermore, we have done relatively little in past years to assure the development of needed managerial talent for leadership in business and other group enterprises; an adequate supply of this talent was taken for granted. Today there is a growing recognition of the importance of managerial activities and of the opportunities and needs for developing talents for effective managerial performance in all organized activity.

DEVELOPMENT OF THE MANAGER CONCEPT

The role and nature of management in our society vary constantly with changes in the social, economic, and political environments. The scope of management responsibilities varies with changes in economic organization and with changes in social demands upon management. Management activities change as a result of technical developments in industrial processes as well as changes in the social environment. These changes in the role of management can be seen in the concepts of the manager which have been dominant in the past; these concepts illustrate the changing nature of management as they reflect the actual role performed by management and the demands upon management made by individuals and groups in society. It is difficult to distinguish sharply between these concepts and to associate each with a specific period of time. Each succeeding concept has developed gradually from earlier ones, and characteristics of all of them can be identified in the practice and opinion of any given period. We can identify and describe five rather general concepts of the manager which outline the development of our modern concept of management.[1]

Trustee of Society

One of the earliest concepts of the manager entrusted him with the responsibility for leadership and direction of an entire society of people. The manorial system of Western Europe and the plantation society of the Southern States are good examples of this concept. The manors and plantations in these agricultural societies were complete social and economic entities with the manager providing leadership for all activities of the society.

Two considerations provided the basis for the authority and responsibility of the manager as a trustee of this society. First, the manager owned virtually all the economic resources of the society, often including the manpower of the society as slaves. As owner-manager, the plantation master directed all the social, political, and economic activity of the society in the utilization of his economic

[1] For a similar analysis see Reinhard Bendix, *Work and Authority in Industry* (New York: John Wiley and Sons, 1956), especially Chapters 2 and 5.

resources and in the protection of his investment. Second, the manager belonged to a privileged social class as a result of his assumed inheritance of unusual capacities and abilities for leadership in all spheres of activity. As a member of this privileged class, the manager assumed a certain moral obligation for the welfare of the less fortunate members of his society. On these grounds also, the manager's role involved the direction and control of all social activities of the plantation or manor. A modified form of the trustee concept can be found today in small communities dominated by a single large employer, but the essential concept of the manager has changed and management generally is not accorded the authority of the trustee of society nor does it seek that responsibility.

Paternalism

The manor and plantation of the agricultural economy gave way to other forms of economic organization with the development of handicraft manufacturing and, later, the factory system of production. Changes in economic organization brought about by these industrial developments were accompanied by changes in the social and political organization of society. An increasing distinction appeared among the various spheres of social activity and interest. The integrated organization of the manor was broken up as men began to distinguish among their economic, political, and social interests. The resulting distinction between economic organization and other organizations of society and the break-up of the economic organization into a number of small, coexistent, independent units tended to reduce the influence and authority of the manager. The manager's role now was restricted to a relatively smaller society.

The basis of the manager's authority also changed with the development of handicraft manufacturing. It now was based largely upon his skill as a craftsman rather than upon his inheritance of property and social position. This skill as a craftsman could be acquired and was not associated with natural abilities qualifying the manager for leadership in all social endeavor. The scope of the manager's responsibility and authority with respect to his employees in the early stages of handicraft manufacturing was comparable with that of the plantation owner but became more restricted with the development of the factory. The master craftsman in the handicraft stage of manufacturing assumed a trustee or father relationship with his apprentices, assuming responsibility for their moral as well as their vocational development. Apprentices frequently lived with the family and shared in the family life of the master. Managers during the early development of the factory system in New England often recruited young women for work, building dormitories for them and assuming responsibility for their moral and spiritual upbringing.[2] This social and moral solicitude diminished as the factory system grew and took form.

In general, the paternalistic concept of the manager involved a narrowing of the manager's role as compared with the trustee concept. It was restricted both in terms of scope and in terms of the number of people involved. Probably of greater significance in the later development of the concept of management was the changed basis of the manager's authority in the paternalistic concept. The basis of authority changed from a social basis to an economic basis, thus reducing the social influence of the manager.

Champion or Hero Concept

Development of the champion or hero concept of the manager involved a further distinction among the economic, social, and political activities of society and a continued shift toward economic activity as the basis of management authority. In fact, it tended to emphasize achievement in economic activity as the test of ability for social leadership.

The hero concept viewed the manager as the possessor of certain natural abilities required for industrial leadership. Possession of these natural abilities was not restricted to any social class. Individuals of relatively humble origin might possess the necessary abilities and might achieve management authority through hard work and demonstration of their abilities. The Horatio Alger stories of success popular at the turn of the century illustrate this concept of the manager. Rapid growth of industrial activity following the Civil War provided opportunities for employment and advancement. Penniless immigrants on arriving in the country were able to secure ready employment and, in many instances, to rise to positions of economic wealth and power. This also was the era of the common man, with recognition given to the practical man of business affairs regardless of his social heritage. The popular concept of the industrial leader attributed to him personal qualities and attributes of leadership on

[2] For an interesting account of these practices, see Harold U. Faulkner, *American Economic History* (New York: Harper and Brothers, 1954), pp. 294-300.

the basis of his demonstrated success in business. The road to industrial leadership was open to all regardless of heritage, the test of leadership being the individual's success in dealing with problems of organization and leadership of industrial activities. There were enough instances of industrial leaders, such as Andrew Carnegie, who rose to success from humble origin to lend credence to this concept.

The role of the manager in society also changed with the development of this hero concept. Paternalism began to fade as a result of the continuing distinction among various forms of social activity and the growing belief that the common man was capable of managing his own affairs. The recruitment of managers from various classes of society also tended to restrict the role of the manager to economic activities, leaving leadership of social and political activities to those most experienced in them. At the same time, however, the industrial leader who had proven his ability over the years in financial and industrial undertakings often was assumed to possess qualities of leadership for other spheres of activity. Thus economic and industrial success began to replace social heritage as the determinant of social influence, and the succesful manager was increasingly viewed as a champion of the people.

Scientific Management

Development of the scientific management concept caused a change in management authority, the manager's role in society, and the training and development of managers. It began as a means of improving the efficiency of management and economic activities and succeeded in altering the entire concept of management.

Scientific management in the United States is identified with the work and teachings of F. W. Taylor.[3] As a pioneer in scientific management, Taylor tried to improve the efficiency of productive processes through the application of scientific techniques to managing work. He began with an analysis of techniques and methods used by individual workmen in conducting the tasks assigned them. Noting the wide diversity of tasks assigned to positions, the many different techniques used in the performance of similar tasks, and the variations in individual productivity, he advocated the study and analysis of industrial operations for the purpose of discovering the best meth-

[3] See Frederick W. Taylor, *Scientific Management* (New York: Harper and Brothers, 1947).

ods of assigning work and performing work tasks. He argued that industrial operations were susceptible to the same study and analysis that had been employed in science and that this study and analysis could discover certain basic principles for the most efficient organization and operation of industrial activity.

Although first applied to the activities of unskilled workers, the development of scientific management implied several changes in the concept of management. First, *scientific* management implied that management consists less in the practice of an art than in the scientific study of operations and the application of certain principles in the organization and direction of work. The authority of the manager rested less upon personal attributes of leadership and stimulation, and more upon a knowledge of the basic principles of industrial operations. *Scientific* management implied that management was less personal and more of a science than was implied by earlier concepts of the role of management.

Second, the scientific management movement implied that the same methods and techniques which were useful in the study and analysis of unskilled operations might be applied in the analysis of the functions of management; just as certain principles work best in the organization and direction of unskilled activities, so are there basic principles of management which can be discovered through study and analysis. Closely related to this is the implication that management can be taught. Discovery of the principles of work organization and direction would permit the teaching of management in schools. In short, managers can be trained and developed, and society need no longer rely upon a fortuitous reproduction of individuals possessing the natural abilities required for management.

Development of this concept of the role of the manager served to restrict the influence of the manager even more to the economic and industrial sphere. Since management consists of a body of principles and techniques which can be learned, there need be no outstanding natural abilities required for management. There is, then, no reason to believe that the successful manager necessarily possesses unusual political and social insights and abilities. Rather, management can be considered solely an economic resource.

Professional Management

The concept of professional management focuses attention upon the manager's job in society and upon the manager's approach to this job. For example, the functions of management are distinguished sharply from the functions of ownership. The professional manager is an agent for ownership interests, a professional employed to conduct the enterprise in accord with these ownership interests. At the same time, the professional management concept emphasizes the broad social responsibilities of the enterprise and the responsibility of management to society at large. The professional manager is an agent for ownership interests, but he also is an agent for employees, consumers, and citizens in the community who are affected by the activity of the enterprise. Thus, the enterprise is viewed as an economic and social organization with responsibilities to many interests in the community, and professional management has the task of merging all of these responsibilities into one operation. For example, professional management is expected to consider the impact of technological change, pricing policies, and employee-relations practices upon the objectives of the political and social communities in addition to considering the economic implications of these issues. Furthermore, professional management is concerned with the economic implications of social action and is expected to contribute to the shaping of social action conducive to economic development.[4]

The concept of professional management implies also the nature of the approach taken by the manager in carrying out these responsibilities. It implies the existence of a body of knowledge concerning principles of good management which the manager is expected to know and apply in his job. Proceeding from the approach of scientific management, professional management looks to the discovery and application of new principles in management. In short, management is viewed, not as an art, but as a profession for which people can be trained. The efficiency of management, according to this approach, lies in the discovery and application of principles, and not in the intrinsic personal abilities of individuals.

The professional management concept is broadening the manager's role in society, and the manager is again viewed as a trustee of society. His authority as a trustee of society has been modified considerably in comparison with the earlier trustee concept, and the basis for this authority has been significantly altered. The authority of

[4] For illustrations of the professional management concept see Lawrence A. Appley, "Management and the American Future," *General Management Series*, No. 169 (New York: American Management Association, 1954), pp. 3-20; and Harold F. Smiddy, "Present Status of the Work of Managing," *Management Science*, Vol. 2, No. 3, April, 1956, pp. 209-221.

professional management is derived largely from the competence of the profession and the recognition of professional obligations. Thus, professional management recognizes responsibilities which extend beyond the confines of the enterprise and attempts to establish authority through development of a profession rather than through ownership or social class.[5]

This review of the management concept points up the changing role of management and the factors which shape this role. It also points up the many different concepts of management being applied today; examples of all of these concepts can be found in present-day management philosophies and policies. One of the leading organizations in development of the professional management approach is the American Management Association. The General Electric Company provides an example of the application of this concept; this company maintains its own school for the training and development of managers, conducts studies of the work of managing, and maintains an extensive program of community participation. At the same time, the managements of many organizations can be best characterized by the trustee, paternalistic, and champion concepts of management. All of these approaches to management will continue to be operative in the future, although the professional management approach will be the dominant influence in development of the future role of management.

THE ROLE OF MANAGEMENT IN THE FUTURE

Management's role in society is a dynamic role. It is constantly adapting to altered economic conditions, social customs, and non-economic institutions. The role of management also adapts to changes in the concepts, ideals, and behavior of managers. The role of management will continue to adapt to future changes in society, and any attempt to predict this role must be based upon foreseeable changes in the economic and social setting of management.

A major influence upon the state and health of any society and its economy is the population of that society and its rate of growth. The population of society constitutes the potential market for the economy, and changes in the size of the population exert an influ-

[5] For example see Clarence B. Randall, *A Creed for Free Enterprise* (New York: Little, Brown and Company, 1952).

ence upon the economy through changes in market size and co
position. An increasing population, for example, provides a stimul
through an increase in the potential market for goods and services. A declining population, on the other hand, deters economic growth and development. This population also constitutes the basic pool of manpower resources of society and in this sense serves as a force limiting the expansion of economic activity. Population projections for the United States which were based upon Depression experiences suggested a declining rate of population increase, leading many to predict the development of a stagnant economy. Experiences since World War II, however, have led observers to believe that the rates of family formation and birth during the Depression years were freakish, and that we can look forward to a stable or increasing rate of population growth for the next 20 years at least. Population projections for 1965 estimate an increase of 15 per cent over 1955, to provide a population of 190 million. The following 10-year period is expected to result in a similar rate of increase, with a population of approximately 220 million by 1975. This continued population growth is expected to provide a constant stimulus to an expanding economy for increasing the standard of living for the entire population as well as supplying the necessities for the enlarged population. An imaginative and resourceful management will have to provide the increased goods and services desired during the next 20 years.

The population increase predicted for the next 20 years will not serve to relieve the present relative scarcity of labor, however. In fact, available labor resources may be expected to become relatively more scarce during the next 20 years. The predicted population increase will result primarily from new births. Since entry into the labor force occurs approximately at age 20, relatively few of the persons born between now and 1975 will be available for work before 1975. The depressed birth rate of the 1930's has resulted in a relative scarcity of people in the 20-44 age range, which normally constitutes the bulk of the labor force. This shortage will continue until at least 1965, when the postwar babies will begin entering the labor force. Two additional factors, increasing education and a demand for a shorter work week, will serve to limit further the available work force of the future, in addition to the influence of the Depression birth rate. The trend toward increased schooling and postponed entry into the labor force may be expected to continue as living standards improve and as automation and technological change create demands for more highly skilled manpower. A large proportion of the population may be expected to seek higher education and postpone entry into the labor force during the next 20 years, thus restricting the relief expected from the maturation of postwar babies. The trend toward shorter working hours also may be expected to continue as living standards improve. Reduction of daily or weekly hours of work will result in further reduction of the available manpower resources. This predicted relative shortage of manpower resources in the face of an increasing population will pose a number of problems for the management of the future—problems which probably will call for changes in the management role.

One probable consequence of the continuing labor shortage will be the introduction of labor-saving, technological developments in industry. Automation, which has been defined as "the use of machines to run machines," offers the promise of increased productivity with a reduction in manpower requirements.[6] The successful application of automation poses several problems for the management of the future. For example, it is most useful in relatively stable activities; automation processes are not flexible and adaptable to rapidly changing conditions. The instability of many segments of the economy prevents the profitable application of automation at the present time. The role of management in the future must involve more and improved long-range planning if automation is to be applied. Another problem posed by automation, mentioned earlier, lies in the transition from a semiskilled labor force to the skilled labor force required by automation. Any mass displacement of the present labor force with the introduction of automation would be viewed as a social problem and would call forth governmental and social programs for the aiding of these displaced workers. The professional manager recognizes the social responsibilities of management and must work to prevent the mass displacement of the present labor force through automation.

Another consequence of the continuing labor shortage plus the increased education of the population will lie in the competition for manpower resources. A condition of labor shortage obviously contributes to a demanding labor force. Present examples of this may be found in the increases in wage rates during the past few years, the growing package of fringe benefits, and the extravagant lures

[6] See Peter F. Drucker, "The Promise of Automation," *Harper's*, Vol. 210, No. 1259, April 1955, pp. 41-47.

offered by managements in recruiting scarce skills. The current emphasis which is being placed upon education and skill in the economy, as well as in society at large, may be expected to continue with automation and a rising standard of living. It is probable that the labor force of the future will demand more and improved opportunities for personal development within industry. In short, the economic enterprise will be expected to contribute to the satisfaction of employee goals to a greater extent than it does today. The manager of the future will be expected to serve as an agent of the employees as well as of the owners of the enterprise and to conduct the enterprise for the benefit of both employees and owners. The manager of the future will be expected to serve as an agent of all who have an interest in the organization.

A closely related challenge also faces the management of the future. The history of economic development has involved remarkable technological developments in production and, more recently, improvements in marketing and distribution. There has been relatively little development, however, in the organization and motivation of employees. Two of the major challenges facing management in the future lie in the improvement of methods of organization of industrial activities and in the improvement of techniques for employee motivation. Handled properly, these two problems of management could be resolved in such a way as to lead to increased industrial efficiency and productivity which would go a long way toward meeting the challenge of our increasing population.

A further challenge to the management of the future lies in the performance of the social responsibilities of the enterprise. Management during the latter part of the nineteenth century and the early part of the twentieth century did not fulfill its social obligations in the eyes of the general public, with the result that these obligations were assumed by federal and state governments. Much of the growth of governmental activities during the past 50 years stems from concern of the public over such problems. Many of these problems were economic in nature—unemployment, economic insecurity in old age, industrial accidents and disease, substandard wage rates, monopoly and collusion, the development of electric power—and might have been solved or eased through private enterprise. The abdication from social responsibility by management led the public to entrust the government with powers to regulate economic activity and to participate in the economy for the solution of these social problems.

There is evidence that modern professional management recognizes the social responsibilities of management and the enterprise. An example is provided in the recent attempts of farsighted managements to eliminate employment instability in response to demands for a guaranteed annual wage. Management of the future must recognize the economic demands, goals, and problems of society if it is to prevent the eventual assumption of the role of management by the government.

In summary, the manager of the future will be expected to assume broad responsibilities for the conduct of the enterprise as an economic and social institution. Performance of these responsibilities will require an increasingly educated and trained group of managers. Professional training and development take time. We must begin today to prepare the professionally qualified managers for the increasingly complex and responsible role of the manager in the future.

SELECTED BIBLIOGRAPHY

Appley, Lawrence A., "Management and the American Future," *General Management Series,* No. 169 (New York: American Management Association, 1954), pp. 3-20.

Bendix, Reinhard, *Work and Authority in Industry* (New York: John Wiley and Sons, 1956).

Drucker, Peter F., *America's Next Twenty Years* (New York: Harper and Brothers, 1955).

Randall, Clarence B., *A Creed for Free Enterprise* (Boston: Little, Brown and Company, 1952).

Smiddy, Harold F., "Present Status of the Work of Managing," *Managing Science,* Vol. 2, No. 3, April 1956, pp. 209-221.

Chapter TWO

Development of the Management Team

INTRODUCTION

The term *management development* has become a byword in American business and industry in recent years. Interest in management development stems in part from a growing recognition of the importance of managerial leadership and of the need to ensure provision for this leadership. It also stems from a growing acceptance of the concepts of professional management. The possibility that principles of good management exist and can be taught offers great promise for improving managerial performance. Prospective managers can be trained for effective performance, and operating managers can be helped to improve their performance through training. Experiments in management development are being conducted throughout business and industry; not all of these experiments will prove successful. These experiments vary considerably in objectives, methods, and philosophies. In this chapter we review the pressures which have contributed to the concern for management development and which have shaped the various experiments in developing managers. We then discuss development of the management team as a reasonable objective for management development and outline a guide for development of the management team. Each of the elements of this guide is then examined in detail in later chapters.

PRESSURES FOR MANAGEMENT DEVELOPMENT

The concept of management development in its more general usage refers to the training and development of personnel for the exercise of the management functions. It is intended to provide more and better-qualified managerial personnel than would otherwise be available. The objectives of companies embarking upon a course of management development are not identical. There are many objectives of management development. To a large extent, these objectives reflect an awareness of different pressures and influences upon the individual companies. Certain of these pressures are general in the sense that they influence every organization to some extent; other pressures stem from the particular circumstances of the individual organization.

Prestige. Much of the current attention given to management development stems from the fact that it is a fad. An executive reads an article describing the development of managers at General Motors; he lunches with an executive from another company who describes their program of management development; and he understands that a third company has just spent $500,000 installing a program of management development. It soon begins to appear that no self-respecting company should be without management development. In fact, 88 per cent of the companies responding to a recent survey assert that they devote regular attention to management development.[1]

Concern may stem from a particular problem which arises in the organization. The problem may deal with production, personnel, or any other aspect of a company's business. The executive has been hearing about the wonders of management development and seizes upon management development as a panacea for the particular problem at hand.

This is not meant to imply that management development is nothing but a fad and that there is nothing worth while about the concept. On the contrary, all of the results claimed for management development may be true. But, unfortunately, management development is popular at present, and much of the attention given it probably reflects this popularity rather than a sober analysis of a par-

[1] "Current Practice in the Development of Management Personnel," *Research Report No. 26* (New York: American Management Association, 1956).

ticular problem. Several years ago the author was asked by one of the armed services to assist in the establishment of a program for management development or officer development. It was argued that private industry was far ahead of the services in the development of managers, and that the services must catch up. It is interesting now to hear the same reasoning from private industry—we must develop managers in the same manner that the services are doing, because they are far ahead of private industry.

Increasing business population. The business population has been expanding at a rate faster than the population since about 1900, and particularly during the past 15 years. This tremendous increase in the business population has increased the demand for management personnel, in both absolute and relative terms, since the population increase has lagged behind the business population.

Beginning in 1900 with a business population of approximately 1½ million firms, the business population increased 100 per cent by 1930, while the population increased only about 62 per cent. Since 1930, the business population has increased 40 per cent while the population has increased only 29 per cent. Thus, in terms of gross numbers alone, the more rapid increase in the business population, and the consequent demand for employees, has created a relative shortage in the labor force, a shortage that appears particularly in managerial ranks, as we shall see later.

Increasing size of business. Our business population is becoming increasingly one in which employment is concentrated in a small proportion of the entire population of firms. While few figures are available for earlier periods, the picture presented in 1951 was one in which a tiny proportion of the business population provided the vast bulk of employment. Less than one per cent of the enterprises in 1951 (36.9 thousand out of a total of 4,067.3 thousand) accounted for almost 60 per cent of the total employment.[2]

Growth in the size of a firm usually brings about an increasing population of management personnel in the company's structure. Each increase in over-all employment is accompanied by a relatively larger growth in the management ranks of the company. This is necessitated by the hierarchy concept and by the increasing use of staff personnel in larger companies. Thus, increases in the size of

[2] Office of Business Economics, U. S. Department of Commerce. *Business Statistics, 1955 Biennial Edition* (Washington, D. C.: U. S. Government Printing Office, 1955).

firm at the same time that the number of firms is growing suggest increases in the demand for managers at an even faster pace. One observer estimates that executive requirements have increased 46 per cent since 1945, while the business population has increased 34 per cent and the general population 12 per cent.[3]

Decentralization. Another current trend which contributes to the recognition given to management development is the decentralization of industrial operations through the establishment of semi-independent units. Decentralization contributes to the demand for managers by increasing the number of management positions required in the organization. It further calls for management development as management philosophy and responsibilities are altered through decentralization of operations. Management positions are created in the decentralized units which are somewhat comparable to the general top-management positions. The executive of a semi-independent unit of the organization often carries profit responsibility for that unit and functions as a decision-maker, just as the top executive of the organization does. This means an increase in the number of general management positions. Decentralization throughout the economy adds pressure to the demands for management personnel; it is even more direct in its influence upon the individual organization undertaking decentralization and seeking personnel to staff the newly created management positions.

Complexities of management. The task of managing has grown in scope during the past 20 years. The manager of today has a much more complicated task than did his predecessor of several years ago. And it appears that managing will continue to grow in scope. For example, the growth of trade unionism and collective bargaining during the past 20 years has increased the scope of the manager's job; he is required to exercise additional new responsibilities as a result of this relatively new aspect of industrial operations. Another growing aspect of the manager's job concerns relationships with the government. The operations and success of the enterprise depend to an increasing extent upon relationships with various governmental units. These governmental relationships are found in the regulation of the employment of labor, in the offering of securities in the bond market, in the taxation and accounting phases, and in the purchases

[3] A speech by Lawrence L. Ellis at the 25th Mid-Continent Trust Conference reported in the *Christian Science Monitor,* November 17, 1956.

of goods and services. The manager of today is responsible for all of these new relationships.

As the task of the executive has grown in scope and complexity, it has called for an increasing use of assistants and specialists in management. The task of the executive today is too large for a single individual; it must be delegated and shared with a management team.

Management succession. The succession of management is a major concern of every organization. The continued growth and even the existence of the organization over the years depend upon an orderly succession of management. The loss of key executives without adequate preparation of successors is to be prevented at almost any cost. Thus, it is the responsibility of management to prepare its successors.

Questions of management succession are becoming more and more important to most organizations through recognition that adequate backstops have not been prepared for the present management team.[4] This lack of preparation of management successors is illustrated in the age distribution of present top executives in American industry. A survey of 8,000 top executives conducted in 1952 indicated that two-thirds of them were over age 50, and more than a fourth of them were over age 60. Comparison of these results with a similar survey of 1928 indicates that the preparation of management backstops had declined in the intervening years. A larger proportion of top executives in 1928 were in the age range below 50 than was the case in 1952. The increasing tendency toward compulsory retirement at age 65 has kept the proportion of executives in these upper age ranges unchanged. Clearly the problem of management succession calls for the development of managers throughout industry. The problems faced by individual organizations undoubtedly are more pressing than is indicated by the general picture presented here.

Shortage of qualified managers. A further pressure stems from a current shortage of managers—there simply are not enough qualified managers to fill the many growing demands for management personnel. As noted earlier, the increases in business population and enterprise size have provided a growing demand for managers that has outstripped even the population increase. Add to this the fact

[4] Stephen Habbe, "Building New Executives," *Management Record,* Vol. 12, No. 4, April, 1950, pp. 132-134.

that many of the persons in the age ranges from which managers usually are drawn were prevented by the Depression and World War II from acquiring the experience and training required for management. Opportunities for industrial experience and progression were restricted severely by the Depression, and the war drew the majority of these men out of industrial experience for another five years following the Depression. Thus, the population in the age range 35-50 has not had the experience and training normally required to perform as managers.

Looking into the future, this shortage is likely to continue if nothing is done to speed and improve the training of managers. The low birth rates during the Depression years have resulted in reducing the proportion of the population in the age ranges 25-40 for the coming 15 years. The proportion of the population in this age range is under 22 per cent today and will continue to drop to about 17 per cent in 1970, after which time it should increase.[5] Thus, this shortage of personnel in the so-called "productive" age range will provide increasing pressure in the managerial labor market. If only a "normal" proportion of this age range enters the managerial occupations, the relative shortage of managers will be intensified during the coming 15 years. It has been predicted that 25 per cent more executives will be needed in 1965, but that only 5 per cent more will be available unless steps are taken now to increase the rate of growth of the management pool.[6]

Personal objectives. Personal objectives of managers and potential managers also contribute to the pressure for management development. Education, development, and utilization of one's abilities have always been major goals of our society. More attention has been given this objective in recent years as a result of the rising standard of living and per capita income of the country's population. Parents are providing extended education for their children, adults are continuing their education in night school, and employees are seeking opportunities for their continued development and application of abilities in employment. Managers share this concern for personal development, and, to a certain extent, management development reflects this growing concern for personal development.

---

[5] *Current Population Reports, Series P-25, No. 123* (Bureau of Census, U. S. Department of Commerce, October 20, 1955).

[6] Ellis, *op. cit.*

The relative shortage of personnel in all occupations, particularly in management, is forcing many organizations to provide opportunities for personal development as a means of attracting and retaining employees.[7] Recruiting advertisements of different companies point up this competition for employees through the description of the many opportunities for development and growth with the individual firm. The graduating college senior is promised opportunities to continue his education and development with the company, and to experience a number of assignments in the process of determining his career with the company. Whyte reports that graduating seniors more and more are basing their choice of offers upon the educational and developmental opportunities offered by the different companies.[8] In short, management development has been forced upon many companies in the struggle to recruit managers and potential managers to the organization.

Need for improved performance. Competition among enterprises has become more and more a matter of competition among managements. Competition is concerned with imagination, development of new markets, adjustment to changing consumer desires and market conditions, and productivity rather than with mere competition of products. The successful organization wins through its management team. Consequently, there is increasing pressure upon the management team for improved performance by the organization.

It is generally recognized that few, if any, of us ever perform up to our full capacities. Many of us have talent and abilities that have not been developed or utilized to their fullest. The same holds true for most managers. Closely associated with the pressure for improved performance by individual managers and by the entire management team is the pressure for management development.

IS MANAGEMENT DEVELOPMENT NEW?

Why the concern over management development at the present time? It is true that several of the pressures for management development are a result of particular historical ex-

---

[7] Dale Yoder, *15th Annual Upper Midwest Industrial Relations Conference, 1957* (Minneapolis: Industrial Relations Center, University of Minnesota), pp. 33-42.

[8] William H. Whyte, Jr., *The Organization Man* (New York: Simon and Schuster, 1956), pp. 109-110.

periences—for example, the shortage of personnel and the expanding demand for managers—but problems of management succession, expansion, and growth have always been present in business and industry. We apparently have met these pressures in the past without too much difficulty; why need we be so concerned about them at the moment? What have we done in past decades to develop managers, and why aren't these same methods adequate today?

It is certainly true that management development is not new. It is the emphasis being given to management development that is new. Organizations have been concerned with the development of managers for decades, and managers have been developed to meet the needs of business and industry for decades. The general problem of management development is not new; rather, the problem is changed somewhat in nature and is intensified by a number of considerations.

The primary method used in the development of managers in past decades has been described as "letting the cream rise to the top." Personnel were recruited into the organization as rank-and-file employees and permitted to work their ways to the top. This general method of management development has many advantages and undoubtedly worked well in many instances. Individuals who reached positions of top management had experienced most of the types of work in the organization, knew the operations of the entire organization, and had proven their ability at every step of the way. Such a method is inadequate today, however, as a means of supplying the number of competent managers required. In fact, it is our inability to provide the necessary experiences which has so aggravated the pressing current problem of management development. The present situation probably would not be so critical had we been able to provide this experience during the Depression and war years. Part of the current problem is development of a short-cut method of providing this needed experience.

"Letting the cream rise to the top" is no longer adequate for the long-run development of management, either. Our corporate organizations and operations have grown so large that it would require a lifetime today for the individual to acquire experience comparable to that acquired in normal employment progression 50 years ago. It simply is not possible to rely upon a program of unassisted progression or rotation among activities to provide the experience required in the development of personnel for top-management positions.

Clearly, an alternative or modern concept of management development must be fashioned to meet both the current and the long-run needs for qualified management personnel.

RESPONSIBILITY FOR MANAGEMENT DEVELOPMENT

The responsibility for development of competent management personnel is lodged with the board of directors and the management organization of every enterprise. As was pointed out earlier, the major responsibility of management is the establishment, maintenance, and development of the organization, not the conduct of day-to-day operations of the enterprise. Success of the enterprise and the organization lies in the strength of its management team. Consequently, a major responsibility of the present management of any enterprise should be the development of competent and qualified managers able to assume the responsibilities of the present management organization.

Practical reasons also dictate the lodging of responsibility for management development with the top management organization. The process of the development of managers is not likely to receive the support or attention it deserves without top-management support and recognition. Individual units of the organization and individuals within the organization are likely to be most concerned with the day-to-day conduct of their activities and neglect the long-run development of the organization. Only top management can provide the stimulus for development of the management team, and top management must assume this responsibility as part of the responsibility for development of the entire organization.

OBJECTIVES OF MANAGEMENT DEVELOPMENT

The term *management development* has been applied to cover a host of different concepts and activities. In many cases, it undoubtedly has been attached to ideas and programs as a means of making them more marketable, trading on the faddism of management development. The various attempts at management development conducted in different organizations are contributing to a growing uniformity of concept. This process of refinement will continue as additional experience in management development is obtained. An attempt is made here to outline a general concept of management development which integrates the varying approaches to management development and which focuses attention upon the common goals and objectives of these approaches.[9]

We have already reviewed the many pressures upon management which have contributed to a growing concern for management development. Each of these pressures contributes a specific objective for management development. We might summarize the general objectives of management development as they relate to these pressures and state that *management development seeks a continuity of performance and a continuing improvement of performance of management functions in all group activity, now and in the future.* This general statement of the objectives of management development implies certain considerations that help us clarify the specific goals and the role of management development.

First, management development is concerned with the performance of the management functions. While we shall consider these functions in more detail later, at the moment we merely repeat that the primary function of management is the establishment, maintenance, and provision of an organization. It is the planning, staffing, directing, and coordinating of a group of people for the achievement of certain common goals. This function is the key to the entire organization. The success with which this function is performed will determine the growth and even the continued existence of the organization. Responsibility for performance of this function is not centered in a single individual; rather, it is shared by the entire management team. This suggests that management development is concerned with development of the management team.

Management development in past decades might be characterized as "manager development," or the development of individual managers. The management function was more concentrated in a single individual than is the case today, and development of individuals for the relatively few management positions within an organization had more influence upon the performance of the management function than would be the case today. Furthermore, this manager development was relatively unplanned and left up to the individual. In a sense, the Darwinian concept of "survival of the fittest" was applied to management development. The individual who managed

[9] See *Principal Elements of Management Development* (Minneapolis: Industrial Relations Center, University of Minnesota, 1956).

to develop his own capabilities through experience was awarded the prize of the management post.

This older concept of management development is no longer applicable. The organization is vitally concerned with the provision of managers and the performance of the management function. This provision can no longer be left to chance. The sharing of responsibilities among the entire management organization also places emphasis upon the management team. The needs of the management team may be very specific, such as the need for a sales manager or a controller, and such development cannot be left to chance. It is extremely unlikely that qualified managers would be available at the proper time for each specific position on the team if development were left to chance. The concept of management development employed here is the development of the entire management team or organization as a team rather than as a group of individuals.

Mention has been made repeatedly of the need for management development in providing a reserve of qualified managers capable of insuring a continuity of performance of the management functions. The repeated failures and troubles of organizations following the retirement or death of key executives testify to the necessity for providing a management reserve for a smooth succession of managements. Equally important is the objective of improvement in the performance of the management functions. Management performance is a result of the individual performances of managers and of the coordination and cooperation of individuals as members of a team. Thus, one of the objectives of management development includes improved manager performance, and the concept of individual manager performance is included as a part of the larger concept of development of the management team. This manager development must contribute to the improved performance of the entire team and implies planning and coordination of manager development for the achievement of this goal. Improved performance of the management team also can result from many activities affecting the organization and coordination of individual managers' tasks. Thus, operating objectives of management development include improved communications, organization relationships, and delegation of authority and responsibility.

A third major objective of management development implied in the general statement above is the satisfaction of the desires and needs of members of the organization. A successful organization must provide opportunity for the satisfaction of individual members' desires as well as for the achievement of the common goals and objectives of these members. Management development seeks this increased satisfaction through providing opportunities for and assisting in the development of individual capabilities and potentialities within the organization.

In summary, we can say that management development is concerned with the continuous improvement of performance of the management functions through the provision of adequate reserves of capable and qualified personnel to assure a smooth management succession; improved performance of individual managers and improved coordination of efforts within the management team; and increased satisfaction of the desires and needs of individual members of the management organization.

ELEMENTS OF MANAGEMENT DEVELOPMENT

Management development occurs in every organization regardless of intention. Managers are recruited, are assigned to positions, and must adapt to the demands of the job and the organization. Whether recognized or not, the assignments and experiences of managers shape their development, and their assignments as members of the management team shape the effectiveness of performance of this team. The objectives sought through management development might result naturally from the activities conducted in the organization under the direction of the management team, although this is unlikely. A primary characteristic of modern attempts at management development is the planning devoted to improved performance of the management team. The essential elements of a comprehensive program for management development are performed in the natural course of staffing and directing an organization. Management development involves the planned coordination and integration of these elements for improvement of the long-run performance of the entire management team.

The elements of a comprehensive program for management development are the functions performed in building and administering any organization of people. Essentially the same functions are performed in the establishment and maintenance of organizations of non-managerial personnel. A number of principles and guides for the performance of these functions have been developed and now are being adapted for application in the development of the management team. The essential elements of a program for management development are outlined in the remainder of this chapter. The problems involved in the performance of these elements and guides for the solution of these problems are discussed in more detail in later chapters. Each of these elements of management development constitutes the subject of a later chapter.

Organization Analysis and Planning

An effective program for development of the management team must be geared to the existing and future needs of the organization. We must not only determine the general managerial needs of the organization, but we must also know what particular managerial jobs must be filled now or will develop in the future. What is the managerial structure now and what will it become? Organization planning determines future managerial needs, and accurate predictions of future needs are particularly important because of the lead time required in the development of competent managers.

The structure and organization of responsibilities of the management team also have a somewhat more direct impact upon management development as they shape immediate training opportunities and influence team coordination. The organization of jobs, span of control, delegation and decentralization of responsibilities, and relationships among individual jobs all have a direct impact upon team performance. Further, they determine the range of experiences available for training and the ladders for progression within the organization. This structure of responsibilities may encourage or restrict efforts for development; it may facilitate or hinder the utilization of manager talents.

Specific considerations of organization analysis and planning as they bear upon management development are discussed in the following two chapters. Chapter 3 reviews principles of organization and their implications for management development. Chapter 4 explores in more detail the organization of responsibilities into individual management jobs and the implications for development of personnel for these jobs.

Management Appraisal and Inventory

Management appraisal and inventory focus attention upon both the individual manager and the management team in the determination of specific goals of management development. The appraisal is an attempt to assess the degree to which the individual manager's performance and qualifications meet the job standards set forth in the organization structure, and to assess his potential for improved performance of these or other responsibilities. The inventory provides a measure of existing management abilities and potential for development throughout the organization. Gaps between these measures and known or anticipated needs point the direction for specific developmental action. The appraisal and inventory also provide an aid for improved utilization of managers' abilities through improved assignments and improved planning for problems of succession.

Management Compensation

An important factor influencing the development and performance of the management team is the climate within which the various techniques of management development are applied. Special practices for the improved recruitment, training, and utilization of managers will be of little value unless accompanied by a system of rewards and incentives which stimulates interest and effort for development. An organizational climate which encourages risk-taking and interest in self-development, as well as delegation of responsibilities, and coaching for the development of subordinates, will not in itself accomplish the objectives of management development, but it appears to be a necessary condition for this management development.

The appropriate climate for management development is a result of many influences. It depends to a great extent upon the structure of management compensation provided, viewing compensation in a broad sense as including status symbols and perquisites as well as monetary compensation. A number of special devices and techniques for management compensation have been developed in recent years in attempts to provide this desired climate for management growth and performance. These techniques are reviewed and evaluated as influences of management development in Chapter 6.

Management Recruiting

The recruitment of individuals for the management team is an integral element of management development. Recruiting is required to insure an adequate supply of management potential for development and promotion within the management team. Consequently, the success of recruiting activities directly determines and limits the effectiveness of other elements of management development. The efficiency of training and coaching activities is limited by the potential for development of individuals recruited into the organization.

Management recruiting provides a more direct impact upon the development and performance of the management team where it is used to supplement promotion from within the organization and provide managers already qualified for responsible positions. Recruiting success in these instances has an immediate effect upon the performance of the entire team. Various practices for the recruitment of potential managers and qualified management personnel are reviewed and discussed in Chapter 7.

Management Selection and Placement

The selection, placement, and assignment of personnel in management positions have both an immediate and a long-run impact upon the effectiveness of the management team. First, selection and placement decisions have an immediate bearing upon operations at the time of assignment. Mismatching of abilities and job requirements results in underutilization of management manpower, loss of performance by the management team, and dissatisfaction on the part of affected personnel. An equally important consideration concerns the influence of present assignments upon the future performance of personnel. Assignments can be used as methods of providing valuable experience and development for individual managers, if well planned and conducted in the proper sequence and at the proper stage of the individual's development. Assignments which fail to provide proper challenge, as well as those which overwhelm the individual, can be detrimental to his development and future performance. Considerations in the selection and placement of managers are discussed in Chapter 8, along with a review of measures used in the matching of individual capabilities with job requirements.

Individual Development

Individual development is a major concern in management development. It is considered here as a single element of management development, although a large and important element, as a way of emphasizing the relation between individual development and the other elements of management development. Individual development would contribute little to improvement of the management team in the absence of the other elements outlined here.

Development is the growth or activation of something latent and must be largely individual. Each individual will possess different potentialities, and his development of these potentialities will be somewhat more or less advanced than that of other individuals. While common experiences and opportunities can be made available to a group, actual development must be individual in nature.

All of the elements of management development mentioned above come to bear upon the development of individual abilities. For example, the guidance and assistance given the individual manager in his development should be geared to the needs of the management team. It would be of little value to the team to develop abilities which have no relevance for management, or to develop the same abilities in all managers if a variety of abilities is required. Hence, individual development should be planned and guided on the basis of the needs of the organization and the potential of the individual. The structure of the management organization, the management appraisal and inventory, the management compensation structure, and the recruiting, selection, and placement activities all contribute to improved efficiency in the development of individuals for the management team. Chapter 9 outlines the various activities available for individual development and attempts to relate these to all other elements of management development.

Management Development Research and Evaluation

Recent interest in the subject of management development has served to point up a number of problems and unanswered questions. These questions range from very basic problems concerning the nature of a manager's job and the identification of management potential to the evaluation of alternative methods for teaching management skills. The press for guides to the solution of immediate problems of management development has resulted in the application of existing knowledge to these problems. However, the search for answers to basic questions concerning management development and for critical evaluation of alternative practices should continue. Chapter 10 outlines the requirements of such research and suggests several directions for this research.

SUMMARY

In this chapter we have attempted to point out reasons for the current interest in management development, to set forth the nature of management development and what can be expected from it, and to outline a master-plan for management development. We have suggested that development of the management team is the proper concept for consideration of management development, and that this development involves the application of principles of personnel administration within the management organization. We shall examine in later chapters each of the elements of management development outlined here, suggesting guides and concepts useful in framing over-all programs for management development within any organization.

SELECTED BIBLIOGRAPHY

Principal Elements of Management Development (Minneapolis: Industrial Relations Center, University of Minnesota, 1956).

Shartle, Carroll L., *Executive Performance and Leadership* (Englewood Cliffs, N. J.: Prentice-Hall, Inc., 1956).

Chapter THREE

Organization of the Management Team

INTRODUCTION

A major task of management is the coordination of the efforts of people. This coordination of individual efforts for the accomplishment of common goals provides meaning for group activity. In a similar fashion, the concept of the management team achieves practical meaning only as managerial responsibilities and activities are grouped and coordinated for team performance. Organization of the management team has a direct impact upon performance of the management team and should be considered as an element of any comprehensive program for development of the team. At the same time, the organization of managerial responsibilities shapes the assignments of individual managers and thus influences the opportunities for individual development through experience. Development of the management team through organization for improved teamwork is considered in the present chapter. General guides to organization of the management team are reviewed with particular consideration of their implications for management development.

CONCEPTS OF ORGANIZATION

The term *organization* has many different meanings.[1] Let us consider several of these different definitions or concepts of organization.

[1] See Carroll L. Shartle, *Executive Performance and Leadership* (Englewood Cliffs, N. J.: Prentice-Hall, Inc., 1956), pp. 4-5.

Organization as an Entity

A general definition of the term *organization* refers to a complex whole composed of a number of integrated parts. More specifically, the term generally is used to refer to a group of two or more persons whose activities are coordinated for the purpose of achieving a common goal or purpose. The New York Yankees baseball team, for example, is an organization in this sense.

Organization Structure

The term *organization* also is used to refer to the structure of relationships among the people or activities comprising the group. It may be viewed as an ordered guide or plan for the relating of activities and/or people in the achievement of a common goal. The organization structure and the chart which commonly is used to depict this structure, provide a statement of the behavior expected of the people grouped together in the enterprise.

Organization Behavior

The behavior and relationships of individuals within the group do not always conform to the structure or guide for behavior. The term *organization* may be used to refer to the actual behavior of persons grouped together in the enterprise whether or not their behavior conforms to the organization structure. The expression "formal organization" is often used to refer to the organization structure and the expression "informal organization" to refer to the organization behavior. This difference in terms implies that patterns of behavior commonly do not conform to the expected behavior, an implication that we shall deal with more fully later on.

Organization Process

"Organization" also may be used in describing the process of systematically coordinating activities and people. It is the act of defining and grouping the activities of an enterprise in a logical and systematic manner. Activities are grouped and related to other activities to obtain the maximum contribution in achieving the objectives of the enterprise.

ORGANIZATION AS A MANAGEMENT GUIDE

An essential task or function of management is the coordination of the activities of people for the achievement of objectives of the enterprise. Organization is the guide for accomplishing this task. Activities required to accomplish the objectives of the enterprise are defined, grouped and related in a plan or guide for their coordination—the organization structure. This plan or structure then provides the guide for all activities of the enterprise. The organization structure is of little value itself. Its value lies in its usefulness as a means to an end, the objectives of the enterprise. Coordinating the activities of all persons in the enterprise involves communicating the common objectives, issuing directives and instructions for performance, and motivating all members of the enterprise. The organization structure provides a framework for conducting these activities.[2]

The organization structure is a guide for most of the basic responsibilities of management. It provides a blueprint for the selection of people and the staffing of the organization; it provides the guide to communications among members of the organization; it is a directive informing members of their expected performance or behavior as members of the organization; and it provides a method of control over the performance of organization members.[3] The organization structure is evaluated in terms of its contribution to the management task of coordinating activities for achievement of the enterprise objectives; it serves no purpose apart from this.

Several subsidiary considerations should be recognized, however, in planning and shaping the organization structure. For one thing, the personal objectives of individual members of the organization will influence the organization structure. Individuals join the organization and cooperate for achievement of the enterprise objectives if they view this action as a means of furthering their personal objectives. In this sense, Barnard distinguishes between an "effective" organization and an "efficient" organization: the effective organization

---

[2] Chester Barnard, *The Functions of the Executive* (Cambridge: Harvard University Press, 1946), pp. 89-91; and Kenneth E. Boulding, *The Organization Revolution* (New York: Harper and Brothers, 1953), pp. 134-135.

[3] See Paul E. Holden, Lounsbury S. Fish, and Hubert L. Smith, *Top-Management Organization and Control* (New York: McGraw-Hill Book Co., 1951), pp. 6-7.

achieves the goals of the enterprise whereas the efficient organization achieves also the objectives of persons cooperating in the organization.[4] Bakke describes this adjustment of the organization structure in consideration of members' objectives as "the fusion process"; the organization tries to impress a pattern of behavior upon the individual and the individual seeks to impress a pattern upon the organization, each trying to make the other an agency for realization of its goals.[5] While the major purpose and logic of organization stem from the enterprise objectives, there must be consideration of the objectives of members of the organization in the planning of the organization structure. The organization dictated by organization goals and operations requirements must be adapted to facilitate achievement of personal goals in so far as possible.

The contribution of the organization structure to the development and maintenance of a strong management team is an equally important consideration. The grouping of activities within the organization structure determines the number of managers required, the nature of their positions and hence required personal qualifications, the opportunities for varied experience in the development of individual managers, and the opportunities for acceptance of responsibilities and the exercise of authority in training and developmental positions. The survival of the enterprise depends in large part upon its ability to develop and maintain a strong team of managers. The organization structure influences the probabilities of survival through the structuring of management position requirements and through the opportunities for development and progression provided within the enterprise.

GUIDES TO ORGANIZATION

The organization process involves the definition of activities necessary for achievement of the enterprise objectives, and the grouping and relating of these activities in some logical manner. Major activities are grouped into departments and divisions, and specific activities are grouped into individual positions for performance within each department or division. This process has been viewed alternatively as proceeding from a division of activities from

[4] C. Barnard, *op. cit.*, p. 91.

[5] E. Wight Bakke, *The Fusion Process* (New Haven: Labor and Management Center, Yale University, 1953), p. 58.

the general to the specific, or as a grouping of activities from the specific to the general. The first approach begins with the view that responsibility for all activities is lodged with the major executive positions. Elements of the responsibility of the chief executive are successively differentiated into groups and subgroups of responsibilities until the final sets of responsibilities are each sufficient to require the performance of a single individual. The alternative approach begins with the large mass of activities which must be performed. These are grouped into individual positions, and positions are grouped into units for supervision. Positions are created at successively higher levels of management for the supervision of subordinate activities until the responsibilities for over-all supervision can be exercised by a single person, the chief executive. These alternative approaches may be equally useful in the establishment of a philosophy of organization. The usual pattern of growth of the organization structure, however, has occurred through the successive differentiation of activities into subordinate positions.[6] Furthermore, analysis of the organization structure proceeding from the over-all objectives to individual job assignments emphasizes the group endeavor and the logic of relationships in terms of these over-all objectives. Regardless of the concept or theory of organization employed, there are several techniques which have been found useful in the establishment and communication of the organization structure.

Grouping of Activities

Effective coordination of the activities of the management team involves the classification and relation of activities into organizational units. The basic guide to this classification and grouping of activities stated by Henri Fayol concerns "unity of direction." All activities which make the same general contribution to the objectives of the enterprise are grouped together. "Unity of direction" has been interpreted in different ways, and there are alternative guides to the classification and grouping of activities within the management organization. Each guide focuses attention upon a slightly different aspect of the general objectives. All of these guides can be applied in the organization of the management team, each of them being most useful at some particular stage of growth of the enterprise or

[6] See Ernest Dale, *Planning and Developing the Company Organization Structure*, Research Report No. 20 (New York: American Management Association, 1952), pp. 121-122; and Carroll L. Shartle, *op. cit.*, pp. 36-38.

at a particular level within the organization structure. A consideration of these guides to classification and grouping is relevant here, since each implies slightly different managerial needs and each offers slightly different opportunities for development of the management team.

Functional. Organization by function emphasizes the different types of performance or activity within the management team; activities involving similar skills and qualifications for performance are grouped together. The definition of functions is somewhat arbitrary and may range from general classifications such as production, sales, and administrative services to more specific classifications involving research, accounting, purchasing, sales, personnel administration, and transportation. The functional form of organization offers advantages of performance, since it facilitates the specialization of performance and permits the employment of specialists in the different functions. A disadvantage lies in the emphasis placed upon functional and professional objectives as opposed to the more general objectives of the enterprise. Furthermore, the functional form of organization restricts opportunities for experience in general management necessary for development. Functional organization at lower levels of the management structure particularly can be advantageous as an aid to improved performance through specialization. It will be replaced with some other classification guide in top-management organization usually, and development of specialists for the more general top-management responsibilities will then call for special attention.

Product. Organization by product involves the grouping of activities relating to the production and distribution of a product into a single unit regardless of the function performed. Such a basis for organization obviously is appropriate only in multi-product enterprises. Activities within each product unit are then organized on some other basis, such as the functional grouping of activities. Somewhat greater decentralization and delegation of decision-making is possible in the product form of organization than in other forms, since it is relatively easier to establish objective criteria of performance—commonly, profit performance—and, thus, to provide the control necessary for effective delegation of decision-making authority. These profit criteria of performance in product units focus relatively more attention upon the over-all enterprise objectives than do functional criteria of performance, which are more difficult to relate specifically to the enterprise objectives. Furthermore, profit criteria permit the comparison of different organization units and their performance, providing an incentive for development and performance within these units. In general, the product form of organization appears to offer greater opportunities for the development of general management abilities through experience and to permit relatively greater control in the coordination of managerial performance.

Geographic. Organization on the basis of geographic location of activities is advocated where the geographic separation of activities hinders the communication and coordination among organization units. For essentially the same reasons, geographic organization can be used to provide opportunities for the delegation and exercise of decision-making authority. The manager in charge of a geographically separated unit must be delegated relatively greater authority because of communication barriers. Opportunities for geographic organization exist within most enterprises and should be recognized and utilized as opportunities for developmental experience.

Other available guides to organization emphasize the grouping of activities on the basis of customer groups, special processes, machinery, or stages of production.[7] These guides are used less commonly than the three guides already discussed and they do not appear to offer any special advantages for the development of managerial abilities. Any one of them might be selected on the basis of improved coordination of performance in a specific situation, but there appears to be little basis for choice among them as they relate to development of individuals within the team. On the other hand, the current trend away from functional organization and toward product and geographic organization can be explained in terms of both performance objectives and development objectives.[8] The relatively greater decentralization permitted under the product and geographic forms of organization provides increased opportunities for the achievement of both objectives.

Personality and Organization

There is a belief among some managements that the organization structure should be established around the peculiar interests, abili-

[7] "Shaping Company Structure to Its Needs," *Business Week,* No. 1321. December 18, 1954, pp. 66-70.

[8] See Peter Drucker, *The Practice of Management* (New York: Harper and Brothers, 1954), pp. 218-226; and Ralph J. Cordiner, *New Frontiers for Professional Managers* (New York: McGraw-Hill Book Company, 1956), pp. 40-79.

ties, and personalities of individuals within the organization. This might be called the "great man" theory of organization: individuals are thought to make the organization, and, therefore, specific positions and relationships should be established to take advantage of their interests and abilities. It is true that certain individuals have influenced greatly the shape and nature of several successful enterprises—Sears, Roebuck and Company, General Motors, and Ford.[9] However, the organization structure is intended as a guide, a plan for selecting, developing, assigning, and promoting individuals within the enterprise. The structuring of position and relationship assignments within the enterprise on the basis of abilities and interests of present members commits the enterprise to the recruitment, development, and training of individuals identical to these present members.

The organization structure should be recognized for what it is—a plan for action. The organization structure is a plan for the grouping and relating of activities and assignments within the enterprise—not the relating of individuals. It is true that the plan will have to be altered and adapted to fit abilities and aptitudes of members available for assignment, but the plan should not be discarded. Rather, it should be retained as a plan setting forth the goals for staffing, goals which would disappear if the structure were established merely on the basis of interests and personalities of incumbent members.

Informal Organization

"Informal organization" refers to the behavior of members of the organization, behavior which may or may not conform to the planned behavior set forth in the position descriptions and organization manual. Studies of actual working relationships among members of organizations indicate that informal organization is common.[10] There are many possible reasons for development of these informal organizations, some of them relevant in the planning of the organization of the management team.

Studies reported by Scott indicate that members of the organization frequently possess different conceptions of the organization

[9] P. Drucker, *op. cit.*, Chapters 4 and 10.

[10] See Carroll L. Shartle and Ralph M. Stogdill, *Studies in Naval Leadership: Methods, Results and Applications* (Columbus, Ohio: Personnel Research Board, Ohio State University, 1953), pp. 56-68; and Robert S. Weiss, *Processes of Organization* (Ann Arbor: Survey Research Center, Institute of Social Behavior, University of Michigan, 1956), p. 58.

structure, and that these conceptions commonly agree with observed behavior.[11] In other words, members of the organization tend to behave in accordance with what they believe to be the structure of the organization, although these beliefs frequently are not accurate. These different conceptions of the organization may stem from faulty communication of the planned structure, expectations and personalities of the organization members, or requirements of the positions they hold in the organization. Differences between organization structure and behavior may indicate poor coordination of activities in the planned structure, forcing members of the organization to develop an improved set of relationships in behavior in order to achieve the objectives of their positions. Analysis of the informal organization in such a situation might suggest improvement of the structured relationships among positions.

Others point to social needs of the members as the source of the informal organization.[12] Individuals cooperating in a common endeavor are seeking certain personal satisfactions which they believe can be attained through cooperation. If the planned structure of relationship does not permit the attainment of these satisfactions, an alternative set of relationships will arise which contributes to the satisfaction of these goals. Consideration of the goals of group membership, acceptance and participation in the establishment of the organization structure, might contribute to the satisfaction and morale of the entire organization.

Line-Staff Relationships

A source of frequent confusion and irritation within the management organization stems from the application of concepts of line and staff authority in the structuring of the organization. Confusion over the type of authority assigned a position and differences of opinion over the locus of responsibility for specific functions and activities often arise in the sharing of line and staff responsibility and authority. The structure of line and staff relationships is related to development of the management team as it affects performance of the

---

[11] See Ellis L. Scott, *Leadership and Perceptions of Organization,* Research Monograph No. 82 (Columbus, Ohio: Bureau of Business Research, Ohio State University, 1956), pp. 21-60.

[12] See Perrin Stryker, "Problem for the Front Office," *Fortune,* May, 1951; and Morris S. Viteles, "The Human Factor in Organization," *Research and Technical Report No. 17* of the Industrial Relations Center, University of Minnesota (Dubuque, Iowa: William C. Brown, 1955), pp. 19-26.

management team and as it gives rise to special problems and opportunities for development.

The terms *line* and *staff* refer to types of authority, although these concepts usually are generalized to describe responsibilities and positions as well.[13] A single position in the management organization may be assigned either one or both of these types of authority. *Line authority* is considered as the power or authority to command, the power to initiate and carry through activities of the enterprise. *Staff authority* is defined as authority in the preparation of advice and counsel as an aid in the accomplishment of major functions. Several different types of staff authority and positions can be identified in actual practice. We can distinguish, for example, between the concepts of "specialized staff" and "personal staff." The concept of *specialized staff* refers to the functional organization of certain responsibilities and activities as an aid to the major producing units of the enterprise. Specialized staff units are established for purchasing, personnel administration, and similar functional responsibilities. The concept of *personal staff*, on the other hand, refers to specific positions established for the assistance of a single management position. The position of "assistant" often is established to share the responsibilities of the senior manager, the assistant performing as a substitute manager in the absence of his superior and performing assigned responsibilities of his superior's position at other times. The position of "assistant to" usually is structured more as that of a staff aide to the manager, the "assistant to" performing largely administrative matters and participating little if at all in the decision-making aspects of his superior's responsibilities.

The concept of specialized staff authority has been used widely in organization. The application of this concept in organization permits focusing attention upon specific functions and the employment of specialists to perform these functions. Difficulties in the use of specialized staff arise when the assignments of responsibilities and authority are not clearly understood by the line and staff managers concerned. An example frequently occurs in the administration of activities for development of the management team. The entire program for development can be aided considerably with specialized

---

[13] See "Improving Staff and Line Relationships," *Studies in Personnel Policy No. 153* (New York: National Industrial Conference Board, 1956), and "Line-Staff Relationships in Production," *Special Report No. 18* (New York: American Management Association, 1957).

staff services in organization analysis and planning, maintenance of a management inventory, coordination of appraisal activities, recruiting, specialized training activities, and similar activities for development. However, such activities form only part of the entire program for development of the management team. Significant development of the team will occur only as all managers utilize these aids in improved day-to-day management of their subordinates. The assignment of staff responsibilities for management development is too frequently interpreted by line managers as a signal to turn over all responsibility for development to these staff positions. Any creation of specialized staff services should be accompanied with an understanding that final responsibility for over-all management still resides with the operating managers of the organization and that these services are useful only to the extent that operating managers utilize them in meeting their responsibilities.

The desirability of personal staff assignments as aids to performance and to development is debated constantly.[14] It is argued on the one hand that these positions tend to improve performance of the management team by relieving overburdened managers, and that they contribute to the development of incumbents of the positions by providing experience as an understudy. Critics retort that such positions actually hamper performance by introducing a barrier between the manager and his subordinates, thus complicating communication and coordination, and that incumbents of these positions rarely experience challenging and worthwhile developmental experiences. Utilization of personal staff assignments on a temporary basis can contribute to both performance and development goals, however. Such assignments can be used to relieve a manager on a short-run basis, while a continuing need for assistance suggests the need for analysis of the responsibilities of the position and the ability of the incumbent. It would be more desirable for performance to restructure the position, if necessary, than to impose a new level of management in the organization on a permanent basis. Such assignments also can be helpful in introducing a manager to new responsibilities and in developing him for greater responsibility. However, assignments made for this purpose should involve some sharing of responsibilities rather than employing the subordinate solely for staff studies and administrative matters.

---

[14] See Joseph D. Edwards, *Executives: Making Them Click* (New York: University Books, 1956), pp. 97-99, for a review of arguments.

Management by Committee

An increasing incidence of committees can be noted in the structure of management organizations throughout industry, particularly in the higher levels of the management organization. General Motors, Phillips Petroleum, and McCormick and Company, for example, have been dubbed "committee organizations" because of their widespread use of committees in the management organization.[15] Further widespread use of committees in the management organization is indicated by the results of several surveys. A survey by the American Management Association indicates that two-thirds of the 150 companies surveyed maintain at least one standing committee in addition to *ad hoc* committees.[16] A survey of Ohio manufacturing firms reports similar results; 61 per cent of the main plants and 69 per cent of the branch plants surveyed maintain committees within the structure of their management organizations.[17] A number of reasons have been advanced for the use of committees in the management organization—most of them concerning the nature of management responsibilities and the scope of the manager's job. Peter Drucker, for example, suggests that the chief executive's position in most organizations is too large for a single individual.[18] The responsibilities of the position must be shared by other individuals singly or in committees, particularly as the organization grows in size and operations. A case in point is the E. I. duPont Company, which has employed a committee in the performance of the chief executive's functions for over thirty years.[19] Supporting evidence for this explanation is provided by studies indicating greater use of management committees in those organizations where the management span of control tends to be larger than average.[20]

The establishment of committees within the structure of the management organization raises several questions which bear upon the goals of performance and development of the management team. Committees have been found most useful for purposes of co-

---

[15] See Metropolitan Life Insurance Company, Policyholders Service Bureau, *Business Organization* (New York, 1947).

[16] See E. Dale, *op. cit.*, pp. 92-93.

[17] See James A. Healey, *Executive Coordination and Control* (Columbus, Ohio: Bureau of Business Research, The Ohio State University, 1956), p. 254.

[18] P. Drucker, *op. cit.*, pp. 161-168.

[19] See William H. Mylander, "Management by Executive Committee," *Harvard Business Review*, Vol. 33, No. 3, May-June, 1955, pp. 51-58.

[20] J. Healey, *op. cit.*, pp. 186-187.

ordination, planning, and advising and are not recommended for decision-making and action.[21] Committee organization for management development can be quite useful in coordinating the activities of different units, for example, while responsibility for administration and follow-through in development should be assigned to specific positions. Committees also appear most productive when they are established for specific purposes and assignments and then disbanded upon completion of these assignments. The problem of effective control probably is more important in efficient utilization of committees than at any other point in the management organization.

Committee assignments can be utilized effectively in the identification and development of management potential. McCormick and Company, for example, views management development as a major purpose of the committee management of their organization. Committee assignments are used to test ability and potential to perform broad management functions and to provide individual managers with a broader understanding of the organization and with more general experiences than can be obtained in normal assignments. The objective of personal development cannot be divorced from performance objectives in the establishment of committees, however. Committee members are not likely to experience significant personal development unless the committee is assigned meaningful projects. Performance objectives should be paramount in committee establishment, while development objectives can be given relatively more consideration in the assignment of committee members. In short, committee management can be useful in achieving both performance and development objectives if committees are used primarily for coordination within the management team and if controls over the use of committees are such as to establish and maintain them only as necessary.

Span of Control

The span of control, or number of positions and relationships supervised by the individual manager, has an immediate influence upon the shape of the organization structure of the management team. A quite limited span of control gives rise to a hierarchy of more numerous levels of management in an organization than does

[21] E. Dale, *op. cit.*, p. 92.

an extended span of control. Determination of the span of control concept, limited or extensive, which is to be applied in the organization of the management team involves a balancing of considerations affecting managerial performance and development of individual managers within the team. For example, James Worthy, of Sears, Roebuck and Company, advocates a relatively "flat" organization structure with a consequent wide span of control as a means of facilitating communication within the management team.[22] Worthy also argues that a relatively wide span of control prevents over-supervision and cites studies within Sears, Roebuck which indicate that higher morale is achieved in units with wide spans of control. At the same time, considerations of development and training of subordinates tend to limit the number of people that a manager can supervise effectively. The smaller his span of control, the more time a manager will have to devote to coaching and working with subordinates.

Surveys of the span of control in business and industry report spans of control ranging from one to 24 positions.[23] The median span of control within management organizations appears to be approximately six. Interestingly, one survey reports that managers supervising six or more positions spend an average of two more hours a week on the job than do managers with a smaller span of control. Certainly the scope of a manager's responsibilities varies directly with his span of control, although the ideal span of control will vary from one position to another and from one manager to another, depending upon the nature of the assignment and the ability of the individual.

Generally, the span of control of a manager's position should be most limited in those positions which carry heavy responsibility for the development of subordinates. For example, subordinates in relatively structured job assignments will require less coaching and assistance from the manager than subordinates in less structured assignments; as an assignment is changed to provide additional experience and training, the effective span of control of the manager is reduced. Similarly, objective standards of performance tend to reduce the amount of supervision required and permit an enlarged

---

[22] See James C. Worthy, "Organization Structure and Employee Morale," *American Sociological Review*, Vol. 15, No. 2, 1950, pp. 169-179.

[23] See E. Dale, *op. cit.*, pp. 56-60; J. Healey, *op. cit.*, pp. 64-67; and Lydia Strong, "Of Time and Top Management," *The Management Review*, Vol. 45, No. 6, June, 1956, pp. 486-493, for reports of these surveys.

span of control. Frequent changes of policies and practices will call for increased coaching and reduce the effective span of control. Previous training and competence of subordinates also affect the effective span of control, since relatively greater time is required for coaching and training during the initial stages of a subordinate's assignment.

A distinction should be drawn between the concept of "span of control" and the concept of "span of access." The individual manager can make himself available for consultation and discussion with a larger number of subordinates than he can effectively supervise and develop. An organization structure designed for maximum development of the management team should clearly recognize the objectives of development realizable within the limitation of the span of control of the management position; considerations of span of access are much less relevant in organizing for development within the management team.

Delegation

The process of delegation refers formally to the means of putting into effect the organization plan; it is the assignment of responsibility and authority to individuals within the management team. Delegation is a technique for the individual manager's use in achieving the objectives of his assignment through reassignment of activities to subordinates. Delegation is relevant to our discussion as it affects over-all performance of the management team and as it contributes to the development of individual managers within the team.

The individual manager, through delegation, structures the organization unit under his supervision. The coordination of activities under his direction is determined by the assignments he makes, and the opportunities for development of subordinate managers through experience are shaped by his delegation of responsibilities. Achievement of the performance and development objectives of delegation often fails because of improper delegation stemming from misconceptions of the meaning of delegation. For example, responsibility is a charge making one answerable or accountable.[24] It is personal in the sense that it cannot be passed on, reassigned, or transferred. It refers to a relationship between the parties involved. In this sense, respon-

---

[24] See Alvin Brown, *Organization* (New York: Hibbert Printing Company, 1945), pp. 25-35.

sibility cannot be delegated. The manager creates responsibilities of subordinates through his charges to them. On the other hand, authority is the right to act, the power to undertake or refrain from undertaking something. The individual manager presumably possesses the authority necessary to accomplish his responsibilities and, in creating responsibilities of subordinates, relinquishes portions of this authority to subordinates. Thus, authority is delegated or temporarily relinquished, although the superior manager retains the right of recall of authority. Many managers are reluctant to delegate authority, since they cannot delegate or relinquish responsibility. In consequence, the performance of subordinates may be hampered through lack of authority or fuzzy demarcations of authority, and their development in the exercise of authority is thus restricted.

Delegation is essential for the effective development of subordinates. They will experience authority and will have the opportunity to make mistakes only if they are delegated authority. This delegation of authority is facilitated by the establishment of proper controls by the superior manager. The establishment of performance standards for assigned responsibilities provides a guide for the subordinate manager and a control for his superior. The delegating manager can easily check upon the exercise of authority and retain his control over it. At the same time, this check upon performance facilitates development of the subordinate, as it points up needs for improvement and permits the delegating manager to gauge the readiness of subordinates to accept additional responsibility and authority. Delegation does not occur in a vacuum. Delegation is conditioned by the attitudes of delegating managers and the abilities of subordinate managers. It is part of the manager's job to gauge his subordinate's readiness for accepting responsibility and exercising authority and to tailor delegation to the ability and readiness of the subordinate. The entire management team should accept the idea that mistakes in the exercise of authority will be made by subordinate managers, and that it is the opportunity to make such mistakes which spurs the individual to the development of his potential. A manager will effectively delegate to his subordinates only if his superior in turn sets the tone for this delegation. Effective organization of the management team is characterized by a framework of responsibility and authority which challenges the abilities of managers and provides opportunities for their development.

Organization Chart

The organization chart is a pictorial statement of relationships among responsibilities and activities within the enterprise. Boxes in the chart signify units of responsibility and authority, whether the boxes ultimately refer to departments, divisions, positions, or specific responsibilities. Lines connecting these units of responsibility and authority indicate the nature of responsibility and authority relationships within the organization. Special symbols often are used to indicate specific types of relationships among the units within the organization; solid lines may indicate delegated authority, broken lines may indicate a reporting relationship, and colored lines may indicate consultative relationships. Regardless of the specific symbols used, the major purpose of the chart is to provide an over-all indication of the coordination of activities within the enterprise and the relationships established to facilitate this coordination.

Charting the organization structure serves several useful purposes. For example, the chart serves as a check upon the logic of established relationships. The fact that some organizations cannot be illustrated in a clear fashion indicates that these organizations do not have any systematic coordination of activities and that whatever coordination occurs is accidental.[25] The organization chart also serves as a guide to expected or planned relationships among positions; it provides a map or guide for growth. The chart provides all members of the organization with a clear statement of the relationships they are expected to maintain in the conduct of their work. In this sense, the chart is more useful as a guide to individual activity in large organizations than in small ones where there are fewer relationships to be kept in mind. And, in fact, organization charting is found somewhat more frequently in enterprises with branch establishments than in single-unit, smaller organizations.[26]

Some managements have avoided organization charting because of a resistance to the formal establishment of relationships within the organization. They fear that organization charting reduces the flexibility and free coordination of activities within the enterprise. An organization structure will arise within every group, whether the structure is planned or unplanned. In the absence of a clear statement of planned and expected relationships, individuals within the

[25] See P. Holden and others, *op. cit.*, pp. 93-94.
[26] See J. Healey, *op. cit.*, pp. 116-117.

group will establish the relationships they feel most desirable from a personal standpoint. The resulting structure of relationships normally will not provide the most effective structure of relationships for group activity, since the basis for its establishment has been a personal one rather than one based upon consideration of the organization objectives.

The organization chart has been feared at times also because of the feeling that it is a chart of status and prestige relationships. Prestige may be associated with different levels and positions on the chart despite the fact that the chart is intended to depict only relationships of authority and responsibility. A circular organization chart has

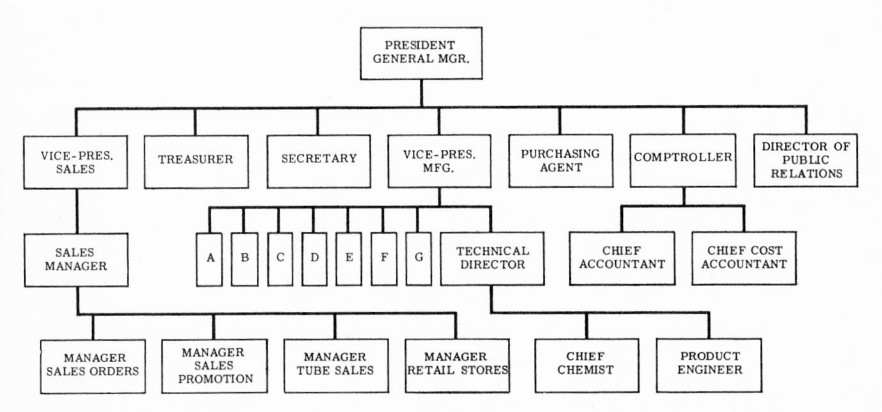

Fig. 1. Traditional-Type Organization Chart. (From C. G. Browne, "The Concentric Organization Chart," *Journal of Applied Psychology,* Vol. 34, No. 6, December, 1950, p. 376.)

been developed and is used by several companies as one way of avoiding the prestige implications of different levels in the traditional organization chart.[27] Another method of charting the organization structure does away with boxes and lines completely and substitutes instead a table of functions and positions, indicating the extent of responsibility of each position with a system of check marks.

Any association between organization charting and rigidity of relationships stems primarily from management philosophy rather than from the chart itself. The organization chart is a guide to relation-

[27] See C. G. Browne, "The Concentric Organization Chart," *Journal of Applied Psychology,* Vol. 34, No. 6, December, 1950, pp. 375-377.

ships and depicts the relationships considered essential to efficient coordination of the management team. The organization structure should be adapted to any change in conditions which calls for an altered set of relationships, and the chart should be changed as a means of communicating the change in the structure of relationships.

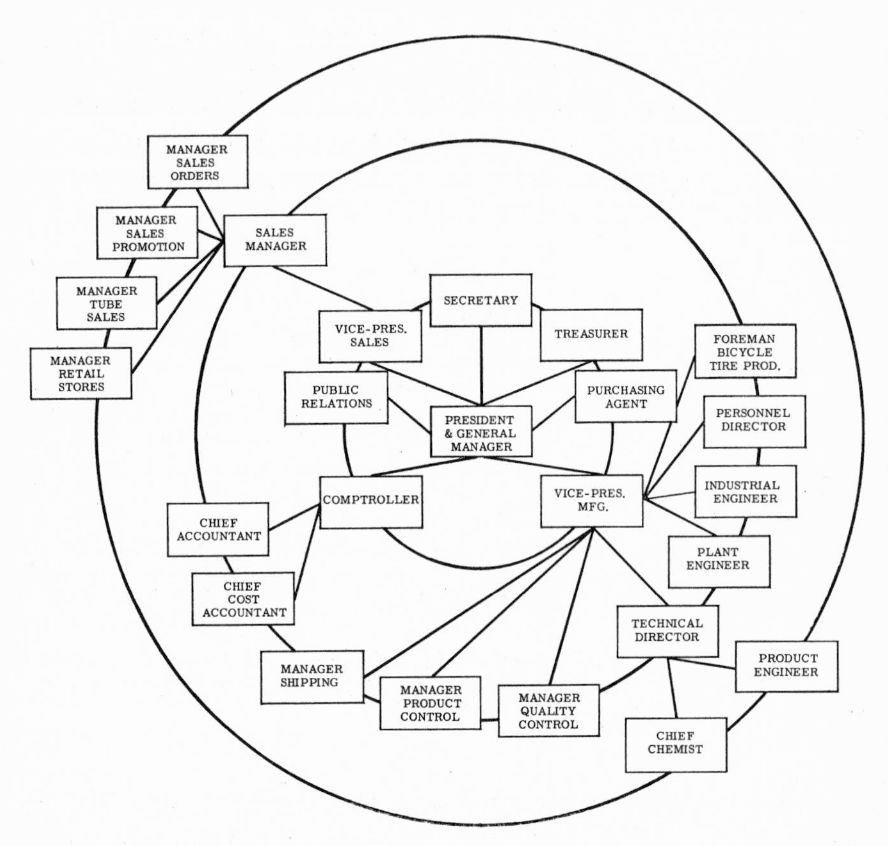

Fig. 2. Concentric Organization Chart. Note: Circles indicate echelon level; black connecting straight lines indicate flow of authority. (From C. G. Browne, "The Concentric Organization Chart," *Journal of Applied Psychology*, Vol. 34, No. 6, December, 1950, p. 376.)

Organization Manual

A number of companies utilize manuals in the communication of the planned organization structure to members of the management team.[28] This manual usually contains statements of the principles

[28] See the organization manuals of the American Enka Company and the Standard Oil Company of California as examples.

Executives' SPECIFIC FUNCTIONS . . .

RESPONSIBILITIES TO OTHER EXECUTIVES

	Board	President	Vice-Pres., Finance	Vice-Pres., Marketing	Director, Advertising	Legal Counsel	Vice-Pres., Manufact.	Vice-Pres., Personnel
Establish over-all objectives	B	A	E	E		E	E	E
Approve over-all plans	B	A	E	E		G	E	E
Direct over-all operations	B	A	G	G		G	G	G
Approve expansion plans	B	A	E	E		F	E	F
Coordinate line and staff	B	A	E	E		E	E	E
Decide on tax matters		B	A			G		
Coordinate budget	F	B	A	E			E	
Determine financing needs		B	A					
Determine marketing policies		B		A	G			
Over-all sales forecast	F	B	F	A			F	
Coordinate product expansion		B	E	A			E	
Plan advertising	F	D	E	B	A		G	F
Administer legal matters		B	G			A		

A Actual job responsibility
B General supervision
C Direct supervision
D Decide on specific points
E Must be consulted
F Must be notified
G May be called in

Fig. 3. Linear Organization Chart. (From *Business Week*, April 6, 1957, p. 187.)

applied in development of the organization structure, charts of relationships within the organization structure, and individual position descriptions. The manual tries to explain the organization structure as well as describe it and to communicate individual position assignments.

The organization guide or manual is helpful in promoting understanding and appreciation of the responsibilities of all members of the management team, in preventing the overlapping or conflict of assignments, and as a guide to development and performance of individual managers. Each manager has available his own position description as well as descriptions of more responsible positions. An understanding of the responsibilities of all management positions is helpful to the individual manager in the performance of his present assignment as well as in the guidance of his personal development for future assignments.

Position Description

The position description is the final product in the delineation of responsibilities within an organization. It is a directive or statement of expected behavior of an individual within the management team. This statement defines the objectives of the individual assignment, outlines tasks and responsibilities, and indicates relationships with other assignments in the management team. It is a detailed statement of authorities and responsibilities described more generally in the organization chart, and it should be consistent with this chart of organization structure.[29]

The position description is a specific aid in the development of the management team. It is a definition of the goals of management development as it outlines standards of performance which guide the selection, development, placement, and promotion of managerial personnel. The collection of position descriptions of an organization thus provides a guide to development of the entire management team. Furthermore, the individual position description provides a guide for the development of the individual manager assigned to the position. It provides both a directive for performance and a guide

[29] See C. L. Bennet, *Defining the Manager's Job, The AMA Manual of Position Descriptions* (Research Study No. 33) (New York: American Management Association, 1958), 437 pp., for a guide to the preparation of management position descriptions and their use, as well as for illustrations of descriptions of managerial jobs.

GENERAL MANUFACTURING MANAGER

Plan, direct, and coordinate all manufacturing activities of the Division to meet schedule, design, and quality requirements at lowest practicable cost and with sound labor relations.

Specific Functions:

——— Select, train, and supervise the personnel needed for his organization.

——— See that assigned products are manufactured in quantities to meet production schedules.

——— See that design and process specifications are adhered to in production.

——— See that quality standards are adhered to in production.

——— Formulate and insure maintenance of an active program of cost reduction.

——— Formulate and insure maintenance of an active program of shrinkage reduction.

——— Review and approve production plans.

——— See that operations are adjusted to meet required changes.

——— See that manufacturing facilities are maintained in proper operating condition.

——— Promote the standardization and improvement of production methods.

——— Consolidate, review, and approve manufacturing cost budgets and permanent property budgets.

——— Promote good industrial relations, employee morale, and community relations.

——— Insure that proper procedures are used by the plants in the inspection of purchased materials.

——— Insure that proper procedures are used by the plants in the control of materials in-process.

Fig. 4. Example of a Functional Job Description. (From *Manual for Management Development,* Training Section, Industrial Relations Department, Sylvania Electric Products, Inc., January 1953.)

for improved performance, in addition to serving as the basis for appraisal and evaluation of individual performance.

Managerial participation in the preparation of position descriptions is a useful aid to development of the management team through improved understanding of the functions of the management team and the contributions of individual positions to team performance. Annual review of the position description and preparation of specific performance objectives for the coming year by the individual manager and his superior strengthen the importance of the position description in management development by focusing attention upon performance objectives and the achievement of these objectives. Performance objectives agreed upon by the manager and his superior become the guides for action during the coming year and the basis for appraisal of performance during the year.[30] Participation by the manager in the development of his position description and performance objectives provides him with an improved understanding of his specific job assignment and its relationship to other assignments of the management team and should contribute to improved individual and team performance.

EVALUATION OF ORGANIZATION PERFORMANCE

The performance of every organization and its component parts is under constant evaluation by those in contact with the organization. Much of this evaluation is informal and almost unconscious; much of it is never expressed or communicated. The general process of this evaluation is relatively standard despite the informality of the process. The person making the evaluation brings to his contact with the organization certain expectations or desires concerning performance, and he measures the achievement of these expectations in making his evaluation. The irate customer, for example, is upset because a purchased article does not measure up to his expectations or because the article he wishes is not in stock. On the other hand, an employee of the organization is pleased about his job assignment or compensation. All approaches to evaluation follow this same general pattern in attempting to measure the achievement of specified objectives through the performance of the organization.

The process of evaluation of organization performance aids in

[30] See Peter F. Drucker, *The Practice of Management* (New York: Harper and Brothers, 1954), pp. 121-136.

achieving more effective direction and control of performance.[31] An evaluation can be conducted only after determination of the relevant objectives against which performance is to be evaluated. This determination and communication of organization objectives provides a unity of direction to efforts of the management team which is lacking without clearly specified objectives. Furthermore, periodic measurement of the achievement of objectives serves as a constant reminder of these goals and as a prod to improved effort in their achievement. The determination of criteria to be applied in the evaluation of organization performance is one of the most critical and most difficult steps in evaluation. It is important because the criteria chosen become directives for future action. Individuals responsible for the performance which is evaluated will direct their efforts to the achievement of satisfactory performance as defined by these criteria. Consequently, the criteria applied in evaluation should reflect accurately the primary performance objectives of the organization. The determination of acceptable criteria for evaluation is difficult because of problems in the definition of organization objectives and in the construction of measures which accurately reflect the achievement of these objectives.

Various criteria can be suggested for the evaluation of organization performance. We might, for example, evaluate performance of a business organization in terms of objectives of the owners, objectives of members of the organization, objectives of customers of the organization, or the general objectives held by society at large. Selection of any one of these sets of objectives does not significantly reduce the problem, however. Determination of ownership objectives might be relatively simple in the case of an individual owner, but determination of ownership objectives in the case of a publicly held corporation is impossible. Similar difficulties are faced if we attempt to specify the objectives of organization members, customers, or society. In a very real sense, the objectives of all of these interests are relevant and can be combined conceptually in a single over-all objective of organization survival. Achievement of the objectives of these various interests is required for the continuing survival of the organization. Survival can be measured only after the fact, however, and the concept of survival power is more relevant in the evaluation of a going concern. The determination of what constitutes survival

[31] See Ralph J. Cordiner, *New Frontiers for Professional Managers* (New York: McGraw-Hill Book Company, 1956).

power of an organization is a very real and basic question that deserves considerably more study than it has received. Some attempts have been made to determine objectives of those associated with business organizations and thus define the performance requisite for survival.[32] Considerably more study is needed, however, before we can specify the ingredients of survival power with any degree of assurance. Historical studies of successful and unsuccessful organizations would be helpful as a first step in the identification of general factors which have been important in the survival of organizations. Factors important to survival in the future are never exactly the same as those important in past survival, but the identification of general factors which have been important in different periods of the past would aid considerably in the identification of measures of survival power for the future.

Current practice in the evaluation of organization performance usually focuses attention upon specific performance considered necessary in the achievement of over-all organizational objectives.[33] Measures applied within the organization in the evaluation of component parts of the organization attempt to measure achievement of directives of the unit or the contribution of unit performance to over-all objectives. Such measures are relatively arbitrary and can be specified to direct performance as desired. For example, a procedure for the evaluation of depot performance within the Air Material Command periodically altered the criteria for evaluation and so directed attention at specific performances as considered necessary by superiors.[34] Measures for the evaluation of component organization units include turnover, absenteeism of employees, achievement of production and cost goals, backlog of unfilled requisitions, productivity, and

[32] See Bernard Bass, "Ultimate Criteria of Organizational Worth," *Personnel Psychology,* Vol. 5, 1952, pp. 157-173; Alvin Brown, "Judging the Effectiveness of Organization," *Advanced Management,* Vol. 20, No. 1, January, 1955, pp. 13-15; and Basil S. Georgopoulos and Arnold S. Tannenbaum, "A Study of Organizational Effectiveness," *American Sociological Review,* Vol. 22, No. 5, October, 1957, pp. 534-540.

[33] For examples see Fred H. Blum, "Social Audit of the Enterprise," *Harvard Business Review,* Vol. 36, No. 2, March-April 1958, pp. 77-86; Basil S. Georgopoulos and Arnold S. Tannenbaum, *op. cit.;* Rensis Likert, "Measuring Organizational Performance," *Harvard Business Review,* Vol. 36, No. 2, March-April 1958, pp. 41-50; Jackson Martindell, *The Scientific Appraisal of Management* (New York: Harper and Brothers, 1950), 278 pp.; and Marvin D. Dunnette, Dallis K. Perry, and Thomas A. Mahoney, *Criteria of Executive Effectiveness* (Air Force Personnel and Training Research Center, Lackland Air Force Base).

[34] See Marvin D. Dunnette *et al., op. cit.*

employee morale and attitudes. The range of possible criteria varies with the range of general objectives and directives of the units concerned. It is important in selecting these relatively specific performance criteria that the criteria actually measure performance which is controllable by those responsible. For example, productivity measures might be satisfactory as measures of desired objectives in a specific instance; but unless productivity can be influenced and controlled by the manager in charge of the performance, this evaluation serves little purpose in the direction of activity or in measuring the contribution of the manager. Rather, measurement of uncontrollable performance will tend to frustrate those responsible for the performance and direct their effort into fruitless attempts to control that performance. We shall return to discuss these problems of evaluation in somewhat more detail in Chapter 10.

SUMMARY

The structure of responsibilities within the management team has a direct influence upon the effectiveness of coordination of managerial performance, and most guides to performance are based upon considerations of the performance objectives of the enterprise. The organization structure is more than a guide to present performance, however. It also is an effective guide to development of the management team, and it directly influences this development whether intended or not. The organization structure shapes managerial recruiting efforts, it determines the abilities and experiences needed for effective managerial performance in the organization, and it controls the development of these abilities through the structure of managerial assignments. Considerations of long-run performance objectives dictate the need for shaping the organization structure for a guide to development of the management team as well as for a guide to present performance of this team.

SELECTED BIBLIOGRAPHY

Barnard, Chester, *The Functions of the Executive* (Cambridge, Massachusetts: Harvard University Press, 1946).

Dale, Ernest, *Planning and Developing the Company Organization Structure,* Research Report No. 20 (New York: American Management Association, 1952).

Drucker, Peter F., *The Practice of Management* (New York: Harper and Brothers, 1954).

Holden, Paul E., Lounsbury S. Fish, and Hulbert L. Smith, *Top-Management Organization and Control* (New York: McGraw-Hill Book Company, 1951).

Wasserman, Paul, *Measurement and Evaluation of Organizational Performance: An Annotated Bibliography* (Ithaca, New York: Graduate School of Business and Public Administration, Cornell University, 1959).

Chapter **FOUR**

The Functions of Management

INTRODUCTION

The study and analysis of the work of managing are relatively undeveloped. For many years managing was regarded as an art, a set of guides and principles developed by individual managers through their experience. The development of the professional manager concept discussed earlier has been accompanied by a growing interest in the study of management and its functions. The increasing concern over development of the management team also has contributed to the attention given to the analysis and definition of managing and the jobs of management. Attempts to develop individual managers into a strong management team assume that the practice of management is understood and can be taught, that there are principles and guides to managing which can be specified, and that experience alone is not the only method of acquiring the ability to manage. These attempts at management development also imply a statement of goals, a definition of what is involved in principles of good management; this definition is sought in studies of the functions of management. A knowledge of the jobs and functions of management is needed in management development. Effective coordination of the management team, recruitment, selection, and placement of individual managers, coaching, counseling, and training of subordinate managers, and appraisal and compensation of members of the management team, all require knowledge of the functions and responsibilities of management.

A number of rather basic questions concerning the nature of the functions and responsibilities of management arise in the design and operation of a plan for development of the management team. These questions include:

1. What are the functions of management?
2. How similar are the functions of management in manufacturing, retailing, government, and the military?
3. How similar are the functions of management in large and in small companies?
4. How similar are the responsibilities and functions of management positions at different levels in the structure of the management organization?
5. How unique are management positions?
6. Can we provide a common training and development process for all management positions, or must these be tailored for each position?

Few of these questions have been answered satisfactorily to date. We shall review the present state of knowledge concerning the functions of management and the course of study of these functions in this chapter.

APPROACHES TO THE STUDY OF MANAGEMENT FUNCTIONS

The term *management function* has become relatively standardized in management literature; it refers to activities or responsibilities which are characteristic of the general nature of managing and of management positions. Approaches to the study of these functions can be classified as theoretical or philosophical, and empirical in nature. The theoretical or philosophical approach involves the consideration of management responsibilities and duties in the abstract and the formation of general classifications of functions to encompass all of the duties generally characteristic of managing. This approach typically considers the entire management organization as the proper unit for study and does not distinguish among different positions within the organization. The theoretical approach has been applied in the development of very general overviews or philosophies of management as a single function common to all organized effort. The empirical approach, on the other hand, involves actual observation and study of the activities of managers in different positions of management. Individual managers are observed or are asked to describe their specific activities and responsibilities, and these descriptions then are used in the establishment of more general descriptions of managing. Both of these approaches are necessary in the study of management functions. The theoretical approach is useful in the establishment of a system of concepts to facilitate the collection and analysis of specific information, and the empirical approach for the testing of general theories and the determination of facts. Neither approach alone is sufficient to provide the required knowledge concerning the nature of managing and of the composition of management positions. Alone, the theoretical approach provides an untested system for classification of management responsibilities, and the empirical approach provides a number of unrelated descriptions of the activities and responsibilities of management positions. Together, they can provide a set of standardized and comparable descriptions of the functions performed in individual management positions that are useful in the understanding of different positions, as well as of the more general functions of the entire management team.

FUNCTIONS OF THE MANAGEMENT ORGANIZATION

The theoretical or philosophical approach is most common in the study of managing. Individual managers or students of management have been concerned with establishing order in the many activities of managing and with providing guides to managing. They have attempted to outline the general functions of management, thinking of the management organization as a whole rather than considering individual management positions. Those using this approach generally rely upon their experience in management or upon general observations of management in the development of their theories. Consequently, while there is some general agreement among the different philosophical descriptions of the functions of management, each emphasizes those activities and functions which appear most important to the writer, and there are numerous minor differences among the different theories. The concepts and ideas about the functions of management are constantly being rearranged by writers with slightly different approaches to management or with different experiences.

One of the early management theorists was Henri Fayol, a French industrialist of the late nineteenth and early twentieth centuries. Fayol was concerned with the existing lack of principles and guides for managing, and sought to provide a theory of managing with principles which might be employed in executive action.[1] He formulated a general order of functions and activities of industrial operations based upon his experiences in industry and government. Fayol identified six major areas of activity of the industrial organization, all required in successful performance: (1) technical or production activities, (2) commercial or trading activities, (3) financial activities, (4) security or protective activities, (5) accounting activities, and (6) managerial activities. Thus, Fayol identified a group of activities of the industrial organization as managerial in nature and a group of activities as necessary to the success of the enterprise, such as the production of goods and services. Fayol's primary concern was with the managing activities, and he continued his analysis in this area. Fayol reasoned that management was necessary for all undertakings involving the organization of activities and people. He felt that the elements or characteristics of managing were universal and applied to all instances of management. Managing was defined in terms of five functions or, as he called them, "elements" of management: (1) planning, (2) organizing, (3) commanding or directing, (4) coordinating, and (5) controlling. Fayol then specified 14 "principles of work" to serve as guides in the execution of these elements of managing: principles concerning the division of labor, organizations, authority and responsibility, the staffing of the organization, and the direction of individual efforts within the organization. Many of these principles and concepts are embodied today in our modern theories of organization and management. In fact, Fayol recognized many of the problems faced today in the development of managers and attempted to outline an approach for the selection, training, and development of managers. Fayol's contribution to the science of management lies in the attention he gave to the study of managing; he focused attention upon the need for both a general theory of managing and one concerned with principles for management action. His general theory and classifications of industrial and managerial

[1] Henri Fayol, *General and Industrial Administration* (London: Sir Isaac Pitman & Sons, Ltd., 1949), 110 pp.

activities provide little in the way of descriptions of actual managerial performance, although they do provide a method for classification of the performance.

The study of managing in the United States usually is traced to the early leaders of scientific management, F. W. Taylor and the Gilbreths.[2] These pioneers in the study of work were concerned primarily with the analysis of non-managerial operations and activities. Their main contribution to the science of management was the attention they focused upon the desirability of systematic study and analysis of work for the determination of principles and guides to action. The Gilbreths did, however, speculate about the general nature of work and industrial operations and established a general system for the classification of work. They identified 13 different processes of work involved in a complete industrial organization: (1) financing, (2) advertising, (3) marketing, (4) distributing, (5) selling, (6) accounting, (7) purchasing, (8) manufacturing, (9) planning, (10) teaching, (11) charting, (12) maintaining, and (13) filing. They did not specifically recognize management as a separate process or activity in this system, implying that managing is required for each of the processes and that managing activities might be classified under the same system of processes.

An English contemporary of the Gilbreths, Oliver Sheldon, also was concerned with the analysis of work and the establishment of a system for classification of activities.[3] Sheldon, an industrialist, was more concerned with management than were the Gilbreths, and his approach tended to follow that of Fayol in the establishment of a philosophy of management. Sheldon employed a very general system for classification of managerial activities, emphasizing broad, general types of activities or functions. He described management in terms of three general functions: (1) "administration," involving the establishment of corporate policy and the coordination of activities of the organization; (2) "management," or the execution of policy within limits established in the administrative function; and (3) "organization," as the formation of a machine of management for the execution of policy. In a sense, Sheldon was discussing three differ-

---

[2] Frank B. Gilbreth, "The Classification of Work," in *Proceedings of the Society of Industrial Engineers, 1924* (Chicago: A. O. Horn Company, 1924), pp. 105-109: and Frederick W. Taylor, *Scientific Management* (New York: Harper & Brothers, 1911), 287 pp.

[3] Oliver Sheldon, *The Philosophy of Management* (New York: Pitman Publishing Corp., 1923), 296 pp.

ent levels of activity and associating a different general function with each level, "administration" referring to the top-level direction of the enterprise, "management" referring to the general direction of activities in accordance with general policy directives, and "organization" referring to the activities undertaken in the staffing and direction of specific operations of the enterprise.

Students of government also have been concerned with the functions or activities of administration and management within the government. One of these, Luther Gulick, suggested a classification of activities into seven different functions of management, a classification which is quite similar to those suggested for industrial management functions.[4] Gulick and other students of management believe that the functions and principles of management are generally the same throughout organizations, whether they be industrial, service, military, or governmental. The seven functions identified by Gulick include (1) planning, or the outlining of things to be accomplished and the methods for accomplishment of them; (2) organizing, or the establishment of a formal structure of authority; (3) staffing, including the recruitment and training of a work force; (4) directing, or making decisions and giving orders; (5) coordinating and relating the various processes of work; (6) reporting and communicating with superiors and subordinates; and (7) budgeting, including fiscal planning, accounting, and control. Gulick's functions of management are quite similar to those of Fayol and, in fact, were based in large part upon an understanding of the work of Fayol, which was largely unknown in the United States prior to the 1930's. Gulick has added three functions—staffing, reporting, and budgeting—to the more general functions named by Fayol. These additions probably reflect in large part a different emphasis recognized by Gulick in his consideration of political and governmental processes.

Another American contributor to the developing science of management was Mary Parker Follett.[5] Follett's major contribution lies in her attempt to expand the concepts of scientific management to include managerial work. She argued that managers and executives could be trained for their positions, and that a first step in this training and development would be the study and analysis of managers'

---

[4] Luther Gulick, "Notes on the Theory of Organization," in *Papers on the Science of Administration,* Institute of Public Administration, 1937, pp. 1-45.

[5] See H. C. Metcalf and Lyndall Urwick (editors), *Dynamic Administration: The Collected Papers of Mary Parker Follett* (New York: Harper & Brothers, 1941), 314 pp.

jobs. She sought facts about the jobs of managers and their activities to replace the traditions, guesswork, prejudices, and stereotypes which characterized our knowledge of management. Her work offers little in the way of a systematic organization of management activities, although she offers many insights into the complexities of human relations involved in the management of an organization. Follett specifically identifies three rather broad and general functions of executives: (1) anticipating future events of interest to the organization, (2) formulation of the purpose of the enterprise, and (3) organization and coordination of activities within the enterprise. This identification of functions parallels the functions suggested by Sheldon. Probably the most relevant insight of Follett was the belief that management jobs could be studied and described, rather than in her suggestions about the content of management jobs.

A related contribution to knowledge and understanding of the work of management was provided by Chester Barnard in *The Functions of the Executive*.[6] Barnard's career as a business executive convinced him of the need for a comprehensive theory of management, for fundamental principles explaining management action and providing guides for the development and performance of managers. He was concerned with the development of a general theory of management rather than with the precise study and analysis of management positions advocated by Follett. Barnard drew upon his experiences in industry and the public service in formulating a theory of the work of the executive. His major concern was with the organization as an entity and the functions involved in successful achievement of organization objectives. Barnard views an organization as two or more people cooperating for the achievement of a common purpose. A successful organization requires the careful formulation of goals and purposes, the establishment of a system of communication and cooperation, and the recruitment and motivation of members of the organization. He identifies the work of the executive, or managing, as the establishment and maintenance of the organization or accomplishment of three major functions involved in building and maintaining an organization. In a sense, the work of managing is that of coordination, which is achieved through the establishment of common purposes, the establishment of an organization structure

---

[6] Chester I. Barnard, *The Functions of the Executive* (Cambridge, Massachusetts: Harvard University Press, 1947), 296 pp. Also see *Organization and Management* (Cambridge, Massachusetts: Harvard University Press, 1948), 244 pp., by the same author.

to facilitate cooperation and communication, and the recruitment and motivation of people to accomplish the work of the organization. Barnard discusses these different functions of managing, outlining problems and offering guides and insights drawn from his experience. The three functions of the executive suggested by Barnard are not new; they closely parallel the functions suggested by Follett and others. Rather, Barnard's contribution lies in the interest stimulated by his general theory and the specific insights and principles suggested in his discussion of these functions. He attempted to provide a general theory of management applicable to all management positions and a general framework for the analysis and study of individual management positions.

A more recent contribution which is somewhat similar to Barnard's was made by Herbert Simon.[7] Simon also is concerned with the role of the manager in the organization. He analyzes the behavior of organizations and finds that the role of management or administration is essentially that of organizing and allocating responsibilities among members of the organization and facilitating communication among positions in the organization. Simon's theory also is essentially a theory of organization with a consideration of the role of administration in the conduct of an organization rather than a theory of management performance. He also attempts the development of a general theory rather than an analysis of specific responsibilities and functions of management positions.

The theories already discussed are essentially individual contributions. They represent the ideas of individual observers. Although these theories were influenced in many instances by the concepts and ideas of others, each theory was intended as an individual contribution rather than as an attempt to synthesize earlier observations. The nature of this development explains the conflicting and overlapping functional classifications of the work of managing. A masterful attempt to synthesize the thinking and concepts of earlier writers on management has been performed by Col. Lyndall Urwick. Urwick has attempted to combine the functional classifications of others and to eliminate the seeming conflict of definitions.[8] He has

[7] See Herbert Simon, *Administrative Behavior* (New York: The Macmillan Company, 1950), 253 pp.

[8] Lyndall F. Urwick, *The Pattern of Management* (Minneapolis: University of Minnesota Press, 1956), 90 pp.; also see *Leadership in the 20th Century* (New York: Pitman Publishing Corporation, 1957), 85 pp., by the same author.

taken the concepts of Taylor, Fayol, Follett, and Mooney and Reilley and combined them into a single system for classification of managerial activities. Urwick points up for the first time the distinction between functions of the management organization as a whole and functions of individual management positions. He recognizes that functions of the management organization need not be performed by each member of the management. Rather, he maintains, they may be allocated among individual management positions in a number of combinations. The functions of the management organization include: (1) forecasting events concerning the organization, (2) making plans for the accomplishment of objectives, (3) organizing responsibilities into individual positions, (4) directing and motivating performance, (5) coordinating the efforts of organization members, (6) controlling the performance of individual members, and (7) the general function of communication involved in the performance of each of the other functions. He recognizes that responsibility for performance of these functions for the whole organization may be assigned to individual management positions in varying combinations of responsibilities. Hence, not all managers need share these general functions in equal degrees. Urwick does identify four functions of leadership, however, which he feels are found in every management position. The individual manager, according to Urwick, must: (1) represent and embody the organization unit to members of the unit as well as to outside people, (2) initiate whatever measures are necessary for the continued healthy life of the organization, (3) administer the functions of the management organization within his unit by arranging for their performance and by imposing order in their performance, and (4) interpret reasons for actions as a means of providing enthusiasm and motivation. In so far as each manager is responsible for a unit of the large organization, he will be responsible for the general management functions within his unit as a part of his administration or management function. Although his approach is largely philosophical, Urwick contributed to the development of a more specific system of definition and classification of management functions through his analysis and synthesis of earlier concepts. His recognition of the distinction between functions of the management organization and functions of individual managers also contributes to a more realistic description of the work of managing.

More recent writers show little tendency to agree on a consistent set of definitions of the functions of management.[9] Although these writers usually define from four to six functions, they disagree with each other in the definition of functions and on the specific activities which are included under each. There also is frequent overlapping of definitions within the set of functions identified by any single writer resulting from hazy and indefinite descriptions of the functions. Definitions of functions vary considerably among writers, although the titles of functions imply similarity in treatment of the work of management. In general, these writers are agreed that responsibilities of the management organization include the establishment of an organization structure, with the assignment of responsibilities and the delegation of authority to individual positions; the establishment of objectives for the entire organization and directives for units within the organization; recruitment, staffing, training, and motivation of organization members; and control of activities and operations through a system of checks and evaluation. They differ in the functional classification of these activities and the emphasis to be given to each.

One empirical study of the functions of the management organization stands out among the many philosophical approaches to the subject.[10] Top management personnel in 31 industrial enterprises were interviewed in an attempt to determine the activities and functions of the management organization. Three separate "zones" of management were identified by the authors of this study—the trusteeship function, the general management or administrative function, and the divisional or departmental function. The trusteeship function is identified with the boards of directors and includes the general responsibility for insuring that effective use is made of the company's assets. The general management function includes functions of the management organization as a whole. The major responsibilities identified within the general management function include the planning and clarification of objectives of the organization,

[9] For example, see Ralph C. Davis, *The Fundamentals of Top Management* (New York: Harper & Brothers, 1951), 810 pp.; Harold Koontz and Cyril O'Donnell, *Principles of Management* (New York: McGraw-Hill Book Company, 1955), 652 pp.; William H. Newman, *Administrative Action* (Englewood Cliffs, N. J.: Prentice-Hall, Inc., 1951), 468 pp.; and Robert Tannenbaum, "The Manager Concept: A Rational Synthesis," *The Journal of Business,* Vol. 22, 1949, pp. 225-241.

[10] See Paul E. Holden, Lounsbury S. Fish, and Hubert L. Smith, *Top Management Organization and Control* (New York: McGraw-Hill Book Company, 1951), 253 pp.

the establishment of a sound plan of organization, the provision of fully qualified people for all key positions, and the establishment and maintenance of effective means of control of the business as a whole. The divisional or departmental function concerns the execution of policies and practices.

The general theoretical or philosophical approach to most of the early study of management and the work of managing was necessary as a first step. This theoretical analysis has provided a general outline of the activities of managing and a general functional classification which is useful in focusing attention upon these activities in the study of managing. A changed approach to the study of management would be useful at this time, however. Further classification and argument over the definitions of functional classes serve little purpose at this point. Rather, what is needed is more precise information about the actual activities and performance of managers. A shift in focus from the general functions of management to the actual practice of management and the activities of various management positions is indicated as the most profitable area for future study.

FUNCTIONS OF THE MANAGER

The preceding section considered the general functions of managing an organization—the functions that must be performed by the management team of the organization. It also was noted earlier that it is not necessary for every management position to perform these functions; it is sufficient that they are performed, whether by one manager or by all. It is possible that one or several managers bear the responsibility for staffing the entire organization, and that other managers carry the responsibility for planning the organization. The functions of the management organization indicate what managers might be expected to perform, not what they necessarily are expected to perform individually. These descriptions of general functions of the management organization are of little specific value in the establishment of management development goals, or in the selection, appraisal, and compensation of individual managers. We must discover how the responsibility for these functions is allocated among the management positions. While it is possible that all management positions carry responsibility for performance of each of the general management functions, it is equally possible that the degree of responsibility for various functions varies among positions, some positions carrying a high degree of responsibility for one function and little or no responsibility for others.

One source of information about individual management position responsibilities is the position description provided in company organization manuals or defined for management compensation purposes. An example of the former is the *Management Guide* of the Standard Oil Company of California.[11] Management position descriptions are not common, however, even in some of the largest corporations. There is a hesitancy among managers to commit to writing the authority and responsibility delegated to a subordinate manager. Many managers feel that "the man makes the job" and hesitate to accept descriptions of their own assignments or to provide position descriptions for their subordinates' positions. Furthermore, management position descriptions, where available, usually are of little value in understanding or comparing different positions, particularly among different organizations. Many of these descriptions contain only a broad general statement of the scope of authority and responsibility of the position; others contain long, detailed lists of specific responsibilities. Such descriptions may be quite adequate when understood in the context of the organization structure and company policy and objectives, but they provide little help in understanding the content of managers' positions. Management position titles are even less meaningful for a study of the work of managing or in grouping similar management positions. Two positions with the same title in one organization often involve quite different responsibilities and authority. Titles are even less meaningful in the comparison of positions in different organizations.

Executives throughout industry have in recent years become interested in defining the functions of management and in determining the qualifications necessary for management. This interest is shown in the articles and speeches of executives describing their concepts of the work of managing. *Fortune* magazine asked a number of executives the question, "Who is an executive?" in the search for a definition

[11] Also see C. L. Bennet, *Defining the Manager's Job, The AMA Manual of Positive Descriptions,* Research Study No. 33 (New York: American Management Association, 1958), 437 pp.

of the work of managing and the qualifications for management.[12] Answers to this survey provide descriptions of the executive's work as seen by the executive. The action and behavior described in answers suggested that five general functions were common to the work of the executives surveyed. These functions were (1) participation in the establishment of over-all goals and policies, (2) making decisions that significantly affect profits, (3) coordination of several major corporate functions, (4) development and maintenance of an organization of subordinates, and (5) delegation of authority and responsibility. The survey concludes that all management positions involve performance of these general functions and that the primary difference between the executive and subordinate managers is one of degree—the executive's responsibility in each function is broader than that of his subordinates. Other descriptions of the top management functions by company presidents and others tend to support the conclusions of this *Fortune* survey.[13] They generally state that the top executive of the organization is responsible for the broad, general functions of the management organization—the establishment of goals, the development of an organization, and the staffing and motivation of subordinates. This is not surprising, however, since the president or chief executive is at the top of the management organization and might be expected to view the functions of the management organization as the responsibilities of his own position. It is unlikely, though, that subordinate managers share the concern and responsibility of the chief executive for these general management functions.

Several attempts have been made to obtain more objective information about the work of managing and the duties of management positions than is provided in the general descriptions by managers. One technique which has been employed in these studies seeks to identify those actions which are critical to successful per-

---

[12] Perrin Stryker, "Who Is an Executive?" *Fortune,* Vol. 52, No. 6, December, 1955, pp. 107-109, 228-232.

[13] For example, see Peter F. Drucker, "Chief Executive and Board," *Dun's Review and Modern Industry,* July 1954, pp. 33-34 ff.; Benjamin F. Fairless and others, "What Should a President Do?" *Dun's Review,* July 1951, pp. 13-15 ff.; Herman W. Steinkraus and others, "What Should a President Do?" *Dun's Review,* August 1951, pp. 21 ff.; Morris G. Fuller and others, "Assuring the Company's Future: What the Chief Executive Should Be Doing Today," *General Management Series No. 175* (New York: American Management Association, 1955); and C. R. Hook, "For Executives Only: A Look at the Man Himself," *Management Record,* Vol. 14, No. 5, May 1952, pp. 170-172.

formance of responsibilities of the position.[14] Applying this technique to one specific job, superiors, incumbents, and subordinates of the job are asked to describe the incidents which have characterized the best and the poorest performance of managers they have observed in the job. These incidents are grouped into broad categories and tabulated, those categories with the largest number of incidents being identified as the "critical incidents" of the job which are demanded for successful job performance.

The application of this technique in the study of two groups of managers, officers of the USAF and research executives, revealed that, while the critical requirements of the two jobs have much in common, there are noticeable differences between the jobs.[15] The categories of incidents discovered in these studies concern (1) handling administrative details, (2) supervision, (3) planning and direction, (4) acceptance of organization responsibility, (5) acceptance of personal responsibility, and (6) proficiency in a specialty. Supervision appeared most critical as a job requirement for the research executives, while planning and directing were most critical for the USAF officers. These findings suggest that the critical elements of performance vary from one managerial job to another despite similarities in general managerial responsibilities. The critical-incidents approach to managerial job description provides little information about the over-all structure of managerial jobs, however, although it is useful in isolating critical elements of managerial performance. Knowledge of both over-all and critical managerial job requirements is necessary for most activities of management development. For example, planning of objectives and work scheduling may be common to all managerial assignments and may occupy a large portion of the manager's time. However, performance of these responsibilities might appear critical to successful performance of only a portion of managerial positions. The critical-incidents approach, while helpful and useful in developing an understanding of managerial job requirements, does not provide the over-all description of the manager's job necessary for management development.

There has been little objective study made of the work of the man-

---

[14] See John C. Flanagan, "Defining the Requirements of the Executive's Job," *Personnel*, Vol. 28, No. 1, July 1951, pp. 28-35, for a description of the critical-incidents technique and its application.

[15] *Ibid.*

ager. Among those that have been made, there is a lack of comparability, as well as shortcomings in individual studies. Nevertheless, most of the few studies available provide information and insights useful in understanding the work of managing. One area of study has concerned the work of foremen in industrial plants.[16] Information in these studies has been collected through self-descriptions of performance and through the use of job analysis. These studies indicate that a major proportion of the foreman's activity concerns other people—superiors, peers, and subordinates—and involves close contact with them. His job is marked by a constant pressure of operations in his organization unit, pressures that call for spending a large amount of time concerned with the operation and maintenance of machinery. Most foremen also spend some time in the actual operation of machinery, although the most effective foremen tend to spend least time operating machinery. Relatively little of the foreman's activity can be classed as administrative, that is, in the sense of planning and organizing activities under his direction. Rather, the foreman's job is characterized by a concern for the work being performed in his unit of the organization.

Similar studies of the performance of higher-level managers reveal certain general and expected differences when compared with the performance of foremen.[17] The amount of time spent at work tends to increase with the level of the manager in the organization, company presidents and major executives spending an average of 54 hours a week. Much of this time also is spent in contact with others, either in conferences, phone conversations, or direct discussions. The higher-level managers spend relatively more time on administrative work—the planning and organizing functions—and they spend less time in performing the work of the organization. These higher-level managers also tend to spend more time reading, both at the office and at home, than do the foremen. The higher-level managers spend an average of six hours a week in

---

[16] See U. S. Army, Adjutant General's Office, Personnel Research and Proceedures Branch, "Activities and Behaviors of Production Supervisors," *Report 946* (Washington, D.C., April, 1952); Robert H. Guest, "Of Time and the Foreman," *Personnel,* Vol. 32, No. 6, May, 1956, pp. 478-486; and Frank J. Jasinske, "Foreman Relationships Outside the Work Group," *Personnel,* Vol. 33, No. 2, September 1956, pp. 130-136.

[17] See "How To Succeed," *Business Week,* April 9, 1955, p. 128; Lydia Strong, "Of Time and Top Management," *The Management Review,* Vol. 45, No. 6, June, 1956, pp. 486-493; and "The Management Poll," *Fortune,* Vol. 34, No. 4, October, 1946, pp. 5-6 ff.

reading reports and business literature. A study of the behavior of city managers reports results similar to those found for the higher-level business managers, city managers spending an average of 54 hours a week at their work, most of this time spent in talking with citizens, subordinates, and public groups.[18]

A Swedish economist, Sune Carlson, conducted a small study of the behavior and action of executives in an attempt to replace the theorizing and speculation about the functions of the executive with actual descriptions of the work.[19] Nine managing directors of Swedish companies cooperated with Carlson in maintaining logs of their activities for a four-week period. The information obtained in the study was relatively objective and provides some new insights into the manner in which top executives perform their responsibilities for the organization. Carlson's most interesting findings concern the conditions surrounding management performance. He found that the executives spend an average of almost ten hours a day in their jobs, most of this time spent in conferences. These executives spent relatively little time alone, and even this small amount of time was so punctuated with interruptions that the average length of time periods when the executive was alone was 14 minutes; even this period was broken frequently by phone calls. The general picture of the executive emerging from this study is that of a man who spends his entire day communicating with others, usually to obtain information. One interesting observation in the study indicates that very little time is formally scheduled for meetings or communications with subordinates of the executive; much of his contact with subordinates occurs through committee meetings where they are present or in *ad hoc* accidental meetings. Carlson's study tells us more about *how* the executive accomplishes his objectives than it does about the functions and responsibilities of the executive. The study suffers from the limitations of many studies of the time patterns of managers in that attention is focused upon observable behavior and in that it does not attempt to measure the purpose or objective of this behavior.

The studies reported above are of relatively little aid in answering the questions posed at the beginning of this discussion—what is the work of managing, and what are the differences and simi-

---

[18] See "Safeguarding Managerial Time," *Public Management*, Vol. 23, September 1941, pp. 259-264.

[19] Sune Carlson, *Executive Behavior* (Stockholm: Strombergs, 1951).

larities of the work of managers in different organizations, levels, and positions of management? Several of these studies have provided insights into the manner in which managers act in the performance of their work, but they add little to our knowledge of the actual work of the manager. The most comprehensive studies of the work of managing and the differences and similarities of management positions have been performed at the Ohio State University and at the University of Minnesota. Each of these studies is examined in some detail below.

Ohio State Leadership Studies

The Ohio State leadership studies represent years of intensive study of leadership performance in naval situations.[20] Despite obvious differences between situations of naval leadership and business management, many of the findings of these studies carry implications concerning the work of business management. The techniques and methods developed in these studies also are applicable in the study of business management and promise the start of intensive study of the work of business management.

The Ohio State researchers began with the premise that leadership performance is influenced by the requirements of the situation as well as by the characteristics of the individual leader. They hypothesized that the situation is of more influence than are the characteristics of the leader. They then sought to measure leadership performance in a number of different situations and to compare the differences in performance associated with differences in the situation and with differences in characteristics of the leader. Most of their studies were conducted with naval officers and concern performance in positions of naval leadership. The basic problem investigated here is quite similar, however, to one of the questions posed earlier concerning management—what are the different performances called for in management positions?

Shartle and his associates at Ohio State focused attention upon several different aspects of the work situation and officer performance in their description of leadership performance or what they called "administrative performance." In general, they described the status of the officer and of the position within the organization,

[20] Ralph M. Stogdill and Carroll L. Shartle, *Methods in the Study of Administrative Leadership,* Business Research Monograph No. 80 (Columbus, Ohio: The Ohio State University, Bureau of Business Research, 1955).

time spent by the officer in various responsibilities or functions, and behavior of the officer toward his subordinates. Forty-six different specific measures were used in the description of these various aspects of performance and the position.

The performance of 470 different naval officers in various installations was described using these measures. Performance descriptions of "all officers having the same assignment in the same type of organization" were grouped together and averaged as a single pattern of performance for that specific position. The specialty assignments of the officers were used in this grouping of officers; the researchers apparently felt that position titles and classifications within the Navy were reliable enough to consider these positions as involving the same responsibilities. This averaging was performed to eliminate differences in performance due to minor differences in the positions and differences among the officers and thus provide a single characteristic measure of performance within the specialty. One hundred and twenty groups of positions, each with an average performance pattern, resulted from the grouping and formed the basic information for the study.

Results of the analysis of the 120 performance patterns indicate that these patterns represent variations of eight basic patterns of performance, each of the eight basic types being characterized by certain performances. It is concluded from this that the administrative performance characteristic of positions of naval officership varies with differences in the specialty assignment and in the organization unit of assignment.

The differences in performance patterns among officers in the same assignment were compared with differences among different specialty assignments and organization assignments. It was found that the differences among specialty assignments were largest, indicating that the situation is a relatively more important determinant of administrative performance than is the individual.

Another of the Ohio State studies followed a number of officers through several assignments, noting changes in administrative performance associated with changes of assignment. The researchers attempted to predict the performance patterns of officers in new assignments from a study of their performance patterns in previous assignments and a study of the performance patterns of the previous incumbents of newly assigned positions. Results of the study were inconclusive, although the authors of the study express the beliefs that officers attempt to carry their individual patterns of performance with them into new assignments and that consideration of these patterns and the performance patterns associated with various positions might improve the assignment of officers in the Navy. In short, individuals can be characterized by the patterns of performance which they attempt to impose upon their assignments. Assignments of managers should match these individual patterns with structured job requirements.

Certain reservations concerning the application of these findings and the application of techniques used in these studies to business management must be mentioned. First, the obvious differences between naval and business environment must be considered. The naval environment is highly structured, whereas the business management environment is quite flexible in certain respects. Consider, for example, the grouping of positions on the basis of specialty title and organization. Shartle and his associates apparently felt that naval position responsibilities were sufficiently structured and known to warrant this grouping; they were not studying the responsibilities of the position, but the performance of the position incumbent. The use of job titles in industry for the grouping of similar positions would result in a hodge-podge of responsibilities. Little is known about responsibilities of various positions of business management, and titles certainly are not standardized. Rather, titles reflect individual preferences, tradition, prejudice, and considerations of prestige instead of responsibility of the position.

Another reservation must be expressed concerning the measures of administrative performance employed in these studies. Examination of the 46 measures used indicates that certain of them measured aspects of the position other than performance level of the position in the organization, for example. Some concern the responsibilities or functions of the position, others describe methods employed by the officers in performance of the responsibilities, and still others concern attitudes of the incumbents toward delegation of authority and responsibility. The combination of all of these measures into a single pattern confuses performance, attitudes, and position characteristics. The direct application of these measures in the study of the nature and requirements of management positions does not appear desirable because of the overlapping and confusing mixture of position, attitude, and performance measures.

Certain of the performance measures do suggest an approach to the study of management positions, however. These are the measures of officer allocation of time among different areas of responsibility or different functions. Fourteen categories of responsibility were defined in the Ohio State research as administrative functions which cut across all positions of leadership. These categories are defined as: [21]

Inspection of the Organization—Direct observation and personal inspection of installations, building, equipment, facilities, operations, services, or personnel—for the purpose of determining conditions and keeping informed.

Investigation and Research—Acts involving the accumulation and preparation of written information and data. Usually prepared and presented in the form of written papers.

Planning—Preparing for and making decisions which will affect the aims or future activities of the organization as to volume or quality of business or service. Including thinking, and reading, as well as consultations and conferences.

Preparation of Procedures and Methods—Acts involving the mapping of procedures and methods for putting new plans into effect, as well as devising new methods for the performance of operations under existing plans.

Coordination—Acts and decisions designed to integrate and coordinate the activities of units within the organization or of persons within units so as to achieve the maximal over-all efficiency, economy, and control of operations.

Evaluation—Acts involving the consideration and evaluation of reports, correspondence, data, plans, decisions, or performances in relation to the aims, policies, and standards of the organization.

Interpretation of Plans and Procedures—Acts involving the interpretation and clarification for assistants and other personnel of directives, regulations, practices, and procedures.

Supervision of Technical Operations—Acts involving the direct supervision of personnel in the performance of duties.

Personnel Activities—Acts involving the selection, training, evaluation, motivation, or disciplining of individuals, as well as acts

[21] Ralph M. Stogdill and Carroll L. Shartle, *Methods in the Study of Administrative Leadership,* Business Research Monograph No. 80 (Columbus, Ohio: The Ohio State University, Bureau of Business Research, 1955), pp. 52-53.

designed to affect the morale, motivation, loyalty, or harmonious cooperation of personnel.

Public Relations—Acts designed to inform outside persons regarding the program and functions of the organization, to obtain information regarding public sentiment, or to create a favorable attitude toward the organization.

Professional Consultation—Giving professional advice and specialized assistance on problems of a specific or technical nature to persons within or outside the organization.

Negotiations—Purchasing, selling, negotiating contracts or agreements, settling claims, and so forth.

Scheduling, Routing, and Dispatching—Initiating action and determining the time, place, and sequence of operations.

Technical and Professional Operations—The performance of duties specific to a specialized profession.

Checks upon the allocations of time provided by officers indicate relatively satisfactory reliability of the measures and relatively satisfactory agreement of the estimated allocations with logs of time spent in the areas of responsibility. Results of the Ohio State research suggest the possibility of applying a similar type of measure to the study of responsibilities of management positions. Such a study would appear to provide more meaningful information than is obtained in measures of time spent in physical activity and continued speculation about the responsibilities and functions of managers.

In summary, results of the Ohio State studies cannot be applied directly in answering questions about managing and management positions. They do suggest certain avenues of approach to the study of management, however. They suggest that management positions can be described and measured in a meaningful manner. They also imply that there are differences among the jobs of management, that different responsibilities and functions are emphasized in different jobs, or that managing is not a single, general function. At the same time, the Ohio State studies suggest that management positions can be grouped into jobs with common characteristics and responsibilities. The identification of these groups and the description of their responsibilities or functions would go a long way toward answering the basic questions involved in management development. This would permit the development of techniques for management development which are based upon sound understanding of the goals of development which must include improved performance of the functions of management.

University of Minnesota Studies of Management Development

Studies of management development at the University of Minnesota's Industrial Relations Center, like the Ohio State studies, include investigations of managers' jobs. These studies parallel the Ohio State studies in several respects, although there are important differences in approach. The Minnesota studies, for example, concern the positions of managers in private business and industry which are not so structured as positions of naval leadership. Further, the Minnesota studies investigate methods of grouping positions into common managerial job types, while the Ohio State studies began with common job types and investigated differences of responsibilities, attitudes, and organizational structure associated with these job types. The Minnesota studies investigate the questions "What are the responsibilities of managers' positions?" and "What position similarities, important for management development, exist among these positions?"

The approach to managerial position analysis and description developed at Minnesota is similar to that of the Ohio State studies. Management positions are analyzed and described in terms of the relative proportion of time spent in performance of various functional classifications of management responsibilities. Eight functional categories of managerial responsibility are defined in the Minnesota approach to management position analysis. This functional classification encompasses all of the responsibilities performed by the management organization, and thus includes the responsibilities performed by any member of the organization. These functions include:

Planning—Determining goals, policies, and courses of action. Work scheduling, budgeting, setting up procedures, setting goals or standards, preparing agendas, programming.

Investigating—Collecting and preparing information, usually in the form of records, reports, and accounts. Inventorying, measuring output, preparing financial statements, record keeping, performing research, job analysis.

Coordinating—Exchanging information with people in the organization other than subordinates in order to relate and adjust programs. Advising other departments, expediting, liaison with other managers, arranging meetings, informing superiors, seeking other departments' cooperation.

Evaluating—Assessment and appraisal of proposals or of reported or observed performance. Employee appraisals, judging output reports, judging financial reports, product inspection, approving requests, judging proposals and suggestions.

Supervising—Directing, leading, and developing subordinates. Consulting subordinates, training subordinates, explaining work rules, assigning work, disciplining, handling complaints of subordinates.

Staffing—Maintaining the work force of one or more units. College recruiting, employment interviewing, selecting employees, placing employees, promoting employees, transferring employees.

Negotiating—Purchasing, selling, or contracting for goods and services. Tax negotiations, contacting suppliers, dealing with sales representatives, advertising products, collective bargaining, selling to dealers or customers.

Representing—Advancing the general interests of the organization through speeches, consultation, and contacts with individuals or groups outside of the organization. Public speeches, community drives, news releases, attending conventions, business association meetings.

Any functional classification of managerial responsibilities is arbitrary and might be defined to include any number of functions. The eight-function classification of the Minnesota studies was chosen as fulfilling the criteria of logic and practicality. Since managers are asked to analyze and classify their job activities into the functions employed in the analysis, it is necessary to select a classification which is sharp and clear, which includes all possible activities, and which is not so detailed that managers have a difficult time apportioning their time among the functions. Several functional classifications were prepared and tested in the analysis of managerial positions. In general, classifications with relatively few functions were difficult to use because of problems of definition and of distinguishing among them. They also tended to cover up differences of time allocation which appeared in more refined allocations.

Classifications with a large number of functions also were discarded because of the difficulty of estimating reliably the relatively small amounts of time spent in each function. Managers using the eight-function classification appeared to encounter least trouble with this classification and are able to provide reliable estimates of the time spent in each function. Furthermore, managers applying this approach report that the classification "makes sense," an important criterion in the selection of an approach to be used widely.

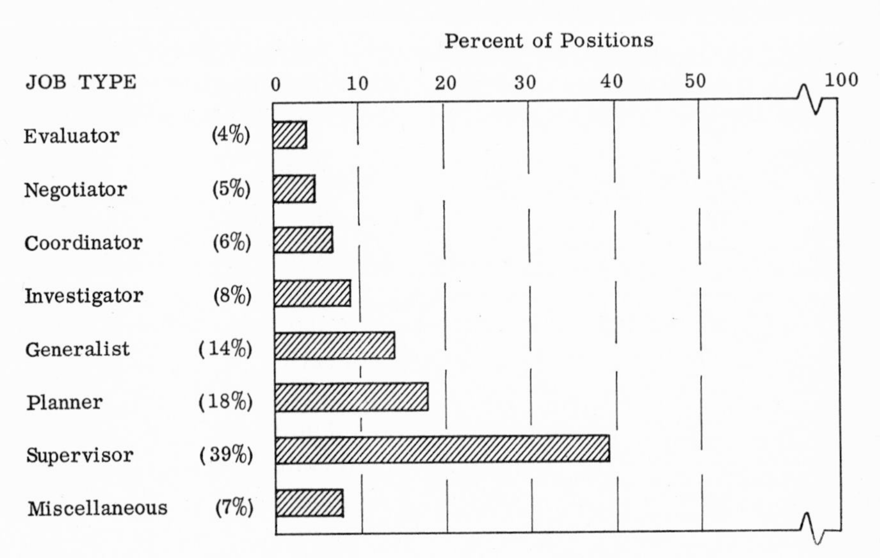

Fig. 5. Distribution of Management Positions among Major Job Types. ($N =$ 348.)

Manager position descriptions obtained in the Minnesota studies are compared and grouped on the basis of similarity of profiles of time allocation among the eight functions. One analysis of almost 350 position descriptions obtained from managers in different company-size groupings, industries, and levels of the organization indicates that a majority of positions involve a relative concentration of time in any one of six of the eight functions. Seventy-nine per cent of these positions involve a concentration of time in planning, investigating, coordinating, evaluating, supervising, or negotiating. An additional 14 per cent of the positions are "generalist" positions involving approximately equal proportions of time in most of the functions. Figure 5 shows the distribution of positions among these job types. The largest single job group includes positions with a relative concentration of time in the supervising function; none of the positions in this sample involves a concentration of time in the representing function.

Use of this relatively simple method for the classification of management positions into basic job types assumes that the resulting job types are relevant to management development. The identification of different job types on the basis of time allocation among managerial functions assumes that the distinction among time patterns is relevant to the selection, placement, compensation, and training of managers. The probable relevance of this classification is suggested through a further analysis of the positions in this sample. Managers were asked to rank the relative contribution of responsibilities in each function to effective performance of the over-all position responsibilities; this ranking is correlated closely with the allocation of time, the greatest time being spent in performance of the most important functions. Thus, the fact that most time is spent in performance of responsibilities of a given function and that this performance is judged most important in over-all effective performance suggests that selection and training requirements for job types might vary. Furthermore, the level in the management organization where the job type is likely to be found and the amount of compensation paid positions within the job type vary considerably among job types. Evaluating and generalist positions are likely to be found at higher levels in the management organizations, and investigator and supervisor at lower levels. Table 1 indicates the ranking of job types on the basis of average

Table 1

RANKING OF MANAGEMENT JOB TYPES ON THE BASIS OF

Organization Level	*Salary*
1. Evaluator	1. Evaluator
2. Generalist	2. Coordinator
3. Coordinator	3. Generalist
4. Planner	4. Negotiator
5. Negotiator	5. Planner
6. Supervisor	6. Investigator
7. Investigator	7. Supervisor

level of positions and average salary of positions classed within the job type. Salary and organization level of the job types appear closely correlated in this sample. Further analyses are under way to determine the association of personal characteristics with the different job types, and the background and training associated with the different job types. Differences found in these analyses will indicate the relevance of these job types for management development and will indicate the importance of distinguishing among these job types in the selection, placement, compensation, and training of managers. Further studies will be required to determine the difficulties encountered by managers transferring from one job type to another, as well as the requirements common to all management job types.

SUMMARY

An understanding of the functions of management and the patterns of responsibility for these functions assigned to management positions is vital to all aspects of management development. Systematic study and analysis of the functions performed in management assignments have been undertaken only recently, and we know relatively little about the similarities and differences of managerial assignments or the personal characteristics and training necessary for effective performance of these assignments. Results of recent studies of managers in business and military organizations indicate that the following functions are found in an analysis of managerial positions:

Planning. Determining goals, policies, and courses of action; work scheduling and routing; budgeting; preparation of procedures and methods; programming.

Investigating. Collecting and preparing information, usually in the form of records, reports, and accounts; research.

Coordinating. Exchanging information, consulting, and advising others in the integration of activities and programs.

Evaluating. Inspection, assessment, and appraisal of proposals, performance, activities, and operations of the organization.

Supervising. Directing, leading, and developing subordinates; interpreting plans and procedures.

Staffing. Maintenance of a work force through recruitment, selection, placement, promotion, and transfer of employees.

Negotiating. Purchasing, selling, or contracting for goods and services; settling claims.

Representing. Advancing the general interests of the organization through compacts with individuals and groups outside the organization.

Technical and Professional. Performance of non-managerial duties specific to a specialized type of work.

Every managerial assignment involves some combination of these functions, and recent studies suggest that relatively similar combinations of these functions are found among managerial assignments. In short, managerial assignments can be grouped into job types. There are important differences in performance required of different job types, although the performance required within each job type is common to all. These studies suggest that the scope and nature of problems of development of the managerial team are larger and more complex than commonly realized. For example, it is suggested that effective development of the management team will involve greater consideration of the differences among managerial assignments and the grouping of assignments into job types for the purposes of selection, training, placement, appraisal, and compensation. It appears that the key to effective development of the management team combines an improved understanding of managerial functions and the relating of development activities to these functions.

SELECTED BIBLIOGRAPHY

Barnard, Chester, *The Functions of the Executive* (Cambridge, Massachusetts: Harvard University Press, 1947).

Carlson, Sune, *Executive Behavior* (Stockholm: Strombergs, 1951).

Fayol, Henri, *General and Industrial Administration* (London: Sir Isaac Pitman and Sons, 1949).

Simon, Herbert A., *Administrative Behavior* (New York: The Macmillan Company, 1950).

Urwick, Lyndall F., *The Pattern of Management* (Minneapolis: University of Minnesota Press, 1956).

———, *Leadership in the 20th Century* (New York: Pitman Publishing Corporation, 1957).

Chapter **FIVE**

Management Appraisal and Inventory

INTRODUCTION

Planning for management development begins with the definition of general goals and objectives and proceeds to the identification of more specific operating targets. The general objective of improved utilization of existing management resources and improved development of adequate resources for the future must be translated into fairly specific goals of management development activities. These more specific objectives are implied in the structure of the management organization; the number of personnel required is indicated in the number of manager positions, and the various skills and performances required are indicated in the manager position descriptions. Organization analysis and planning provides this statement of management development objectives.

Management-development planning rarely occurs in an unstaffed organization. The more common situation involves planning for the improved utilization and development of managers within an operating organization. Therefore, planning for management development must take account of the existing staff of managers and their capabilities as well as the goals implied in the organization structure. Development planning in this instance aims at the maximum development and utilization of the existing staff in filling the needs of the organization, as well as possible recruitment, development, and utilization of additional staff members. The adequacy of existing resources and their utilization within the organization must be constantly examined in an effective program of management development. This periodic examination is required to assure maximum utilization in the planned adapting to shifting objectives as the organization changes and in the evaluation of management-development activities.

The measurement and evaluation of individual managers and the appropriateness of their assignments are an established responsibility of managers. The performance of this evaluation has always been necessary in the making of decisions concerning management personnel actions such as assignment, promotion, and salary determination. Although necessary, these evaluations have not always been so accurate or reliable as they might have been. The need for accurate and reliable measurement and evaluation of managers and their assignments for management-development planning has resulted in the formalization and improvement of measurement and evaluation techniques. Formalized techniques of management appraisal and inventory are recognized as necessary in management-development planning, as are aids for specific development activities and management personnel actions.

The term "management appraisal" is applied to the measurement of the individual manager, his adequacy in the present assignment, and his potential for improvement in this or other assignments. Comparison of existing skill levels of individual managers with requirements of individual positions provides a basis for decisions concerning the most effective utilization of individual managers; comparison of their appraised potentials and position requirements provides a basis for individual development planning.

The term "management inventory" is applied to the auditing of the entire management staff, accomplished through a summation of individual management appraisals. This inventory serves the same functions in the planning for development and utilization of the entire staff as the appraisal serves in the consideration of the individual manager. All individual appraisals are considered in the planning of individual assignments and individual development for maximum long-range utilization of the management staff. The appraisal and the inventory serve essentially the same purposes of management development at different levels of consideration—one at the level of the individual manager and his position, and the other at the level of the entire management team and organization.

The management appraisal and inventory are multi-purpose techniques useful in various aspects of management development. As pointed out above, they are necessary in the planning for development and utilization of the management staff and the individual manager. Comparison of successive applications of these techniques provides an evaluation of progress in management development. They are useful also in the application of different activities for the development and utilization of individual managers. For example, results of the appraisal and inventory are used in the identification of training needs, the determination of compensation, the assignment to positions, and individual coaching by superior managers. Both techniques are useful also in direct stimulation of concern and interest in management development, that is, in manager development of subordinates and individual self-development. Various applications of appraisal results will be mentioned in the discussion of the appraisal and inventory techniques in this chapter. The primary consideration in this chapter, however, is centered upon the techniques of appraisal and inventory; more detailed discussion of the uses of the appraisal and inventory for various actions is presented in later chapters.

THE MANAGEMENT APPRAISAL

The management appraisal is a technique which may be employed for any one or more of several different purposes. The general application of the appraisal technique concerns the evaluation of individual managers. Depending upon the specific purpose of the appraisal, criteria for evaluation are specified and then applied in the evaluation. Although the exact nature of the appraisal varies somewhat with the intended purpose, the appraisal usually attempts to measure the manager's present performance, to identify the degree of his present skills and abilities, and to determine his capacity for further development. The measures and evaluation obtained in this appraisal are necessary for the inventory of performance, abilities, and potential of the management staff and are useful in over-all management-development planning. They also are directly useful in the development and utilization of the individual manager.

Appraisal Purpose

The management appraisal is a technique or a tool of management. It is a means to an end rather than an end in itself. It is a very flexible and adaptable tool which can be fitted to serve any or several of a number of different purposes. The appraisal is an attempt to obtain evaluative measures of the individual manager. The desired measures should vary according to their intended use; possible measures are not all equally useful for all purposes. The effectiveness and value of the appraisal in any situation depends upon the degree to which it aids in the accomplishment of the intended purpose.

There are a number of possible uses of management appraisals—of possible purposes for which the appraisal should be designed. Many of these purposes are listed below in the order of their recognition by companies participating in a recent study of the management appraisal.[1]

> The most common appraisal objective appears to be the identification of individual and group needs for training and development. These needs are indicated in appraisal of present performance and in the comparison of individual abilities with plans for future staffing and assignment.
>
> Salary determination and adjustments for individual managers frequently are made on the basis of appraised performance.
>
> Replacement planning and individual assignments employ appraisals of present performance and potential for development in matching the individual and the position.
>
> The management inventory used in planning the development and utilization of the entire management team is built from appraisals of the abilities and potentials of individual managers.
>
> The stimulation and motivation of individual managers for improved performance and self-development frequently are provided through informing the manager of the results of his appraisal.
>
> Morale of the management staff may be improved through a belief in the intent of top management to be fair in all personnel

---

[1] See Thomas A. Mahoney, Wallace Dohman, and Thomas Jerdee, "Applying Yardsticks to Management," *Personnel,* Vol. 33, No. 6, May 1957, pp. 556-562.

decisions. The performance and use of management appraisals is an indication of this intent to be fair.

Since the management appraisal can be useful in various applications, a problem arises in the design of an appraisal approach appropriate for an organization. An appraisal approach can be designed for a single primary purpose or as a general-purpose tool to be used in a number of different applications. The general-purpose tool approach recognizes the wide applicability of appraisal concepts, but it is less likely to achieve the benefits desired in each application than an approach specific to the application. The Esso Standard Oil Company recognizes this conflict between the desire for an approach specific to each application of the management appraisal and the desire for use of the appraisal in many different applications occurring in the management appraisal program of the organization.[2] Esso has developed a comprehensive program of management appraisal using four different approaches to appraisal, each developed for a specific application. For example, one appraisal technique is used for the analysis of individual strengths and weaknesses for training purposes, another is used for salary purposes, a third is used in the evaluation and comparison of performance within the department, and a fourth is used in the identification and appraisal of potential ability. A program such as this combines the specific approach with the recognition of the widespread applications of appraisal results in a way that is superior to either the general-purpose appraisal or the single appraisal for a specific purpose.

Appraisal Considerations

The management appraisal is an attempt to measure factors concerning the individual manager which are useful in the development and utilization of his management abilities. The relevant factors may be measureable in quite objective terms, although subjective judgments frequently are required. In either case, various criteria or yardsticks are applied in the appraisal. The adequacy of any criterion or yardstick is measured in terms of certain accepted standards; the management appraisal should be subjected to these same considerations. An adequate management appraisal should meet the following conditions:

[2] For a description of this company's approach to management appraisal see *Research Report on Systems for Management Appraisal,* Esso Standard Oil Company, 1958.

Relevance. An adequate yardstick must measure something useful. "Relevance" refers to the degree of agreement among knowledgeable persons that the yardstick actually measures the desired subject, and that this measurement is useful for one or more desired purposes. A yardstick which measures accurately some useless subject would be of little value; the management appraisal is of little value unless it measures something useful for management development.

Reliability. Reliability or consistency of results is necessary for an interpretation of any particular result of the application of the yardstick. Two types of consistency are demanded of an adequate yardstick. The first type is test-retest reliability, or consistent measures of the same subject over a period of time. The second type is inter-rater reliability, or consistency of results when the yardstick is applied by different people. Both forms of reliability are necessary in the management appraisal if any confidence is to be placed in the individual appraisal, and if appraisals performed by different persons are to be compared.

Objectivity. An objective yardstick is one which can be applied directly to the measured object and which requires little personal judgment of the differentiation between various degrees specified in the yardstick. For example, a count of the rejects of a machine operator is an objective measure, whereas a judgmental distinction between "good" and "superior" quality of production is much less objective. Objectivity is related to reliability of the yardstick; the more objective the yardstick, the more likely that it will be reliable in its application.

Lack of bias. There are a number of possible sources of bias or extraneous influences, each of which affects the results obtained from the yardstick. Bias in the application of the yardstick or in the interpretation of results may arise from differences among people or from varying situations. This bias may be systematic and appear whenever one person applies the measure or in every situation of a particular type, or the bias may appear randomly distributed among the results. Any error in the application of the criterion or in interpretation of the results obviously affects decisions based upon these results.

Practicality. An adequate criterion must appear practical and usable to those who will be applying it and interpreting its results. An impractical-appearing yardstick is an immediate potential source of bias; the people applying and using the yardstick are not motivated to be conscientious in its use and may even seek to influence directly the results obtained with the yardstick. The technical superiority of a yardstick is of little practical value unless those using it accept it as practical and seek to employ it effectively.

Relevance and practicality are perhaps the most critical considerations in the evaluation or design of a program of management appraisal. The management appraisal is the basis of most, if not all, management development. Since much of the actual development of individuals will occur through relationships with their superiors in day-to-day job performance, it is highly important that the appraisal be acceptable to these line managers. Lawrence Appley has pointed out that a major contribution of an appraisal program lies in its making management people "appraisal-conscious." [3] The development and use of the appraisal make these people alert to the performance, qualifications, and potentials of their subordinates, and also tend to sharpen their judgments. Therefore, it is argued that the relevance and practicality of the appraisal yardsticks are more important than the technical considerations. Appley argues further that the typical line manager is not sufficiently sophisticated and trained in the use of the appraisal to appreciate the technical considerations or to use superior yardsticks as effectively as might be desired. This is not to imply that technical considerations of the appraisal yardstick are unimportant and can be neglected. The technical considerations of reliability, objectivity, and lack of bias are quite important in determining the confidence that can be placed in appraisals. They are particularly important in large organizations, where appraisals of different people must be compared in making personnel decisions. These considerations are subordinate only to the relevance and practicality of the yardstick and should be developed as far as possible while maintaining acceptance of the appraisal program by the line managers directly involved. The failure of many technically superior yardsticks of appraisal does not stem from an inconsistency with the above considerations; they stem in large part from a lack of consideration of the practicality of the yardstick and a failure in explaining the yardstick to the managers using it. The line manager usually is not averse to improving the yardsticks; he merely wants to understand the methods employed.

[3] Lawrence Appley, *Management in Action* (New York: American Management Association, 1956), p. 282.

Program of Management Appraisal

The concept of a formalized program for the appraisal of management personnel is of relatively recent origin. It has received widespread recognition only since the need for management development became apparent. While many organizations developed programs of merit rating or appraisal for non-managerial personnel a number of years ago, these programs were rarely extended into the managerial levels. The relatively recent development of formal systems of management appraisal does not mean that management personnel were not appraised and evaluated until recently. Every manager continually notes and compares the performances and mistakes of subordinates almost unconsciously. Furthermore, appraisals are called for in almost all personnel actions—promotions, transfers, discharge, training, and compensation. The informal appraisal meets few of the requirements of an adequate criterion or yardstick, however. It tends to be unduly influenced by recent events, possesses little reliability, tends to be quite subjective, and is subject to extreme bias. Recognition of the need for management development, of the influence of all personal actions upon management development and utilization, and of the need for adequate appraisals in the efficient use of these activities has led to the development of more formalized programs of management appraisal. The more formalized management appraisal programs of today are intended to provide the base needed for efficient management development.

Formal programs of management appraisal are found in slightly more than half of the companies contacted in a large survey by the Bureau of National Affairs during 1956.[4] Fifty-eight per cent of companies with more than 1,000 employees have such programs, and 55 per cent of smaller companies formally appraise their managerial staffs. A much more limited study of companies in St. Paul, Minnesota, reveals much the same pattern and also illustrates the relationship between the formal appraisal program and conscious management development.[5] Management appraisal practices of companies with a stated policy of management development were compared with those of companies without such a stated policy. Approximately 55 per cent of the former conduct formal appraisals

---

[4] Bureau of National Affairs, "The Executive," *Survey No. 37, Personnel Policies Forum,* July 1956.

[5] See T. A. Mahoney *et al., op. cit.*

of both management performance and potential, whereas only 46 per cent of the latter formally appraise performance and only 23 per cent appraise the potential of their managers. Formal programs of management appraisal can be expected to become more common as more companies seek improvement of their management organizations.

Formal management appraisal programs generally are similar in several respects. For one thing, the same general criteria or yardsticks of appraisal tend to be applied throughout a single organization. This general standardization of criteria facilitates comparison of appraisals from different units of the organization. Such comparison is of particular value in decentralized organizations as a means of spotting particular skills and potential within any one unit for transfer to another unit. Other similarities concern the timing of appraisals, review of the appraisal, and counseling of the person appraised. Appraisals generally are scheduled for particular times as a means of prodding the person or persons responsible for the appraisal and of insuring performance of the appraisal. Some provision usually is made for a review of the appraisal by a single individual or by a committee as a check upon bias and accuracy. Although somewhat less common, provision usually is made for discussion of the appraisal with the person appraised. Beyond these general similarities, there is little agreement among companies on specific aspects of the management appraisal. There is a great deal of variation among yardsticks applied and among the methods of performing the appraisal.

Management appraisal yardsticks. The selection and definition of yardsticks or criteria for the appraisal of managers are critical to the success of the entire appraisal program. Each of these yardsticks, as well as the over-all appraisal, are judged in terms of the requirements of relevance, objectivity, reliability, lack of bias, and practicality mentioned above. In general, the management appraisal has sought two types of measures: (1) some measure of present effectiveness, and (2) some measure of potential for development. These two general types of measure provide an inventory of existing skills and abilities, identification of strengths and weaknesses, and prediction of the extent of potential development of abilities.

Specific yardsticks for the appraisal of managers should be sought in the duties and responsibilities of the management staff. The overall concern of management development is present and future performance of the management team; relevant criteria must be related to this performance. Two alternative approaches have been used in the definition of specific criteria related to performance of the management team. The first of these deals with managers' personal characteristics, traits, and abilities considered essential for performance of management responsibilities. An attempt is made in the development of yardsticks to identify personal traits, characteristics, and abilities required of managers. The appraisal seeks a measurement of the extent to which each of the characteristics is developed in the individual manager; the appraiser observes the behavior and performance of the person being appraised and judges from this the existing degree of each characteristic appraised. The appraisal of characteristics is translated back into performance predictions in the planning of individual assignments. The second approach to definition of appraisal yardsticks is much more directly related to individual performance. Specific aspects of performance to be appraised and expected standards of performance are defined. The appraiser notes directly the degree to which actual performance measures up to the expected performance. Predictions of potential for development and future performance in other positions are made through direct comparison of appraised performance of responsibilities in one position with responsibilities of another position. The major advantage of the trait-appraisal approach lies in its acceptability to managers. Individual managers, particularly those in top management positions, appear to be fond of hypothesizing lists of traits and characteristics required of managers.[6] The major disadvantage lies in the error possible in the selection of essential characteristics and also in later attempts at prediction of performance from the appraised characteristics. Also difficult is the accurate appraisal of subjective characteristics commonly selected for appraisal—character, initiative, integrity, and self-confidence. The performance approach is much more direct, as it lessens the possibility of error in the selec-

[6] For example, see Joseph M. Dodge, "Some Special Characteristics of Successful Management," *Advanced Management,* Vol. 20, No. 4, April 1955, pp. 5-8; John M. Fox, "What It Takes to Be a Manager," *Advanced Management,* Vol. 22, No. 6, June 1957, pp. 18-21; J. Elliott Janney, "Company Presidents Look at Their Successors," *Harvard Business Review,* Vol. 32, No. 5, September-October 1954, pp. 45-53; Frederick G. Macarow, "The Anatomy of Business Leadership," *The Management Review,* Vol. 46, No. 2, February 1957, pp. 88-96; James H. Rand, Walter H. Wheeler, and Robert H. Morse, Jr., "What Makes a Good President," *Dun's Review and Modern Industry,* Vol. 65, No. 2321, January 1955, pp. 43, 74-75.

tion of factors to be appraised and in the interpretation of appraisal results. The appraisal of performance, in comparison with specified performance standards, is more objective, tending to improve the objectivity and reliability of the appraisal results.

Early attempts at the appraisal of managers usually employed the characteristic or trait approach. A list of characteristics or abilities was drawn up for appraisal, and the appraiser sought to measure the degree to which each was characteristic of the person being appraised and to predict the individual's capacity for developing each ability. These judgments were made on the basis of observed performance or other behavior of the individual manager being appraised. For example, an appraisal form used by the Trumbull Electric Company lists 17 personal characteristics under the headings of knowledge of work, mental qualifications and judgment, energy, character, leadership, and administrative ability. Each of these characteristics is appraised individually, and these individual appraisals then are summarized in an estimate of future capabilities.[7] This approach to appraisal possesses a certain amount of face validity which makes it acceptable to those employing it. Managers are used to thinking of management as a common set of responsibilities which requires the possession of a standard set of abilities. Furthermore, people tend to judge and appraise others in terms of rather general concepts of personality and character. However, the trait approach is limited in its practical value by several considerations. Traits or characteristics selected for appraisal should be (1) important to the performance of all positions where the appraisal is applied, (2) easily observable and identifiable by the appraiser, and (3) clearly distinguishable from each other.[8] We have already discussed in an earlier chapter the myth of a common management job and the variations among management positions.[9] Recognition of this variation makes it difficult to select any set of characteristics as important in the performance of all management positions. The wide variation among lists of characteristics and abilities which have been devel-

---

[7] See the report by F. M. Oglee in *The Development of Executive Talent,* M. Joseph Dooher and Vivienne Marquis (editors) (New York: American Management Association, 1952), Chapter XXXV.

[8] Reign Bittner, "Developing an Employee Merit Rating Procedure," in *Rating Employee and Supervisory Performance* (New York: American Management Association, 1950), pp. 20-34.

[9] Also see Myles L. Mace, *The Growth and Development of Executives* (Cambridge: Harvard University Press, 1950), pp. 20-21, for consideration of this problem.

oped and applied in the appraisal of managers fails to indicate any general agreement upon concepts of the manager's job and the required abilities for performance of this job. It is difficult also to observe each trait. The appraising manager is limited to observation of the performance of the person being appraised. The trait or ability must be defined and measured in terms of performance if the appraiser is to observe it directly. While the general concept implied by each listed trait or ability may be recognized by all, it is difficult to distinguish among traits and then measure each reliably without first agreeing on precise definitions in terms of performance. Lacking these definitions, each appraiser is likely to interpret each general trait in a slightly different manner.

The trait approach is relatively common in the appraisal of managers, despite the shortcomings noted above.[10] The general usage of this approach probably reflects several influences. The first of these is the face validity mentioned above and the ease of obtaining acceptance and agreement upon general concepts of ability desired of managers. This usage probably also reflects laziness. A common method of developing an appraisal program is to observe what other companies are doing and then borrow their concepts and measures for installation in one's own firm. The trait approach was particularly common in early attempts at the appraisal of managers. Its perpetuation is due in part to uncritical acceptance of yardsticks being used in one company for installation in another.

Examination of the traits and abilities used as yardsticks for the appraisal of managers illustrates several of the points made above. Traits and abilities commonly applied as yardsticks are grouped under the headings of personality, leadership, character, and intellectual characteristics. Any grouping of these measures is arbitrary, owing to the difficulty of definition of each measure. The grouping does serve, however, to point up the nature of these measures. Numerous additional characteristics might be listed if we were to consider all of the articles written about the qualities of leadership and management, or all of the speeches given by top management officials. Most of the characteristics listed here and mentioned in articles and speeches are recognized as generally desirable personal characteristics regardless of the situation. It is difficult, if not impossible, to point up the specific need for each characteristic in various

[10] See Mahoney *et al.*, *op. cit.*

Table 2

MANAGEMENT APPRAISAL YARDSTICKS—TRAITS AND ABILITIES

Personality Characteristics	*Character*
Motivation	Integrity
Social acceptance	Responsibility
Self-confidence	Honesty
Emotional balance	Dependability
Energy	
Adaptability	*Intellectual Characteristics*
Social sensitivity	Common sense
Forcefulness	Ability to learn
Ambition	Analytical ability
Initiative	Open-mindedness
	Originality
Leadership Characteristics	Judgment
Ability to inspire	Knowledge
Ability to delegate	
Administrative ability	

management positions or to identify the degree of each characteristic required for successful performance in these positions. An appraisal of traits and abilities has little practical value unless these yardsticks are operationally definable and useful in management development activities.

The second general approach taken in the establishment of yardsticks for the appraisal of managers deals directly with measures of manager performance. This general approach involves the identification of performance standards for management positions, the direct measurement and comparison of actual performance with these standards, and the prediction of potential and future performance on the basis of observed performance. Variations among the performance yardsticks established for appraisal stem largely from the particular method applied in the identification of relevant measures. For example, attention might be focused upon the performance of the unit supervised by the manager or upon personal performance. It might be argued that the manager's responsibility is performance of the unit supervised, that it is this performance that is important, and that appraisals should properly be concerned with the performance of the organizational unit.[11] It is certainly true that performance of the organizational unit is of major concern in a control of operations. A good case can be made, however, for placing

[11] See Carroll L. Shartle, *Executive Performance and Leadership* (Englewood Cliffs, N. J.: Prentice-Hall, Inc., 1956), Chapter 6, for discussion of this point.

major emphasis upon personal performance of the manager in the appraisal for management-development purposes.[12] There are many aspects of any manager's assignment which cannot be altered by the manager. He is assigned responsibility for an organizational unit which usually is already staffed and operating. He steps into a situation structured by operating policies, personnel assignments, and customs and traditions developed by his predecessors. He may be able to alter certain of the limiting factors, but he will be restricted in the degree to which he can build the situation he desires. Performance of the unit is affected by the factors he is permitted to alter and those that cannot be changed. A more accurate appraisal of the individual manager's performance and potential might well be obtained through measurement of personal performance and those aspects of organizational performance which are under his control. Certainly any realistic appraisal based upon organizational performance must recognize the unalterable conditions beyond the control of the manager which affect organizational performance.

One method which has been employed in the appraisal of managerial performance is similar to the generalized trait or ability approach to management appraisal. This method attempts the definition of generalized performance yardsticks for the appraisal of performance in various management positions. Selected areas of responsibility are suggested as common to all management positions, and measures of performance of these general responsibilities are sought in the appraisal. Typical performance responsibilities which are employed include organization and planning, motivation of subordinates, training, direction and supervision, coordination, and general administration. A major shortcoming of this approach lies in the fact that management positions vary in responsibilities and standards of performance. While certain general areas of responsibility may be common to most management positions, the degree of responsibility and expected performance standards for each will vary among different positions. This general performance approach, however, does focus attention upon elements of performance rather than upon generalized personal characteristics and does represent an improvement over the appraisal of characteristics.

A second method employed in the appraisal of performance in-

---

[12] See S. Rains Wallace, "Contributions to Business and Industry," in *Planning for Progress* (Pittsburgh: American Institute for Research, 1956), pp. 13-20.

volves the "critical incidents" approach.[13] This approach, described briefly in a previous chapter, attempts to identify specific acts of behavior which have been critical to the success or failure of incumbents of specific jobs. These critical incidents are used as the yardsticks for appraisal. Critical incidents are identified by first grouping individual positions into jobs or groups of positions with similar responsibilities. Information is then collected concerning specific acts of job incumbents which have been critical to their success or failure in the job. This information is then analyzed to determine the specific behavior which characterizes effective and ineffective performance of the job. The factors of behavior which emerge from this analysis are then used as yardsticks in the appraisal of present job incumbents.

The critical-incidents technique is a relatively sophisticated research technique for the identification of specific behavior characteristics of effective and ineffective performance in any job group. It appears to be useful in this connection in the identification of yardsticks for the appraisal of performance and in the identification of factors important in training for effective performance of the job. However, there are several considerations which tend to limit the practical value of the technique in identifying yardsticks for management appraisal. The technique does require research sophistication for the understanding and application of the technique. Furthermore, it requires the collection of large numbers of critical incidents—something which would be difficult for a job with few positions or incumbents. A more serious consideration concerns the grouping of positions into jobs. Any grouping of positions into jobs in the absence of adequate position descriptions would be suspect. The precision of identification of critical incidents for the appraisal of performance depends upon the similarities of positions grouped together. The grouping of relatively dissimilar positions into jobs either as a result of inaccurate position descriptions or in an attempt to build up the number of positions and people involved would result in the identification of critical incidents common to all positions and might cause one to overlook specific incidents which are much more critical in individual position performance. The technique identifies

[13] See, for example, American Institute for Research, *The Development of Job Analysis Procedures*, No. 4, June 1951; and John C. Flanagan, "Defining the Requirements of the Executive's Job," *Personnel*, Vol. 28, No. 1, July 1951, pp. 28-35.

that behavior which differentiates the effective from the ineffective job incumbents. Knowledge of the additional performance requirements and appraisals of this performance may be quite important in the identification of training and development needs and in the assignment of individual managers to positions of responsibility.

A third method of establishing yardsticks for the appraisal of managerial performance involves the development of specific performance standards for each management position.[14] Quite specific descriptions of responsibility are prepared for each position. The standards expected in the performance of these responsibilities are spelled out as objectively as possible, indicating the specific evidence considered in the evaluation of performance. An appraisal approach used in the Bemis Bag Company illustrates the practical application of performance standards in management appraisal. Position descriptions prepared for each managerial assignment indicate the performance expected in the assignment. Each manager is appraised by comparing his performance with the standards outlined in the position description. These descriptions can be supplemented with statements of goals to be achieved during each appraisal period, and can be altered periodically as well to take account of changing responsibilities. General Mills, for example, bases its management appraisal upon performance objectives jointly established by each manager and his superior. These objectives are established for each appraisal period, and the appraisal then consists of measurement of actual performance and comparison with the previously established standards.

Much of the value of these individual performance standards lies in the opportunity to develop highly objective yardsticks; it is easier to specify objective performance standards for individual positions than for a large group of related but different positions. It is possible, with highly objective standards, for the individual manager to appraise his own performance and to obtain the same results as his appraisers do. The appraisal then becomes more an analysis of performance than an evaluation, and the appraiser's role becomes more like that of a coach trying to help the appraised manager improve and less like that of a critic. Results of the appraisal in this case have obvious relevance in the identification of individual needs for train-

[14] For examples, see Walter R. Mahler and Guyot Frazier, "Appraisal of Executive Performance, the 'Achilles' Heel' of Management Development," *Personnel*, Vol. 31, No. 5, March 1955, pp. 429-441; and Douglas McGregor, "An Uneasy Look at Performance Appraisal," *Harvard Business Review*, Vol. 35, No. 3, May-June 1957, pp. 89-94.

ing and development. For all of these reasons, the use of objective performance standards in the appraisal of managerial performance is likely to be accepted as practical and useful by the managers involved in the appraisal. There are two considerations, however, which tend to restrict the use of these yardsticks. First is the difficulty of developing acceptable objective performance standards. It is difficult to find objective measures of performance for many management positions, particularly those with staff responsibilities. Care must be exercised to avoid focusing undue attention upon relatively routine responsibilities where it may be easier to objectify performance measures at the expense of more important responsibilities for which objective measures are not readily available. A second drawback of the individual performance standards lies in the lack of comparability of appraisals among managers in different positions. The variation of performance standards among positions makes it difficult to predict the probable performance of an individual in a new assignment where the performance standards differ from those of his present assignment. Direct comparison of the qualifications of two individuals being considered also is hampered by the fact that they have been appraised against different performance standards. The use of individual performance standards for the management appraisal consequently has greater application in the improvement of present performance than in the planning of future assignments and development for these assignments.

An approach to management appraisal developed at the University of Minnesota Industrial Relations Center suggests an improvement in the definition of individual performance yardsticks.[15] This approach involves the description of management positions in terms of the areas of functional responsibility described in an earlier chapter. Specific responsibilities and the objective standards expected in their performance are grouped under the functional areas of investigation, planning, evaluation, coordination, supervision, staffing, negotiating, and representing. Individual appraisals involve the comparison of performance with the standards specified for the position. This is done in the same manner that any set of individual performance standards is applied. The particular value of this approach lies in the standardized classification of responsibilities which facilitates

---

[15] Thomas A. Mahoney and Coenraad Mohr, "A Guide to Management Appraisal and Management Development," *Mimeographed Release No. 8*, University of Minnesota, Industrial Relations Center, 1956.

the comparison of appraisal results. While specific performance standards differ among positions, the standardized classification of responsibilities makes the desired comparisons easier. For example, different positions might have different responsibilities for "coordination" and different standards of performance for these responsibilities. However, comparison of performances in "coordinating" is necessary in the assignment of managers and is facilitated by the classification of specific responsibilities into common groups. Preliminary experience with this method of defining management appraisal yardsticks indicates that it can provide relatively objective yardsticks which are relevant in management development and which are accepted as practical and useful by the people involved. In general, the development of specific individual performance standards involves more cooperation and work by line managers than is required for the development of other standards of appraisal. Cooperation and interest generally is obtained more easily for the development and use of these standards than for other standards, however, because of their apparent practicality and value. This participation of line managers in the development of standards of appraisal also is valuable in so far as it creates a greater consciousness and awareness of the purpose and value of the management appraisal.

Management appraisal techniques. A primary consideration in any management appraisal program is the establishment of criteria or yardsticks for the appraisal. Equally important is the method employed in comparing the individual manager with these criteria and in measuring different degrees for each criterion. Many of the various techniques for comparison and measurement have been developed in conjunction with specific types of appraisal yardsticks and are commonly associated with them. However, each of the techniques discussed here might be adapted and applied in the measurement of the various types of yardsticks discussed above.

The simplest and easiest of the various measurement techniques to apply is a ranking form of measurement. This technique involves the direct comparison of individuals rather than the comparison of each individual with a set scale of measurement. In general, the ranking approach merely involves the establishment of a standard for comparison, followed by the ranking of individuals in terms of this standard. One ranking technique, the alternation-ranking technique, presents the appraiser with a list of individuals and a stand-

AR-PP-1

ALTERNATION RANKING REPORT (Present Performance) CONFIDENTIAL

IMPORTANT: Before you begin read carefully the instructions on the back of this form. | DATE:

CLASSIFICATION OF GROUP BEING RANKED

DEPARTMENT | RANKER: | DO NOT WRITE IN THIS SPACE

EMPLOYEES TO BE RANKED (DO NOT LIST MORE THAN 30)	EMP. NO.		
		1 - HIGHEST	
		2 - NEXT HIGHEST	
		3 - NEXT HIGHEST	
		4 - NEXT HIGHEST	
		5 - NEXT HIGHEST	
		6 - NEXT HIGHEST	
		7 - NEXT HIGHEST	
		8 - NEXT HIGHEST	
		9 - NEXT HIGHEST	
		10 - NEXT HIGHEST	
		11 - NEXT HIGHEST	
		12 - NEXT HIGHEST	
		13 - NEXT HIGHEST	
		14 - NEXT HIGHEST	
		15 - NEXT HIGHEST	
		15 - NEXT LOWEST	
		14 - NEXT LOWEST	
		13 - NEXT LOWEST	
		12 - NEXT LOWEST	
		11 - NEXT LOWEST	
		10 - NEXT LOWEST	
		9 - NEXT LOWEST	
		8 - NEXT LOWEST	
		7 - NEXT LOWEST	
		6 - NEXT LOWEST	
		5 - NEXT LOWEST	
		4 - NEXT LOWEST	
		3 - NEXT LOWEST	
		2 - NEXT LOWEST	
		1 - LOWEST	

INSTRUCTIONS FOR ALTERNATION RANKING ON PRESENT PERFORMANCE

Read these instructions all the way through before ranking anyone.

On the other side of this sheet is a list of employees who are doing various types of work. All of them may be performing satisfactorily, but some are almost certain to be doing a better job in their own particular type of assignment than are others in their kind of assignment. (For example, individual A, in a job of relatively high responsibility, might be considerably less effective in performing it than is individual B who performs a somewhat less responsible job. In such a case, B would rank higher than A in terms of his contribution to the company as a job-performer.) Information is needed as to which employees on the list are doing the best work, and which are not doing as well as others.

You may use your own judgment as to what makes one employee better than another. Many factors may be considered: dependability, ability to do the work, willingness to work, cooperation, ability to get along with people, and any others which you think are important. In making your decisions, use your own personal knowledge of the individuals and their work. Do not depend on the opinions of others. Your judgments will be treated confidentially.

NOW PROCEED AS FOLLOWS:

A. First, eliminate those you cannot rank:

1. Look over the list of names on the other side of this page and draw a line through the name of any person whose work you do not know well.

2. Look over the list again and draw a line through the name of any person whose work in your opinion is so different from most of the others that you do not think he (or she) can be compared with them.

B. Second, proceed with your ranking:

1. Look over the list of remaining names and decide which one person you think is the best on the list. Draw a line through his name and write it in the blank space marked "1-Highest" at the top of the page.

2. Look over the remaining names and decide which one person is not as good as the others on the list. Draw a line through his name and write it in the blank space marked "1-Lowest" at the bottom of the page. Remember, you are not saying that he is unsatisfactory; you are merely saying that you consider the others better.

3. Next, select the person you think is best of those remaining on the list, draw a line through his name and write it in the blank space marked "2-Next Highest."

4. Next, select the person you think is not as good as the others remaining on the list, draw a line through his name and write it in the blank space marked "2-Next Lowest."

5. Continue this ranking procedure (selecting next highest, then next lowest) until you have drawn a line through each name on the list.

Fig. 6. Alternation Ranking Report (front and reverse). (From Employee Relations Department, Esso Standard Oil Company.)

ard for comparison. (See Figure 6.) The appraiser then selects the outstanding individual for first rank and selects the least outstanding individual for the last rank. Among those remaining on the list, he then proceeds to identify the most and least outstanding individuals alternately until the entire list has been ranked. The ranking need be performed only once where a single criterion for appraisal is specified. The same approach can be applied where a number of criteria are identified, a single ranking being performed for each of the criteria. The alternation-ranking technique is relatively simple to apply and, probably for this reason, is acceptable to those performing the ranking. It also has been found to be one of the more reliable appraisal techniques and is used widely in securing appraisals for research purposes. However, difficulty in the interpretation of rankings and in the combination of multiple-criterion rankings makes the approach relatively unacceptable for purposes of management counseling and training.

Other techniques of measurement for management appraisal entail the development of standards by which each manager is measured. A common technique uses a scale with varying definitions of degrees for each yardstick applied. These definitions are ordered to represent a continuum to the appraiser, who selects the appropriate degree for the person appraised. (See Figure 7.) The scale technique has been used widely in the appraisal of a manager's personal characteristics and abilities. The scale technique is not considered reliable as a measurement technique, because it is associated with the appraisal of personal characteristics which are difficult to define and order by degrees. The scale technique's reliability could be improved when used in the appraisal of more objective yardsticks.

A more complicated method of measurement, the forced-choice technique, attempts to eliminate the personal bias of the appraiser. (See Figure 8.) Several statements illustrate different degrees on each appraisal yardstick. These statements are arranged in groups of four or five. Each statement is repeated among a number of different statements. The appraiser must consider each group of statements and choose the most descriptive and least descriptive statement in each group. Each statement is weighted, and these weights, and the comparisons made in the appraiser's choice of statements combine to provide an over-all appraisal score for each person appraised.[16] This method may achieve greater objectivity

[16] See L. Huttner and R. A. Katzell, "Developing a Yardstick of Supervisory Performance," *Personnel,* Vol. 33, 1957, pp. 371-378; and M. W. Richardson, "Forced-Choice Performance Reports," *Personnel,* Vol. 26, 1949, pp. 205-212.

than other methods, as the rater is forced to compare specific descriptions of behavior or characteristics rather than develop an over-all rating. For the same reason, appraisers often resent the approach and try to choose among alternative statements by assumed relationships with the desired over-all appraisal. Experience with the

This performance review is designed to provide supervisors with a uniform basis for making fair and impartial appraisals of the performance of employees.

It is intended to be of benefit to employee and supervisor alike. Among the objects to which this review is an aid are:

(A) To weigh the employee's fitness--for his or her present position, for transfer or promotion to another position or for increased compensation.
(B) To determine how employee's performance can be improved.
(C) To place each individual in the work to which he or she is best suited.

DIRECTIONS

1. As each factor is considered, be sure to compare this person with all the other employees in similar positions.
2. In assuming standards for this individual, be sure they are appropriate to his or her job level and not those applicable to higher or lower job levels.
3. When rating an employee, call to mind instances that are typical of the employee's work and personal characteristics. Do not be influenced by exceptional or uncommon circumstances.
4. Give thought and consideration to your ratings. Be sure that they represent your best judgement. Do not allow personal feelings to influence your rating--be objective.
5. After rating the factors below, answer the questions on the reverse side.

QUANTITY OF WORK Consider volume of work produced consistently	Unsatisfactory output ☐	Limited. Does just enough to get by ☐	Average output ☐	Above average producer ☐	Exceptional output ☐
QUALITY OF WORK Consider accuracy and neatness	Very poor ☐	Not entirely acceptable ☐	Acceptable accuracy and neatness ☐	Very neat and accurate ☐	Exceptionally neat and accurate ☐
COOPERATION Consider cooperation with associates and supervisors	Entirely uncooperative ☐	Reluctant to cooperate ☐	Adequately cooperative ☐	Very cooperative ☐	Unusually cooperative ☐
DEPENDABILITY Consider amount of supervision required and application to work	Unreliable and inattentive ☐	Needs frequent supervision ☐	Generally reliable and attentive to work. Follows instructions carefully ☐	Very reliable and conscientious, needs little supervision ☐	Extremely reliable and industrious ☐
ABILITY TO LEARN Consider ability to understand and retain	Very limited ☐	Requires repeated instructions ☐	Learns reasonably well ☐	Readily understands and retains ☐	Unusual capacity ☐
INITIATIVE Consider originality and resourcefulness	Lacking ☐	Routine worker ☐	Occasionally shows initiative ☐	Better than average ☐	Outstanding ☐
JUDGMENT Consider ability to evaluate situations and make sound decisions	Poor ☐	Not always reliable ☐	Good in most matters ☐	Reliable ☐	Decisions most logical and well founded ☐

Fig. 7. Illustration of a Scale for Management Appraisal.

DIRECTIONS

To fill out the form properly, you must consider each of the blocks separately. Read all five statements in the first block; then pick out the statement that is MOST descriptive of the supervisor on whom you are reporting. Under the word MOST, circle the letter that appears before the statement that you have selected.

Then from the four remaining statements, pick out the one that LEAST describes the supervisor, and under the word LEASE, circle the letter that goes with that statement. Do the same thing for each of the thirty blocks. You may rightly feel that none of the statements in a block is an exact description of the man, but it is necessary that you make the best choice that you can. Consider each block as an independent unit. Since the comparisons are different from block to block, it is not necessary to refer to previous marks in order to be consistent.

PART I

SUPERVISORS PERFORMANCE REPORT

NAME OF SUPERVISOR BEING RATED

MOST	LEAST	1
A	A	Displays temper often.
B	B	Makes very few mistakes.
C	C	Is not open to new ideas.
D	D	Makes no attempt to demonstrate his own skills.
E	E	Has plenty of drive and energy.

MOST	LEAST	2
A	A	Has more drive than leadership.
B	B	Needs very little supervision.
C	C	Not as tactful in reprimanding as he should be.
D	D	Inclined to make snap decisions.
E	E	Came up through the ranks.

MOST	LEAST	3
A	A	Tends to make positive statements which subsequently prove to be incorrect.
B	B	Not anxious to assume additional responsibility.
C	C	Feels his own educational limitations.
D	D	Expects instructions to be carried out without having to follow up to see that the work is done.
E	E	Makes complete analysis of every problem.

MOST	LEAST	4
A	A	Has good ideas.
B	B	Has a poor memory.
C	C	Does not follow his job through.
D	D	Seldom lays off for any reason.
E	E	Shy.

MOST	LEAST	5
A	A	Gives men the benefit of any doubt.
B	B	Gets angry when criticized by superiors.
C	C	Adequate training for his job.
D	D	Very formal in his dealings with his men.
E	E	He is ready for the job ahead of him and he will do a good job at it.

MOST	LEAST	6
A	A	Ready and willing to assist any employee in any phase of the work.
B	B	Puts off job as long as possible.
C	C	Not capable of correcting his faults.
D	D	Does not "polish apples" for his superiors.
E	E	Level-headed and calm in handling tense situations.

MOST	LEAST	7
A	A	No particular administrative ability.
B	B	Observes Company's rules.
C	C	Inaugurates systems for handling details.
D	D	Attempts to look after all details himself.
E	E	Industrious.

MOST	LEAST	8
A	A	Is not open to new ideas.
B	B	Gives excuses.
C	C	Makes very few mistakes.
D	D	A good judge of a man's ability.
E	E	Attempts to demonstrate his own skills.

MOST	LEAST	9
A	A	Methodical.
B	B	Not respected by subordinates.
C	C	Possesses rare judgment as to exactly the amount of responsibility he should assume.
D	D	Agrees with all Company policies.
E	E	Loud-mouthed.

MOST	LEAST	10
A	A	Gets a job done with minimum effort.
B	B	Doesn't praise work of men to superior.
C	C	People avoid him as much as possible.
D	D	Unable to advance higher due to general attitude.
E	E	Doesn't like to be pushed around.

MOST	LEAST	11
A	A	Firm in convictions.
B	B	Has ability to use other people and their knowledge to best advantage.
C	C	Seldom takes over-all Company viewpoint.
D	D	Feels he should only have to work eight hours a day.
E	E	Checks work of men excessively.

MOST	LEAST	12
A	A	Individualist.
B	B	Learns quickly.
C	C	Gives impression of having plenty of time to handle problem at hand.
D	D	Needs help in making routine decisions.
E	E	Fails to recognize ability when a good job is done.

MOST	LEAST	13
A	A	Always willing to accept new and varied responsibilities.
B	B	Is not a good diplomat.
C	C	Better liked by superiors than by subordinates.
D	D	Backs his men up only if they are in the right.
E	E	Admits errors if shown to be wrong.

MOST	LEAST	14
A	A	Has relatively few leadership characteristics.
B	B	Does not trust judgment of those under him.
C	C	Looks to his men to know details of newer operations.
D	D	Thinks well on his feet and in emergencies.
E	E	Can compromise.

MOST	LEAST	15
A	A	Displays imagination in handling new problems.
B	B	Sloppy in appearance.
C	C	His men do not respect his ability as a supervisor.
D	D	Knows all the short cuts.
E	E	Quiet.

MOST	LEAST	16
A	A	Not dependable.
B	B	An extremely good organizer of personnel.
C	C	Doesn't always follow safety policies.
D	D	Neat in dress and appearance.
E	E	Too easy at times.

MOST	LEAST	17
A	A	Makes decisions too quickly.
B	B	Quite often works a lot of overtime.
C	C	Is willing to do anything he asks a subordinate to do.
D	D	Has little enthusiasm for training classes.
E	E	Handles very few details.

MOST	LEAST	18
A	A	Reluctant to assume any responsibility that he can avoid.
B	B	Frequently expects too much of a man.
C	C	Satisfied with present assignment.
D	D	Participates actively in training classes.
E	E	Always on the job ahead of time.

MOST	LEAST	19
A	A	Observes his men very closely.
B	B	Not capable of handling more responsibility.
C	C	Is an excellent organizer.
D	D	Jealous of associates who get ahead.
E	E	Has manner of being positive in statements.

MOST	LEAST	20
A	A	Capable of holding a higher position.
B	B	Personally sees that work is safely carried out.
C	C	Agreeably reverses opinion on decision when proved wrong.
D	D	He is against ideas which are not his own.
E	E	Requires direct guidance of superior.

MOST	LEAST	21
A	A	Supports Company policy even when not in agreement.
B	B	Has ability to go higher.
C	C	At times attempts to make machines out of men.
D	D	Is a poor instructor.
E	E	Not willing to give up.

MOST	LEAST	22
A	A	Bogs himself down in detail work.
B	B	Judgment stands up.
C	C	Poor organizer of work & personnel.
D	D	Will not permit his superiors to overrule him without argument.
E	E	Gives subordinates full credit for ideas.

MOST	LEAST	23
A	A	Backs up Company decisions when made.
B	B	The quality and quantity of work he produces is consistently high.
C	C	Does a poor job because of a very bad attitude.
D	D	Too tolerant of shortcomings of immediate subordinates.
E	E	Takes unnecessary chances in regard to safety.

MOST	LEAST	24
A	A	Explains all details of job to men.
B	B	Recognizes skills and abilities of others.
C	C	Possesses skill in planting ideas in the minds of others and giving them full credit for the ideas.
D	D	Attempts to handle too many things at one time.
E	E	Lacks technical knowledge.

MOST	LEAST	25
A	A	Oversteps authority.
B	B	Is not very good at explaining things so that others can understand.
C	C	Capable of accepting greater responsibility.
D	D	Suggests methods to superiors for better-ing working conditions.
E	E	Backs up his men whether right or wrong.

MOST	LEAST	26
A	A	Has plenty of drive and energy.
B	B	Makes no attempt to demonstrate his own skills.
C	C	Displays temper often.
D	D	Gives excuses.
E	E	A good judge of a man's ability.

MOST	LEAST	27
A	A	Will not tolerate false statements from employees.
B	B	Avoids special handling of any routine work.
C	C	Gives help to subordinates at times when it is not needed.
D	D	Sometimes gives wrong impression.
E	E	Able to stand off and gauge the general features of problems.

MOST	LEAST	28
A	A	Constantly reviews qualifications and classifications of his men.
B	B	Supervises his men's work in too much detail.
C	C	Not sufficiently aggressive.
D	D	Reverses decisions only for excellent reasons.
E	E	Long experience in general refinery operations.

MOST	LEAST	29
A	A	Delegates a little too much responsibility.
B	B	Obtains considerable satisfaction from prestige of his position.
C	C	Has plenty of initiative.
D	D	Shows real interest in personal affairs of subordinates.
E	E	Probably better suited to a job in which judgment is not involved.

MOST	LEAST	30
A	A	Should devote more time to programming work.
B	B	Does not command full respect of men because of lack of ability in handling them.
C	C	Gets rattled when talking to superiors.
D	D	Recognizes limitations of individuals.
E	E	No forseeable limitations in ultimate advancement.

Fig. 8. Supervisors Performance Report, Form O (Directions and Part I). (Reprinted by permission of Richardson, Bellows, Henry and Company, Inc.)

forced-choice method indicates that appraisers can identify the rationale underlying alternative statements and select those which will produce the over-all result the appraiser desires.

A third method might be called the essay technique of management appraisal. Using this technique, the appraiser is asked to describe in writing the performance, abilities, or characteristics of the person being appraised. The appraiser is asked to provide this description for each of the yardsticks applied, but no scale or continuum of degrees is provided for the evaluation of the description. Relatively specific yardsticks may be applied, as when the appraiser is asked to describe the punctuality of the appraised person; or, as is more common, the yardsticks may be general, as when the appraiser is asked to describe the major weaknesses of the appraised manager. Three general yardsticks are specified in a management appraisal program developed by the American Management Association—performance, personal qualifications, and potential. The major feature of the technique is the lack of any attempt to have the appraiser evaluate the appraised manager either in relation to other managers or in comparison with a predetermined scale. Rather, the appraiser is asked to analyze and describe the appraised manager. Probably because the technique seeks an analysis rather than an evaluation, it appears quite acceptable to the managers concerned. The use of appraisal results is limited, however, by the lack of standardization among appraisals. It can be quite useful in individual development for the present position. However, it is much less useful in personnel actions requiring either the comparison of appraisals or the matching of appraisal results with position responsibilities.

Position performance standards have already been discussed as yardsticks for the management appraisal; they must also be considered among the techniques of measurement. The establishment of objective performance standards for each position automatically prescribes the method of measurement; performance is measured in exactly the same terms as it is specified in the standards. Objective performance standards are possible only when objective measures of performance are available or can be developed. In such a case, the appraisal is provided automatically as performance measures become available. These yardsticks and the implied measurement technique appear to satisfy the usual requirements placed upon any appraisal. Probably the major objection to them lies in the possibility that the desire to specify and apply objective performance standards may result in the establishment of irrelevant standards merely because they are easily measured. In this instance, the goal and purpose of the position responsibilities might be subordinated to the easily measured but less relevant factors of position performance.

Management Appraisal Process

The process of management appraisal is at least as important in achieving the purposes of the appraisal as are the yardsticks and measures employed. Decisions concerning the positions covered in the appraisal program, the selection of appraisers, and the frequency of appraisal are important in shaping the appraisal results; perfect instruments and techniques of appraisal are of little value unless they are also applied correctly. Furthermore, certain benefits are sought in the appraisal process completely apart from the information obtained in the appraisal. These benefits include such things as an increased understanding of position responsibilities by the person being appraised and the stimulation of interest in management development by both the appraiser and the appraised manager.

A consideration which is basic to the entire appraisal process concerns the positions to be covered in the program, that is, which managers are to be appraised? As a general principle, based upon the purposes of the management appraisal, all members of the management team should be appraised. Performance of all managers, from the first-line supervisor through the president, is important to the over-all success of the organization, and the appraisal is designed as an aid in the improvement of this performance. As a practical matter, however, the appraisal is applied more frequently at middle- and lower-level management positions than at top-management levels. For example, slightly less than half of the appraisal programs of companies in St. Paul, Minnesota cover all members of the management organization; the usual exceptions in remaining firms are members of top management, with occasional exclusions of research directors and branch managers.[17] This exclusion of members of top management from the appraisal stems in part from the difficulty of specifying relevant standards for appraisal and the difficulty of locating persons who are in a position to appraise top management. The reluctance of members of top management to submit to an ap-

[17] Mahoney *et al.*, *op. cit.*

praisal also is a factor. The inclusion of top management positions in the appraisal program does provide an example and set the tone for appraisal at lower levels, and it would appear desirable on these grounds if no others. Furthermore, the practice is found in enough organizations to indicate that the problems involved are not insurmountable.

Another basic question in the appraisal process concerns the appraiser—who shall perform the appraisal? Three alternative levels of positions might be considered in the designation of appraisers: the superiors, peers, or subordinates of the individual being appraised. Only one of these, appraisal by superiors, is considered seriously, however, in most management appraisal programs. For example, a Bureau of National Affairs survey of management appraisal programs reports that the appraisal is conducted by a single superior or by a committee of superior managers in almost all cases.[18] Two less extensive surveys also report that appraisal by superiors is most common, the single exception being appraisal by peers.[19] The appraisal by peers is practiced most frequently at the top executive or company officer level where superior managers available to conduct the appraisal are limited in number. The most common practice entails appraisal by the individual's immediate superior, either alone or with the aid of a committee of managers also superior to the appraised manager. The justification for this practice lies in the beliefs that the appraisals of subordinates are a management responsibility and that the most valuable application of appraisal results stems from their influence upon the relationships between an individual manager and his subordinates.[20] There also is a certain amount of fear that appraisal by peers and subordinates would produce biased results based upon criteria other than consideration of the appraised individual's contribution to the organization.

Consideration of appraisal by peers and subordinates should not be discarded automatically, however. Certain limited experiences with these appraisals suggest that they may be of value in supplementing the appraisal by superior managers. Both subordinates and peers have observed the appraised manager in situations and be-

[18] Bureau of National Affairs, *op. cit.*

[19] See Joseph A. Litterer, "How 47 Companies Measure Their Executives," *Personnel Journal,* Vol. 36, No. 3, July-August 1957, pp. 97-100; and Mahoney *et al., op. cit.*

[20] Appley, *op. cit.,* pp. 282-284.

havior different from that observed by superiors; their appraisals add another dimension to the appraisal by superiors. Peer ratings and appraisals in the service academies over the years have been found to be more valid predictors of later field performance than ratings by instructors and superiors at the academies. This suggests that the peer appraisal measures something different from what is measured by superiors—something that adds to the over-all appraisal.[21] A limited form of management appraisal by subordinates already is being conducted in many organizations through periodic morale or attitude surveys. A unique experiment in the Esso Research and Engineering Company employs direct appraisals by subordinates in a management appraisal approach. Subordinates rate their managers, using a standardized questionnaire. These ratings are combined into a confidential appraisal of the manager and are given to him for his information and guidance. After two years of experimentation, both managers and subordinates are enthusiastic about the approach and report progress in the development of managers as a result.[22] This application of subordinate appraisals in management development indicates the potential value of such ratings as guides to the individual manager's self-understanding and self-development despite common fears about involving subordinates in the appraisal process.

Another consideration in the designation of appraisers involves the question of individual versus committee appraisals. Both the individual and the committee appraisal are used at present in industry with approximately equal frequency.[23] There are advantages and disadvantages to each method which may make either method particularly appropriate for a given organization. The individual appraisal is performed in most instances by the appraised manager's immediate superior. Advocates of the individual appraisal point up the manager's responsibility for the performance and de-

---

[21] See Donald E. Baier, "Selection and Evaluation of West Point Cadets," *American Psychologist,* Vol. 2, No. 8, August, 1947, pp. 325-326; U.S. Marine Corps, Medical Field Research Laboratory, *Validation of Officer Selection Tests by Means of Combat Proficiency Ratings, Progress Report No. 1: The Prediction of Successful Combat Leadership* (Camp LeJeune, North Carolina, January, 1946); S. B. Williams and Harold J. Leavitt, "Group Opinion as a Prediction of Military Leadership," *Journal of Consulting Psychology,* Vol. 11, No. 6, November-December 1947, pp. 283-291.

[22] See Paul W. Maloney and J. R. Hinrichs, "A New Tool for Supervisory Self-Development," *Personnel,* Vol. 36, No. 4, July-August 1959, pp. 46-53.

[23] Bureau of National Affairs, *op. cit.;* and Litterer, *op. cit.*

velopment of subordinates. The sharing of his appraisal responsibilities, they argue, encourages the manager to dodge his responsibility for performance and development of subordinates. It is felt that the appraisal process should build the boss-subordinate relationship and encourage day-to-day coaching and assistance by the superior manager. In this connection, it is argued that "it is better to have the right man do a poor appraisal than to have the wrong man do a good appraisal." It is true that the value of the individual appraisal will vary with the ability of the manager to appraise his subordinates, but a review of all appraisals by the appraiser's superior can aid materially in the correction of bias and error in the appraisals. Certainly it is easier to lodge responsibility for performance of the appraisal with a single person than with a committee. Furthermore, it is often felt that committee appraisals either are dominated by a single individual or else reflect a compromise among the committee members, thus providing little improvement over the individual appraisal at a greater expense.

A variation of the individual appraisal involves what has been called the *field-review method* of appraisal. The management-appraisal approach of the United States Reduction Company provides an example of the field-review method.[24] Each manager is assisted in the preparation of appraisals of subordinates by a staff specialist who assists in the preparation of all management appraisals. This staff specialist meets with the appraising manager and asks for his judgments concerning the performance and/or potential of his subordinate. He questions the manager about each of the appraisal yardsticks and forces the manager to justify his judgments. The staff specialist may then prepare a written appraisal report for approval by the manager, although the manager is held responsible for the final appraisal. Finally, the staff specialist often works with the manager in preparing for discussion of the appraisal with the subordinate and in the later coaching of the subordinate. Participation of the staff specialist in this manner probably aids in the elimination of appraiser bias and error and also contributes to the standardization of appraisals throughout the organization. Something akin to the field-review technique has also been incorporated into many programs of committee appraisal, a staff specialist

[24] See William V. Machaver and Willard E. Erickson, "A New Approach to Executive Appraisal," *Personnel*, Vol. 35, No. 1, July-August 1958, pp. 8-14.

participating in committee appraisals in much the same capacity as in the individual appraisal. Thus, while the field-review technique currently is used more frequently with the individual appraisal, it may be used with the committee appraisal as well.

The committee appraisal is somewhat newer than the individual appraisal, appraisal by the superior manager having been the standard approach in the past. Advocates of the committee appraisal point to several considerations respecting it as improvements over the individual appraisal. For example, there is less likelihood of bias and error in an appraisal where several viewpoints and judgments are brought to bear upon a single appraisal. Furthermore, the participating managers have observed different performances of the person being appraised and are able to provide a more comprehensive appraisal. The participation of each manager in appraisals throughout the organization also tends more to standardize the appraisal than does the use of the individual appraisal method. Various rules may be specified to prevent the common disadvantages of committee assignments. For example, the manager of the person being appraised usually is included in the committee and is assigned responsibility for the scheduling and coordination of the appraisal. Dominance of the committee is prevented, in at least one company, by asking the most junior member of the committee to speak first and requiring the appraised manager's superior to speak last on each point. Compromise and deadlock are prevented by requiring unanimous agreement on any point included in the final appraisal; points which lack agreement are referred to the committee members for further study.

Management appraisals in the Detroit Edison Company are performed by a committee of approximately four people, all superior to the appraised manager and including the manager's superior. The committee discusses the manager's performance, personal qualifications, potential, and current status, and possible action to be taken in his development. Committee procedures are relatively informal and there are no established rules to be followed in the appraisal discussion. A secretary is assigned to organize the results of the discussion, and unanimous agreement of the committee is required in the approval of these results. A final review of the appraisal is provided by the top managers in the organizational unit. The appraisal approach developed and applied in this company is widely recognized and has been copied and adapted for application in a number of organizations.[25]

The size of appraisal committees varies from two to approximately five members, with three members constituting the most common size. Members of the committee must all be familiar with the work of the appraised manager and usually are chosen from positions superior to his in the organization. The appraised manager's superior participates as the person most familiar with the manager's performance and as the person who will be asked to use the appraisal in development of the manager. He may be assisted in the appraisal by managers from line or staff positions who have an opportunity to observe, and work with, the appraised manager. At least one company permits the appraised manager to select his appraisers, and another permits him to review the committee and reject any of the members.[26] This participation of the appraised manager in determination of the composition of the appraisal committee serves to eliminate much of the fear that the appraisal will be biased and incorrect.

The appraisal period in most companies covers an entire year, a new appraisal being made each year.[27] It is not uncommon, however, for more frequent appraisals to be made following a manager's assignment to a new position. Some companies, for example, appraise each manager at the end of six months on a new assignment and each year thereafter. Each appraisal should consider only the period covered since the last previous appraisal. Examination and consideration of past appraisals at the time of appraisal is likely to influence the current appraisal and present an inaccurate appraisal of the current period. Past appraisals may be examined after the appraisal has been completed, and may be quite useful as an indication of progress and improvement made during the intervening period.

Management Appraisal and Individual Development

It has already been pointed out that the management appraisal provides the basis for numerous personnel decisions affecting de-

---

[25] For a more complete description of the Detroit Edison approach, see Virgil Rowland, "Management Inventory and Development: A Case Study," *Personnel*, Vol. 28, No. 1, July 1951, pp. 12-22; and *Improving Managerial Performance* (New York: Harper and Brothers, 1958), 163 pp., by the same author.

[26] Bureau of National Affairs, *op. cit.*

[27] Bureau of National Affairs, *op. cit.;* and Mahoney *et al., op. cit.*

velopment and utilization of the management staff. The appraisal process also affects the development of managers directly and must be considered a technique of management development in and of itself. This direct relationship between the management appraisal and individual development is described briefly here; it is discussed more fully in later chapters.

Each manager is responsible for the performance and development of his subordinates. This responsibility is performed in the day-to-day direction of activities, correction, coaching, and counseling of subordinates. All of the manager's relationships with his subordinates reflect his judgments of their present performance and their potential for development. The management appraisal directly affects the development of individual managers through the impact it has upon the judgments and considerations of the superior manager. It also is common in the appraisal process to direct the appraising manager's thinking toward the steps necessary for improvement and development of his subordinates, and thus further to involve the manager in the development of subordinates. A rather common practice in the appraisal of managers requires the appraiser or appraisers to identify the particular strengths and weaknesses of the person being appraised and then to outline a program of development for overcoming the identified weaknesses. Certain aspects of the recommended program will entail training or development activities outside the appraised manager's present job, but many aspects will concern activities which can be carried on in his present assignment. The inclusion of this planning-for-development as a last step in the appraisal forces the appraising manager to go beyond the identification of weaknesses and to analyze the weaknesses and outline activities to correct them. This analysis and planning should serve to point up to the appraising manager his role in the development of his subordinates and the particular things that he can do to help.

It has been stated by some that the management appraisal is the single most important tool of management development and that its major contribution lies in the focusing of attention upon the relationship of the manager and his subordinates in the development of these subordinates.[28] It is certainly true that the direct impact of the appraisal upon development by making managers

[28] See Appley, *op. cit.*, and Joseph M. Trickett, "Fulfilling Individual Needs in Management Development," *Personnel,* Vol. 33, No. 6, May 1957, pp. 520-526.

aware of the capabilities and weaknesses of subordinates, and by encouraging thought and consideration of methods for development is one of the important contributions of the appraisal.

The Appraisal Review

The appraisal review forms a connecting link between the preparation of the appraisal and its use in management development. The appraisal review provides a check and control over the appraisal results and recommendations as well as the appraisal process. As a general practice, the appraisal review is performed by a manager two levels superior to the appraised manager. Each manager submits appraisals of his subordinates to his superior for approval before the appraisal process is considered completed. This review provides a check upon the judgments of the appraising manager or committee and provides the superior manager with an inventory of the managers under his general supervision. At the same time, the appraisal review provides the superior manager with information about the performance of his immediate subordinates, particularly about their performance in the development of subordinates.

The appraisal review should be more than a review of individual appraisals. Each manager should submit to his superior an inventory of managers under his direction. This inventory should include both the individual appraisals and recommendations for individual development and an over-all report of the performance and potential of subordinates. In this manner, the reviewing manager is made aware of the relative performance of different management positions. This has a direct bearing on the need for replacements, and the availability of qualified managers for assignment to other positions. The reviewing manager is thus provided with the information necessary to better utilize existing managers within the units under his direction. The appraisal review also informs the reviewing manager of suggested plans for development of individuals within those units and permits coordination of the suggested developmental activities. This review also provides the reviewing manager with information useful in his appraisal of subordinates. The use of the appraisal review in this manner provides an incentive for individual managers to follow through in the development of subordinates and to utilize the appraisal for development.

The appraisal review can be useful in performing two functions that are necessary in the appraisal and development of managers. First, it is a control over the appraisal process at each level of the organization. Second, it encourages managers in the development of subordinates at each level, utilizing the judgments and suggestions of the appraisal, and it serves to build up an inventory of management abilities and weaknesses at each level useful both in the coordination of developmental activities and in the efficient utilization of existing abilities throughout the organization's many and varied units.

Post-Appraisal Interview

The post-appraisal interview is a communication of appraisal results to the appraised manager by his boss. It is a specific technique related to individual coaching and counseling for management development, and it is discussed in this connection in a later chapter. It must be mentioned at this point, however, as a step in the appraisal process.

Communication of the appraisal results in the post-appraisal interview is intended to serve several purposes. Perhaps most important of these is the encouragement of communication and discussion between managers and their subordinates, concerning their mutual responsibilities and performance within the organization. This interview and discussion are intended to clarify the subordinate manager's understanding of his assignment, to make him aware of any weaknesses in his performance, and to point up and stimulate his self-development. The post-appraisal interview is also intended to satisfy the desire that most employees have to know what the boss thinks of their performance—how well they are satisfying the boss's demands. Thus, the post-appraisal interview is intended as a last step in the appraisal process as well as a first step in the development of individual subordinates.

Some form of counsel for managers concerning their strengths and weaknesses is practiced in a majority of the companies surveyed by the Bureau of National Affairs.[29] It is interesting to note that more companies report some form of counseling than report a formal program of management appraisal—more precisely, 70 per cent of the reporting companies counsel, as compared with 60 per cent of the companies reporting a more formal program. This difference points up the fact that appraisals of individual managers

[29] Bureau of National Affairs, *op. cit.*

are made and used in personnel actions despite the informality of the appraisal. It also points to the questionable value of much of the counseling of managers, since in so many cases counseling is not based upon a formal appraisal of the individual. A recent study performed for the Psychological Corporation illustrates the need for post-appraisal interviews and also suggests that many appraisal programs are failing in this last step of the appraisal program.[30] Managers in companies having formal appraisal programs indicate more frequently that they know what is expected of them in their present positions than do managers in companies without formal appraisals; 85 per cent of the former and 60 per cent of the latter indicated that they felt sure of their responsibilities. Fewer managers in all companies, however, felt that they knew what their superior thought of their performance; only 24 per cent of the managers in companies without formal appraisals and 60 per cent of the managers in companies with formal appraisals felt sure of their superior's evaluation of their performance. And, finally, a slightly larger proportion of managers indicated that their superiors had suggested improvements in their performance: 34 per cent of the managers in companies without formal appraisals and 64 per cent of the managers in companies with formal appraisals. The results of this study suggest that a formal appraisal program with post-appraisal interviews does aid in the clarification of position responsibilities and in the communication of individual evaluations and suggestions for improvement. However, the appraisal program is far from being so successful in this connection as might be hoped —probably because of a breakdown in the post-appraisal interview and communication between the boss and his subordinate.

The necessity for the communication intended by the post-appraisal interview is widely recognized. The development of individual managers depends to a large extent upon an understanding of responsibilities, a knowledge of particular shortcomings, and a desire for improvement. It also is recognized, however, that the typical post-appraisal interview does not adequately perform the intended functions. Management-appraisal programs are designed too frequently with major emphasis given to the performance of the appraisal and little consideration given to the communication

[30] Walter R. Mahler, "Bringing About Change in Individual Performance," in *Improving Managerial Performance, General Management Series No. 186* (New York: American Management Association, 1957), pp. 11-18.

of appraisal results. The "sandwich" approach to the post-appraisal interview is typical of the procedure suggested for the superior manager; the manager opens the interview with praise for the subordinate, sandwiches in criticism of his shortcomings, and concludes with another layer of praise. Thorough examination of the purposes of the post-appraisal interview and of the nature of the relationship encouraged in this interview is necessary for the establishment of procedures that effectively utilize the appraisal in management development. It is not enough merely to require such an interview as the last step of the appraisal program; rather, the entire program should be designed to facilitate and improve the interview, and careful attention should be given to the establishment of guides for conducting effective interviews.

Common criticisms of the post-appraisal interview concern the hesitancy of managers to discuss appraisals with their subordinates and the questionable value of the discussion in bringing about the desired results. It is pointed out that the appraised manager, being told of his weaknesses, assumes a defensive attitude and may challenge the appraisal results, forcing the superior manager into an embarrassing position. Consequently, the boss will try to avoid any discussion of the subordinate's weaknesses.[31] At the same time, it becomes quite difficult to bring about a desire for change, or an actual change, in the subordinate if he assumes a defensive attitude toward the interview. The "sandwich" approach to the interview is an inadequate attempt to put the appraised manager at ease and overcome this natural defensive attitude.

A reason for a defensive attitude by the appraised manager to the post-appraisal interview can be found in the nature of the appraisal yardsticks and in the approach taken in the interview. The appraisal of personal traits, characteristics, and abilities which has been common in management appraisal does not lend itself to frank and easy discussion in the post-appraisal interview. Most people inwardly resist any criticism of their characteristics and abilities, and most managers dislike being forced to explain and defend criticism of another's abilities. The typical post-appraisal interview in this instance is focused upon the individual, with the

---

[31] For criticism of the post-appraisal interview, see D. E. Balch, "Executive Selection and Inventory," in *Executive Selection and Inventory, Personnel Series No. 171* (New York: American Management Association, 1957), pp. 3-16; and McGregor, *op. cit.*

manager trying to make the subordinate aware of personal shortcomings. It is easy to understand why this discussion might be resisted by superior managers and how it well might fail to bring about the desired changes.

The growing popularity of performance appraisals in place of trait or ability appraisals reflects, in part, the feeling that performance appraisals are both more relevant and more useful in the post-appraisal interview. There is little opportunity for disagreement over appraisal results where objective performance standards are applied; both the subordinate and his boss obtain the same results in comparing actual performance with these standards. Discussion in the post-appraisal interview can be focused upon performance rather than upon the traits and abilities of the appraised manager. An increasingly common approach to this interview involves previous analysis of his performance by the subordinate manager, and his preparation of a program of action for the coming year.[32] The superior manager can then assume the role of coach in the interview, aiding and guiding his subordinate in the improvement of his performance. This approach would appear to be more effective in accomplishing the purposes of the interview. Furthermore, the attention given performance in the present assignment appears more relevant to over-all management development than does concentration upon a general set of abilities of managers.

THE MANAGEMENT INVENTORY

The *management inventory* is a method of taking stock of the management resources of an organization. It is similar to other traditional inventories in that it involves a periodic measurement and accounting of resources on hand—in this case, management resources. The management inventory is an attempt at appraisal of the entire management organization as a team, just as the individual management appraisal evaluates individual members of the organization. The management inventory facilitates the

[32] See, for example, Balch, *op. cit.;* C. E. Gray, "Appraising Professional Personnel: One Company's Experience," *Personnel,* Vol. 33, No. 5, March 1957, pp. 442-451; O. A. Ohman, "Executive Appraisal and Counseling—The Core of Management Development Effort," in *Addresses on Industrial Relations, 1956 Series, No. 24* (Ann Arbor: Bureau of Industrial Relations, University of Michigan, 1956); and Joseph M. Trickett, "Management Appraisals: A Key to Management Self-Development," *Personnel,* Vol. 32, No. 3, November 1955, pp. 234-245.

identification of strengths and weaknesses of the management team as guides to action in improvement of the management staff.

The general purpose of the management inventory is the improvement of the management staff through more efficient development and utilization of staff members. This general objective is sought through the achievement of several more specific purposes of the management inventory:

1. The identification of current weaknesses of the management staff and the measurement of current utilization of management resources provided in the inventory are intended to point up positions which are inadequately staffed and to indicate individuals whose full capabilities are not being utilized. In this manner, the inventory serves to guide action for management development.
2. Current status of the management team, as measured in the inventory, is used in the prediction of future organizational needs and in planning to prepare for these needs.
3. The management inventory is intended to stimulate interest in and concern for management development throughout the management staff. This is accomplished by focusing attention upon the needs of the organization and by pointing up the concern for development and utilization of each manager's capabilities.
4. The management inventory contributes to improved utilization of managers through the construction and maintenance of a centralized accounting of resources useful in the staffing of positions throughout the organization.

The concept of resource inventories is not new; these have been applied for years in the inventory and control of numerous physical resources of production. However, this concept has been applied in the inventory of managers only recently. The major value of the inventory lies in its contribution to improved development of the management organization. The growing interest in the management inventory is largely a consequence of growing concern over management development.

Management Inventory Measures

The general process of inventorying any resource consists of measuring and counting the available resources. The practical usefulness of the completed inventory is influenced to a large extent by the form in which results of the inventory process are summarized.

Several different measures have been developed for use in the management inventory. The three most common of these measures are the coded organization chart, the replacement table, and centralized personnel files.

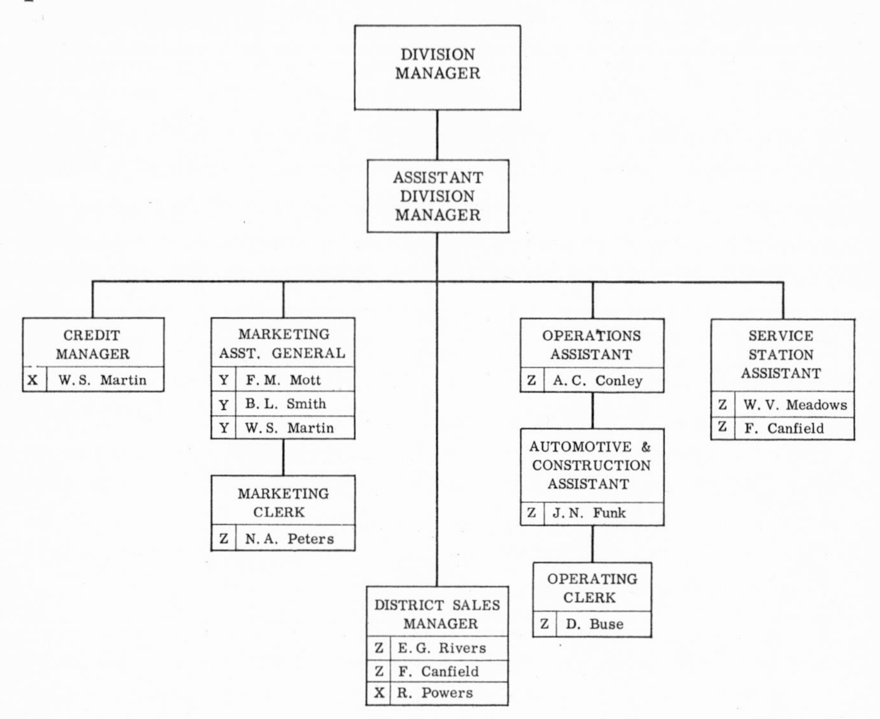

Fig. 9. Replacement Chart. From George B. Corless, "Executive Development Program for Affiliates of Standard Oil Co. (N. J.)," *Personnel Series No. 100* (New York: American Management Association, 1945).

Coded Organization Chart. The coded organization chart is an attempt to illustrate the over-all status of the management organization in one measure. It has been developed to provide a ready reference to the efficiency of performance throughout the organization and to the adequacy or strength of reserves throughout the organization. This summary or measure of the management inventory is prepared by using an enlarged organization chart indicating relationships among the management positions. Special codes, symbols, or colors are then used to indicate the present performance and readiness for promotion of the incumbent of each position in the chart. An example of one such chart is illustrated in Figure 9. Some

HYSTER

HYSTER COMPANY

ORGANIZATION DEVELOPMENT SUMMARY

CONFIDENTIAL

5

DEPARTMENT: ____________

LOCATION: ____________

INCUMBENT	POSITION	PERFORM-ANCE	POTENTIAL	AGE	YRS. WITH CO.	YRS. ON PRESENT JOB	FIRST REPLACEMENT	DATE READY	PERFORM-ANCE	POTENTIAL	AGE	YRS. WITH CO.	YRS. ON PRESENT JOB	SECOND REPLACEMENT	DATE READY	PERFORM-ANCE	POTENTIAL	AGE	YRS. WITH CO.	YRS. ON PRESENT JOB

KEY:

PERFORMANCE:
A—Outstanding
B—Very Satisfactory
C—Satisfactory
D—Questionable
E—Unsatisfactory
F—New on the job

POTENTIAL:
1—Outstanding
2—Very High
3—Average
4—Limited
5—None at Present
6—New on the job

Prepared By: ____________ Date: ____________

Reviewed By: ____________ Date: ____________

____________ Date: ____________

Form No. 765—557

Fig. 10. Organization Development Summary, from the Organization Development Manual, Hyster Company, 1957.

of these charts also indicate the expected retirement date of the position incumbent and the most likely backstop for each position. The specific information coded in the chart and the codes used will vary with each organization. In general, the coded organization chart is intended to provide an over-all summary of the capabilities of the present management staff compared with specific organization assignments. The coded information should include only that information most useful in pointing up inefficient utilization of resources and needs for development within the organization.

Replacement Table. The replacement table is a more detailed presentation of certain of the information contained in the coded organization chart. The coded organization chart focuses attention upon the entire organizational unit portrayed, and the replacement table focuses attention upon individual positions within the organization. In general, the replacement table is intended as a statement of the management reserves available for replacements or backstops in each position of the organization. Each position of the management organization is considered separately. The present incumbent is listed first, with an indication of his performance, his readiness for promotion, and his expected retirement date. Listed after the present incumbent are each of the possible replacements, with indications of their present performance, their readiness for promotion into the position, and other relevant information. Replacements are listed in the order of their readiness for promotion to the position. An example of such a replacement table is presented in Figure 10. These detailed tables provide an indication of the adequacy of reserves throughout the organization and also indicate the spots where development is required or where a surplus of reserves is available. They may also serve as staffing schedules for each position in the management organization.

Centralized Personnel Files. The most detailed accounting of management resources in the management inventory usually is kept in the form of management personnel files. These files contain the most specific information maintained for each member of the management staff. The files are centralized at some point in the organization to facilitate the planning of management personnel actions throughout the organization. They may be consulted, for example, in staffing individual positions. Centralization of the information contained in the files contributes to the efficient utilization of managers throughout the organization; individuals in all organization units are considered available for assignment to other units as such assignments are required for the benefit of the organization or of the individual manager. The types of specific information usually contained in these files include personal history, work experience, and results of management appraisals. The information and files may be organized and indexed on the basis of skills and experiences of the managers or on the basis of appraised potential for various assignments. General Electric and American Cyanamid have developed cross-indexes of managerial qualifications utilizing IBM cards; other companies often use colored tabs on file folders.[33] In summary, the centralized filing of specific information about individual managers provides easily available information useful in planning for efficient utilization of these management resources. This centralized filing and indexing are particularly useful in large companies with a number of organizational units; they facilitate the utilization of managers throughout the organization for the over-all benefit of the organization.

Process of Management Inventory

The process of management inventory involves the measurement, collection, and organization into useful form of information concerning individual managers within the organization. As with the management appraisal, the process of inventorying management resources is quite important in the achievement of certain of the goals of the inventory. The process of the inventory, as well as results, serves to focus attention upon the adequacy of present resources and to stimulate interest in management development.

Certain of the information required in the management inventory is quite objective and a matter of record; it need be organized only once and then occasionally brought up to date. This includes information such as education, work experience, and other personal-history information. This type of information might be obtained at the time of initial employment and maintained by recording all new experiences as they occur. There is a certain value to be obtained, however, through solicitation of this information from the individual manager at the time of the initial inventory and periodically there-

---

[33] For examples, see Stephen Habbe, "Who Gets the Promotion?" *Management Record,* Vol. 29, No. 5, May 1957, pp. 166-168; "Keeping Tabs on Key Men," *Factory Management and Maintenance,* Vol. 115, No. 4, April 1957, p. 113; and "Keeping Tabs on Key Personnel," *Nation's Business,* Vol. 45, No. 12, December 1957, pp. 42-43, 90-91.

after. The importance placed upon the inventory and the concern for management development is brought home to the individual manager when he is asked to provide this information for the inventory; periodic review and revision of his record serve to remind him constantly of the steps taken to insure efficient utilization and development of individual managers.

A relatively common practice in the inventorying of managers involves the assignment of inventory responsibilities to a staff coordinator of management development. This coordinator is responsible for the periodic collection and organization of information in the inventory and for the preparation of predictions based upon the inventory. He may, for example, conduct studies of retirement and turnover in the prediction of vacancies to occur in the organization. This coordinator also is responsible for the centralized management personnel files and the coordination of personnel assignments and actions throughout the organization. The coordinator prepares the coded organization charts and replacement tables for organizational units from the information supplied him in the inventory.

A critical element of the management inventory is provided by the individual management appraisal. It is the appraisal which provides the measures of present performance and promotability of individual managers. As noted earlier, these individual appraisals are added to the inventory through the appraisal review. The staff coordinator may prepare coded organization charts for each organizational unit based upon the last previous appraisal; these are brought up to date in the appraisal review. Each individual manager reports to his superior or to a committee of superiors, explaining the results of the current appraisal of his subordinates and plans for their development. Notation of the current appraisals of performance and potential on the chart points up changes since the previous appraisal and calls attention to both particular needs for development and cases of under-utilization of managers in the unit. Review of these appraisals provides the superior manager an opportunity to familiarize himself with the performance and potential of managers at lower levels of the organization. It further enables the superior manager to spot problem areas in management development and to emphasize the importance of development to his immediate subordinate. Extension of this appraisal review up through the various levels of the organization builds the management inventory until it is complete for the entire organization and serves as a control over management development within each unit of the organization. This phase of the inventory process is perhaps the most valuable aspect of the inventory because of its direct and immediate impact upon management development. In this respect, the process of the management inventory is more valuable than the completed inventory, which is most useful in the planning of specific personnel actions affecting the development and utilization of managers.

SUMMARY

The efficient development and utilization of the management team entails a periodic examination of the capabilities and weaknesses of individual managers and their assignments as members of the management team. The techniques of management appraisal and inventory are intended to provide this periodic assessment. In addition to their value for planning the general development of the management team, management appraisal and inventory both influence management development in several other respects. Performance of the assessment involved in appraisal and inventory provides a direct stimulus to the development and utilization of managers within individual organizational units. The assessments provided in the appraisal and inventory influence management development in the application of various activities of management development; these assessments are used as the basis for decisions concerning training, assignment, and placement of individuals and concerning compensation. In short, management appraisal and inventory are the basis of much of the management development of any organization. The performance of the management appraisal and inventory were discussed in this chapter; later chapters will discuss in more detail the application of appraisal and inventory results in the development of the management team.

SELECTED BIBLIOGRAPHY

McGregor, Douglas, "An Uneasy Look at Performance Appraisal," *Harvard Business Review,* Vol. 35, No. 3, May-June 1957, pp. 89-94.

Mahler, Walter R., and Guyot Frazier, "Appraisal of Executive Performance, the 'Achilles' Heel' of Management Development," *Personnel,* Vol. 31, No. 5, March 1955, pp. 429-441.

Rowland, Virgil, *Improving Managerial Performance* (New York: Harper and Brothers, 1958).

Chapter SIX

Management Compensation

INTRODUCTION

How much should a manager be paid? What are the factors that determine the compensation appropriate for a manager's job? These questions are important and interesting in their own right. Also, these questions about management compensation cannot be divorced from considerations of management development. The structure of management compensation within an organization is an important influence in the development of the management team. The compensation structure is a system of rewards and incentives which expresses the philosophy of the organization and sets the climate for management development. The rewards and incentives provided in management compensation indicate the general goals of the organization and its willingness to reward performance contributing to these goals. Further, the compensation structure is a structure of performance directives to members of the management team, and it facilitates or hinders development of the management team according to the degree of accord between these directives and the objectives of management development. In this chapter we examine the relationships between management compensation and management development and propose several guides to the application of compensation principles in development of the management team.

PROBLEMS OF MANAGEMENT COMPENSATION

Management development was defined earlier as a complex of activities designed to improve present performance and future strength of the management team. Management compensation seeks the same general objectives. The structure of management compensation is a system of rewards aimed at attracting qualified managers to the organization, stimulating managerial performance and development, and retaining the loyalty and interest of members of the management team. A number of other considerations also influence the design of management compensation practices, however, and inconsistencies appear between management compensation practices and management development activities despite the general similarity of organization goals.

Many of the problems of management compensation stem from the lack of an acceptable rationale of management compensation. In general, we lack a clear understanding of what is to be accomplished by management compensation. Nor have we fully grasped the justification for the use of management compensation in accomplishing specified objectives. The rationale for compensation of the owner-manager of past years was based upon his role as an entrepreneur and "risk-taker." The owner-manager supplied capital and managerial talent, and his compensation was determined by the success of the enterprise. The professional manager of today is likely to be an employee, the capital for the enterprise being provided by the stockholders. The rationale of owner-manager compensation based upon profits of the enterprise is no longer adequate. Instead, we need an understanding of what we want to accomplish through managerial compensation and how we can apply compensation criteria developed from these objectives. Much of present practice in management compensation shows the lack of such a rationale. Specific compensation practices have been grouped together into a program for compensation without consideration of the over-all objectives of the compensation program. All of these compensation practices can be made more effective through a unified compensation program than they can when conducted as separate and distinct practices.

The problem of determining the worth of an individual manager is basic to all management compensation. The criteria used in determining compensation tell the manager what is important from the standpoint of the organization and what he must do to achieve success within it. These compensation directives probably are more important in shaping managerial behavior than are the directives communicated through promotion policies, management training, and management appraisal and counseling. In spite of this fact, many companies attempt to divorce management appraisal and development from management compensation. The usual reason given for this centers around the difficulties in defining the criteria for management compensation, and also the difficulties encountered in resolving inconsistencies between these criteria and the objectives of management development. Such an approach denies the importance of management compensation in shaping individual development and fails to realize the potential benefit of management compensation as an aid to development of the management team. Conflict between compensation practices and the goals of development also limits the effectiveness of activities for development of the management team.

Another group of problems of management compensation is related to the influence of general social and economic considerations upon organization practices. For example, continuing inflation, successive wage increases for non-managerial employees, and individual and corporate income tax provisions have all contributed to the shaping of managerial compensation in the years since World War II. Continuing inflation has focused attention in the shaping of compensation upon real income and standards of living. Corporate and individual income tax provisions have directed attention toward forms of compensation which provide a maximum contribution to the manager's real income at a minimum cost to the organization. Increases in managerial compensation have not kept pace generally with wage increases for non-managerial employees—in part because of the relatively greater cost to the organization of equal increases in take-home income. For example, average gross income of supervised employees increased 106 per cent between 1939 and 1950, while average income of top management increased only 35 per cent.[1] As a consequence, managerial salary differentials have been reduced considerably in recent years, particularly in the ranks of middle management. Alternative forms of compensation have been developed

[1] Edward C. Bursk, "Thinking Ahead," *Harvard Business Review*, March 1952, pp. 141-156.

which supplement managerial salaries at a reduced cost to the organization. These alternative forms of compensation are not equivalent in terms of influencing managerial performance and development, however, even when they are equivalent in terms of contribution to the manager's real income. Salary, bonus, and pension plans provide incentives for different types of managerial behavior. Development and application of these alternative forms of compensation have contributed to the difficulties of relating compensation practices to management-development objectives; the task is thereby increased in scope and complexity.

A number of more specific problems arise in the coordination of management compensation and management development. Some of these problems are mentioned as illustrations of the need for coordination, although the types of problems encountered and their solutions vary considerably from one situation to another. One such problem arises in the relating of compensation and training assignments. Any attempt to rotate managerial assignments for training and development purposes runs into difficulties unless it is geared to the realities of the compensation structure. Assignments which would be beneficial in terms of training and development often are impractical because of the consequences in terms of the individual's compensation. Furthermore, assignments to positions with higher or lower levels of compensation usually are viewed as promotions or demotions even though the individual's compensation is not adjusted during the training assignment. Consequently, assignments which would provide desirable training effects often are not carried through in practice. Better planning of assignment rotation to facilitate rotation within levels of compensation, or the development of special compensation provisions for these assignments, would facilitate improved development.

MANAGEMENT COMPENSATION POLICY

A clear understanding of aims and objectives is needed as a first step in the establishment of a sound management compensation program. Many programs for management compensation appear to be patchwork quilts of little bits and pieces which have been added over a period of time without any comprehensive plan. Management compensation policies setting forth the objectives of compensation and the rationale of the organization's approach to compensation are needed to guide the development of an effective compensation program and to evaluate the various elements of the program. Numerous alternative forms and methods of management compensation exist. Many current programs for management compensation have resulted from the unplanned addition of specific methods and techniques over time. It is unrealistic to expect that a sound program would emerge from the selection and combination of elements on the basis of current popularity or needs occasioned by temporary problems. It is not surprising that managers, stockholders, and interested observers attack many existing management compensation practices as gimmicks, in view of the lack of a rationale relating all of the many different practices of compensation.[2] The development of a statement of management policies is a first step in the rationalization of management compensation and in the development of a compensation program which will assist in the accomplishment of organizational objectives. Such a policy statement also is a prerequisite in the coordination of management compensation and development of the management team.

What are the goals of management compensation? What are we trying to achieve through management compensation? Answers to these questions are more often implied in practice than stated in policy. General Dynamics Corporation is one organization which has recognized the need for a rationale of management compensation and the communication of this rationale within the organization.[3] Their answers, and the answers implied in the compensation practices of other organizations, suggest the following goals and objectives of management compensation.

1. *Attract competent managerial personnel.* A rather obvious objective of management compensation is the attraction of competent personnel to the organization. New members of the management team must be recruited constantly to provide resources for expansion and reserves for replacement of present personnel. The prospective

---

[2] See, for example, Arch Patton, "Executive Compensation: Are 'Gimmicks' Necessary?" *The Management Review,* April 1954, pp. 258-259; and "How Much Should an Executive Be Paid?" *Financial Management Series No. 97* (New York: American Management Association, 1951). Also see Perrin Stryker, "How Much Is An Executive Worth?" *Fortune,* Vol. 51, No. 4, April 1955, pp. 108-111, 226-234.

[3] An attempt to develop a rationale for management compensation can be seen in *The Executive Function and Its Compensation,* prepared by the University of Virginia Graduate School of Business Administration for General Dynamics Corporation, 1958. 55 pp.

recruit to the management team, whether a trainee or an experienced manager, weighs many factors in making his decision to join the organization. Compensation is only one of the factors considered. However, compensation is an important factor in the decision, since it largely determines the standard of living available to the manager. It also has certain status and prestige implications. Furthermore, compensation is one of the more objective and easily compared factors considered. The prospective recruit finds it easier to compare the compensation offered by one organization with that offered by competing organizations than to compare other relevant factors. Compensation, thus, assumes more importance in most instances. Compensation also is the factor most easily controlled and shaped by the organization in its attempts to attract competent personnel.

2. *Provide incentives for development.* Development of individual managers within the organization is largely self-development. The organization cannot force development; the most it can do is to provide a climate which stimulates and guides self-development. The compensation and promotion policies are important elements of this climate. Compensation differentials among management positions and levels can provide incentives for development. They will contribute little to desired development, however, unless there is a conscious effort to correlate compensation with promotion practices and to correlate both with the over-all objectives of management development.

3. *Provide incentives for performance.* Management compensation seeks improved performance of the management team through improved individual performance and more effective teamwork. The implementation of practices to achieve this objective requires careful consideration. Compensation differentials and advantages must be closely related to those levels of individual performance deemed critical to effective performance of the management team. Participation of the owner-manager in the profits of the organization in past years provided an automatic incentive to performance which benefited the organization. No such direct incentives are provided automatically in the compensation of the professional manager. They can be provided in modern management compensation, but only if compensation practices are related directly to desired individual and team performance.

4. *Retain qualified managers.* Retention of qualified managers is vital to the maintenance of the management team. As in the recruit-

ment of management personnel, there are many factors which influence the decision to maintain affiliation with an organization and to contribute to its program. In general, the manager must feel that his personal aims and objectives are being furthered through association with the organization, and that it is in his interest to participate in the organization. Compensation is one of the factors most easily shaped to provide the needed link between organization objectives and personal objectives. Through the use of management compensation to achieve this end, the achievement of objectives of individual managers becomes a formal goal of management compensation.

5. *Protect stockholder benefits.* This objective of management compensation is recognized formally less frequently than the objectives already mentioned. It is no less important than the other objectives, however. The recognition of stockholder rights and interests in management compensation practices provides a needed control over management compensation. Management compensation is a tool of the organization to be used in directing and guiding progress toward achievement of the organization's goals. The recognition of stockholder interests in management compensation can be an effective control over the use of this tool.

MANAGEMENT COMPENSATION PRACTICES

Management compensation practices vary in essentially two respects, the form of the compensation and the level of compensation. The number of forms of management compensation constantly increases as new variations or practices are developed to achieve specific objectives more accurately. Competition in recruiting and maintaining a team of competent personnel contributes to this development of new forms of compensation as organizations seek more attractive incentives for highly paid executives. Variation in the amount or level of compensation is somewhat more difficult to observe and compare because of the vast differences between forms of compensation. For example, it is quite difficult to determine pension provisions or stock options which would be equivalent to $1,000 in salary. It is possible that much of the variation noted in managerial salaries and other monetary compensation stems from opposite variations in non-monetary compensation, and that total compensation, if it could be measured, would show less variation. Studies of inter-company and inter-industry levels of compensation usually are limited to a comparison of salary, bonus, and pension payments. These studies indicate rather consistent differences in the amounts paid by organizations in these forms of compensation.[4] For example, levels of compensation vary directly with the sales and profits of the organization. Level of sales apparently is the key factor, since both profit and compensation vary directly with sales. Very definite industry differences also have been noted, the manufacturing industries leading in levels of compensation, with public utilities and transportation compensating at the lower levels. Within manufacturing, the automobile and steel industries consistently provide relatively higher levels of compensation. Again, however, sales may be the key relationship, the industry level of compensation varying directly with the average size of company sales in the industry. An interesting hypothesis suggests that compensation varies directly with sales because the size of the management team also varies directly with sales.[5] As the management team grows in size, the number of levels in the hierarchy tends to grow. Levels of compensation at the supervisory level of management are similar in most organizations, and the maintenance of salary differentials between levels of management results in a larger number of highly paid positions within the larger firms. This explanation thus attributes inter-company and inter-industry differentials to the bureaucratic elements of the organization.

The problems of equating alternative forms of managerial compensation complicate any over-all consideration of the impact of

---

[4] See Grover Amen, "Patterns in Top Management Pay," *Dun's Review and Modern Industry,* Vol. 69, No. 7, May 1957, pp. 68-71; Arch Patton, "Building on the Executive Compensation Survey," *Harvard Business Review,* Vol. 33, No. 3, May-June 1955, pp. 84-90; A. Patton, "What Management Should Know About Executive Compensation," *Dun's Review and Modern Industry,* Vol. 69, No. 4, February 1957, pp. 43-44; A. Patton, "Industry Patterns for Executive Compensation," *Harvard Business Review,* September-October 1955, pp. 121-132; David R. Roberts, "New Facts About Executive Compensation," *The Management Review,* July 1955, pp. 473-489; Dean H. Rosensteel, "Top Management Compensation: AMA's Latest Survey," *The Management Review,* Vol. 45, No. 1, January 1956, pp. 27-31; Jerome M. Rosow, "From the Thoughtful Businessman," *Harvard Business Review,* Vol. 34, No. 6, November-December 1956, pp. 144-145; A. R. Towl, "Patterns of Executive Compensation," *Harvard Business Review,* Vol. 29, No. 4, July 1951, pp. 25-36; "New Survey on Executive Compensation," *Personnel,* Vol. 31, No. 4, January 1955, pp. 287-288; David R. Roberts, "A General Theory of Executive Compensation Based on Statistically Tested Propositions," *Quarterly Journal of Economics,* Vol. 70, No. 2, May 1956, pp. 270-294.

[5] Herbert A. Simon, "The Compensation of Executives," *Sociometry,* Vol. 20, No. 1, March 1957, pp. 32-35.

compensation differentials upon management development. For example, profit-sharing, stock options, pensions, and salary each focus attention upon different criteria of managerial performance and provide incentives to different forms of managerial behavior. Consideration of compensation differentials in terms of some over-all measure of monetary value neglects the essential differences of these alternative forms of compensation. Thus, the following discussion is concerned primarily with a comparison of alternative forms of compensation and their relationship to the objectives of management compensation.

Salary Compensation

Salary is the single most basic element of compensation. Other forms of compensation frequently are combined with salary, but these additional forms merely supplement the more basic program of salary compensation. Salary was for many years the only form of compensation provided managers, the additional forms having been developed in more recent years. Today salary is the most common form of management compensation and forms the basic core of every management compensation program.

Salary compensation is important to the individual manager for several reasons. For one thing, it is the most important single determinant of the individual's standard of living, since salary commonly is the largest single element of compensation and since it is relatively more stable over a period of time than are other forms of compensation. The amount of salary to be paid over a period of a year or more is known, and expenses can be planned around that guarantee. Salary also determines the manager's status and prestige quite apart from its impact upon his standard of living. Salary is a measure of the manager's market value and indicates his relative standing within the community of colleagues. For example, a story is told of a manager who was offered $50,000 a year in salary and an equal amount in deferred compensation. He requested that the entire amount be paid in salary despite tax disadvantages because he wanted to be a "$100,000 a year" manager.[6] In this connection, salary is the most frequently compared element of management compensation. It is used in the comparison of positions within and between organizations because it is so easily measured. Finally, salary is im-

[6] "Ideas Shift on Executive Pay," *Business Week*, No. 398, June 16, 1956, p. 85.

portant to the manager, for it usually determines his eligibility for participation in non-salary programs of compensation as well as the extent of this participation. Both the number and the amount of non-salary elements of compensation, such as bonus and pension, vary directly with the level of salary, these additional forms of compensation reflecting the basic salary structure.

Salary compensation is a major concern to the organization for many of the same reasons. Salary commitments form the largest single element of management compensation cost to the organization and require concern for this reason alone. The importance of salary as a cost to the organization is increased by the relatively fixed nature of the cost—a cost that varies little with the earnings of the organization. Salary also is of concern to the organization because of the importance of salary to the individual manager. Since salary plays a large role in the individual manager's evaluation of job opportunities, salary is an important consideration in any program to recruit, motivate, and retain competent managers. Also, since much of the entire compensation program is based upon the salary structure, the effectiveness of the over-all compensation program depends largely upon the salary component of the program.

The salary component of management compensation is multipurpose, bearing upon all of the objectives mentioned earlier—the attraction, motivation, and retention of personnel. Contrary to most other elements of management compensation, it is not pinpointed to the achievement of any subgroup of objectives. The salary program is designed and evaluated in terms of its implications for the achievement of all of these objectives, and a number of specific practices must be considered in the design of a salary program to aid in their achievement.

The maintenance of competitive salary scales is a significant factor in the attraction, motivation, and retention of managers. The comparison of salary scales by manager recruits is a major element in their evaluation of organizations; the salary scale is considered representative of the organization's philosophy and policies. Once affiliated with the organization, the manager continues to compare his salary with the salaries paid in other organizations and with those received by his business associates. The maintenance of competitive salary scales is necessary to elicit the full cooperation of the manager and to retain him in the organization. In past years, organizations often neglected review and revision of salary scales until forced to do so by the impending loss of a key manager. The growth of management compensation surveys in recent years attests to the increasing attention being given to the maintenance of competitive salary scales. Results of these surveys are consulted annually by many companies in the evaluation of their salary structures; more than half of the companies participating in a recent compensation study indicated their use of these surveys.[7] Existing surveys of management compensation are less than adequate, however, and a number of problems face the organization using them in the evaluation of its salary structure. For example, one problem lies in the identification of competitors for the same management abilities as those required within the organization.[8] The market for rank-and-file employees is relatively easy to identify because of known patterns of employee mobility and movement; similar study is required at the managerial level to identify the limits of markets for managerial employees. The inter-industry salary differentials already noted in management compensation surveys suggest that companies commonly consider industry and, to a lesser extent, company size as the important factors in identifying competitors in salary evaluations. Studies of managerial mobility would be helpful in checking the adequacy of these assumptions. Another problem in the use of survey results stems from the nature of managerial positions. It is difficult to identify comparable management positions among various organizations in a survey of compensation because of variations in the grouping of management responsibilities and the lack of standardization of position titles. Consequently, many surveys report as much variation of salaries within a particular group of positions as occurs between that group and a related group of positions.[9] This problem has led many companies to rely upon surveys of supervisory compensation, or surveys of the compensation of company presidents, arguing that there is less variation in these positions than in middle-management positions.[10] The salary structure of the organization is established through some sort of job evaluation, and the entire structure moves up as

---

[7] "Job Evaluation," *Personnel Policies Survey No. 40* (Washington, D.C.: Bureau of National Affairs, December, 1956).

[8] See Nicholas L. A. Martucci, "Compensation Surveys for High-Level Positions," *Management Record,* Vol. 28, No. 12, December 1956, pp. 418-421 ff., for a discussion of problems involved in the use of compensation surveys and attempts to overcome these problems.

[9] *Ibid.*

[10] See Arch Patton, "Building on the Executive Compensation Survey," *Harvard Business Review,* Vol. 33, No. 3, May-June 1955, pp. 84-90.

supervisory or chief-executive compensation increases. Any adequate solution of the problem of maintaining competitive salary levels requires development of a standardized system of position analysis and classification to facilitate inter-company comparisons of salary. A standardized description such as was described in an earlier chapter might well be attempted in the search for methods to improve existing surveys and gain the maximum return from the cost and effort employed in these surveys.[11] Certainly, existing surveys of managerial compensation are not adequate for any precise comparison and evaluation of the salaries of managers.

The structure of salaries within the management organization also influences the development of a strong management organization. As noted above, this structure of salaries tends to determine the entire structure of compensation, since other forms of compensation generally vary in accordance with the salary structure. The individual manager, observing this structure and its relationship to the organizational hierarchy and responsibility differences, tends to identify the performance and responsibility associated with higher levels of compensation and direct his efforts accordingly. The criteria which determine salary differentials tell the manager what performance is most valuable to the organization and how he should direct his own development; the relative size of these differentials tells him the relative importance of the development of different abilities and provides an incentive to development.

Formal job evaluation is commonly used in the determination of relative value of managerial positions and in the establishment of salary differentials; surveys indicate that approximately 75 per cent of companies in the United States use some form of job evaluation in the establishment of a management salary structure.[12] Among the different methods of job evaluation, the point system is used most frequently. Numerical points are assigned to positions on the basis of the degree to which specific factors are present in each position assignment. The criteria employed in this evaluation vary considerably from organization to organization, reflecting in part the grouping of responsibilities into positions and the relative emphasis placed upon different responsibilities. The selection and weighting of factors to be used in job evaluation for managers is critical; these de-

[11] See Chapter 4.

[12] See Dean H. Rosensteel, "Supervisory Compensation—An Interim Report," *Personnel,* Vol. 33, No. 4, January 1957, pp. 354-361.

cisions point up the responsibilities and abilities considered most important to successful performance of the management team. Application of these criteria in job evaluation establishes the salary differentials which direct efforts of individual managers. Thus, an approach to job evaluation which is successful in one organization need not serve the purposes of another organization with different needs for management development; an approach which is tailor-made to fit the needs of the individual organization is much more likely to be successful than an approach borrowed from another organization.[13] Similarly, the determination of proper salary differentials is a matter of judgment, and will vary from one organization to another, depending upon the job structure, the need for incentives to performance and development, and the rapidity of promotion. Furthermore, these salary differentials should be evaluated periodically to determine their effectiveness and should be revised as necessary to achieve the desired results.

A degree of flexibility is commonly built into the salary program to permit variations of salary with individual performance and thus provide a relatively direct incentive for improved performance within an assignment. Flexibility is provided through the establishment of salary ranges for positions. The salary for a manager is set within this range on the basis of appraised performance in the position; he starts at the minimum salary for the position and progresses within the range as his performance improves. Although the exact size of this range varies from organization to organization, there is a widespread feeling that effective incentives for performance are provided only where the range approximates from 40 to 60 per cent of the minimum salary for the position.[14] The salary range for each position should be sufficiently large to permit about four or five salary increases for effective performance in that assignment. Salary increases of less than 10 per cent each provide relatively little incentive for improving performance. The performance appraisal for salary increases has a direct relationship to management development and can be a powerful technique for stimulating individual

---

[13] A guide to management job evaluation which can be applied in development of a tailor-made approach is presented in Thomas A. Mahoney, Herbert G. Heneman, Jr., and Elda Turnacliff, *A Guide to Job Evaluation: Managerial and and Non-Managerial* (An Experimental Design), Mimeographed Release No. 9 (Minneapolis, Minnesota: Industrial Relations Center, University of Minnesota, 1959), 119 pp.

[14] Dean H. Rosensteel, "Developing Effective Incentives for Management," *Personnel*, Vol. 31, No. 6, May 1955, pp. 520-529.

development and performance. This salary appraisal, with its direct and immediate consequences for the appraised manager, is intended to direct performance and development and should be viewed as an appraisal for management development. However, a sharp distinction is often drawn between the salary appraisal and other appraisals for management development. The salary appraisal is based solely upon performance, while other appraisals consider both performance and potential. Consequently, management personnel transactions, training, and coaching are based upon one appraisal, and compensation increases are based upon a separate and often contradictory appraisal. For example, many organizations which pay an annual bonus to managers have attempted to base this bonus upon individual performance. Many of these organizations have found in practice that there is little correlation between bonus recommendations and performance appraisals. The experience with bonus recommendations reported at Westinghouse is not unusual; here it was found that fewer than 25 per cent of annual bonus recommendations agreed with appraisal ratings.[15] This marked disagreement between managerial appraisals and salary recommendations is not uncommon, although few organizations are willing to admit it publicly. As a result, the distinction between appraisals for management development and appraisals for compensation has been emphasized in many organizations attempting to obtain accurate and reliable appraisals for developmental purposes. This distinction implies that appraisals submitted for salary recommendations, and the consequent adjustments of compensation, have little impact upon the individual manager's development and performance. The fact of the matter is that these salary appraisals are more likely to influence individual development and performance than coaching and counseling based upon appraisals which have no relationship to compensation. The compensation appraisal is a powerful influence in management development and will direct performance and development whether intended to or not. Consequently, the compensation appraisal should be incorporated into the over-all plan for development of the management team rather than ignored as a difficult and touchy subject. Practicing managers who are unwilling to relate the compensation appraisal to management development either are not committed to the objec-

---

[15] See Perrin Stryker, "The Executive Bonus," *Fortune*, Vol. 54, No. 6, December 1956, pp. 127-131, 160-170.

tives of development or do not understand the nature of management development.

Several disadvantages of salary compensation have been implied already in this discussion—disadvantages or shortcomings that call for the supplementation of salary in the design of a compensation program. One of these shortcomings stems from the relatively inflexible nature of salary, limiting its value as an incentive for performance and restricting organization activities through its contribution to fixed costs. Another widely recognized shortcoming of salary as a form of management compensation arises from existing income tax provisions. Progressive income tax rates tend to hinder the building of an estate from salary payments, thus reducing the possible contribution of salary to this personal goal of managers. In so far as building an estate is an important objective of the manager, he must be aided by other forms of compensation. Progressive income tax provisions also serve to reduce the incentive effect of salary increases or to force the organization to expend larger amounts than would otherwise be necessary to provide adequate incentives in take-home compensation. Thus, at higher levels of management particularly, salary is a relatively expensive method of compensation—more expensive than alternative forms of compensation, such as deferred compensation, pensions, and stock-purchase plans. Nevertheless, salary will continue to form the basic element of compensation for most managers despite its disadvantages. And salary practices provide the most direct tie between compensation and management development in most situations. The recognition given compensation as a guide to individual performance and development in structuring the salary program provides the basis for relating supplementary forms of compensation to the objectives of management development.

Salary Supplements

Salary supplements, as the term indicates, closely resemble salary as a method of management compensation. The term also indicates that salary is the basic element of management compensation and that other forms of compensation merely serve to supplement salary in the achievement of specific purposes. Compensation forms which are classed here as salary supplements resemble salary in that they usually consist of monetary or near-monetary compensation, as distinguished from benefits and services. They also tend to be related to responsibilities of the individual position and the manager's performance of these responsibilities. They differ from salary, however, in specific methods of payment and in the determination of scales or rates of compensation. Consideration of salary supplements in management compensation provides an element of flexibility to the compensation program. First, the mere inclusion of a second form of compensation for possible use provides flexibility. More important, however, these supplements are quite flexible in themselves and can be adapted to serve many different interests.

Salary supplements have grown in use during recent years; a recent American Management Association survey indicates that approximately one-half of the companies surveyed use supplements in their management compensation programs.[16] Common forms of supplemental compensation include the bonus, profit-sharing, incentive compensation, stock options, and other stock-purchase plans. The increasing popularity of these supplements probably stems from their relation to specific objectives which cannot be accomplished by salary alone. For example, it was mentioned earlier that salary compensation is characteristic of the professional manager as distinguished from the owner-manager, who participated in profits of the organization. It has been feared by many that salary compensation does not provide sufficient incentive for the professional manager to take an interest in the organization's performance. Salary supplements attempt to provide this incentive by fostering manager participation in ownership through stock-purchase plans or by permitting participation in company profits through profit-sharing. Relating compensation to company profits in these ways also provides more flexibility of compensation, reducing the fixed nature of salary alone. Salary supplements are used to focus attention upon the performance of individual position responsibilities as well as upon over-all company performance. The bonus and other forms of incentive compensation are capable of adjustment with variations in individual performance, thus providing somewhat more specific performance incentives. Certain salary supplements also are used to minimize cost to the company of given take-home compensation for the manager, or to narrow the gap between compensation cost and income to the individual. For

[16] See Dean H. Rosensteel, "Executive Compensation: Developing a Balanced Program," *The Management Review,* Vol. 45, No. 5, May 1956, pp. 388-399.

example, stock-option and purchase plans compensate the manager through capital appreciation, which is taxable at a lower rate than salary income. This consideration is of prime importance in compensating highly paid executives. The president of General Motors, for example, received salary supplements in 1957 which exceeded his salary.[17] Bethlehem Steel is another organization which has made extensive use of bonus and stock-option supplements to salary. It must be remembered, however, that the term "supplement" is used advisedly; these payments supplement salary in pinpointing specific compensation objectives, but they cannot replace salary as the basic form of management compensation.

Salary supplements are more common at higher levels of management than at supervisory and middle-management levels. This difference occurs for several reasons, one of which is the nature of responsibilities assigned at the different levels of management. Top-management responsibilities are much broader, and performance at this level has a greater impact upon the organization than is the case with supervisory and middle-management positions. In so far as salary supplements relate compensation to company performance and seek to provide personal identification with company performance, they have a greater impact at higher-level positions in management. Furthermore, tax provisions which make certain supplements less expensive than salary are most relevant in the design of compensation programs for highly paid positions. Thus, qualifications for supplementary compensation and the amount of supplementary compensation tend to vary with the salary structure. In this respect, supplementary compensation in general serves the same purpose as the salary structure and increases the impact of the salary structure upon the individual manager.

The most common of the salary supplements considered here is some form of bonus plan, although the popularity of the bonus appears to have declined in recent years. Bonus plans were found in approximately 60 per cent of companies during the 1920's, whereas only about 45 to 50 per cent of companies have bonus plans today.[18] This decline in popularity appears related to a shift in na-

---

[17] See Stryker, *op. cit.*, and "Compensation of Top Executives," *Studies in Labor Statistics No. 17* (New York: National Industrial Conference Board, 1956).

[18] See Stryker, *op. cit.*, and "Compensation of Top Executives," *Studies in Labor Statistics No. 17* (New York: National Industrial Conference Board, 1956), 31 pp.

ture of the bonus, the bonus of the 1920's being a form of profit-sharing and the modern-day bonus taking the form of incentive compensation; the profit-sharing bonus is being discarded and, where replaced, takes the form of incentive compensation. Bonus programs attempt to provide incentives by relating compensation to company performance, individual performance, or some combination of the two. The bonus is related to company performance by making the size of the total bonus fund dependent upon company earnings. As an example, McKesson and Robbins provides for the allocation to bonuses of 10 per cent of net earnings after taxes and after subtraction of a fixed return per share of stock.[19] The allocation of this fund among different management positions is difficult, and it is here that dissatisfaction frequently occurs. A common practice in past years involved allocation of the bonus fund in accordance with the salary structure, each manager sharing in the fund in the same proportion as he shared in total salary compensation. This type of bonus is more appropriately termed *profit-sharing*, since it involves nothing more than the allocation of a certain portion of earnings to be distributed among managers on the basis of relative salaries. The advantages and disadvantages of this type of bonus are discussed later under consideration of profit-sharing supplements. It should be noted here, however, that popularity of this type of bonus has declined because it provides little direct incentive for individual performance. Since the bonus varies with company performance rather than with individual performance, it provides direct incentives for individual performance only within those positions which have a direct impact upon company operations. More recently attempts have been made to provide incentives for individual performance as well as company performance with the design of slightly different bonus plans. The General Motors and American Seating Company plans are typical of these newer plans.[20] Bonus funds in both companies depend upon company earnings in much the same manner as at McKesson and Robbins. Allocation of the fund at General Motors is based upon performance of the various divisions and units of the company, and

---

[19] Stryker, *op. cit.*

[20] See Merle C. Hale, "The Bonus as an Incentive in Management Motivation," *Executive Compensation: Company Policies and Practices, Financial Management Series No.* 97 (New York: American Management Association, 1951, pp. 8-11; and R. H. Davis, "How to Set Up a Middle Management Incentive Plan," *Management Methods,* Vol. 11, No. 1, October 1956, pp. 51-58.

finally upon appraisals of the individual manager's performance. At American Seating, performance and costs for each unit are budgeted at the start of the year. The individual manager's bonus depends upon the extent to which he is able to reduce actual costs in achievement of the budgeted performance. Effective incentive compensation requires variation of compensation with variation of an element of performance which can be affected by the individual and by units of the management team. The profit-sharing type of bonus provides an over-all incentive for improved performance of the management team as a unit, but no specific incentives for the individual performance are required in this team effort. The alternative bonus plan attempts to provide incentives for both improved individual performance and improved performance of the management team as a unit.

Bonus plans would appear to have little if any direct impact upon compensation objectives apart from the stimulation of performance. The only influence of bonus payments upon the attraction and recruitment of managers, stimulation of self-development, and the retention of managers would tend to arise from the influence of bonus payments upon the amount of compensation provided, rather than from the nature of the compensation. In short, the fact that a portion of total compensation is provided in the form of a bonus probably has little effect upon these objectives; the bonus contributes to their achievement only in so far as the level of compensation is raised as a result of the bonus.

Profit-sharing is a supplement incorporated in many programs for management compensation. A number of organizations have attempted profit-sharing, although many of these attempts have been failures. Over 1200 profit-sharing plans have been introduced since 1842, only about 40 per cent of them successful enough to last for a relatively long period of time.[21] Approximately one-half of larger companies and one-third of smaller companies surveyed by the Bureau of National Affairs currently employ profit-sharing in their compensation programs.[22] The general purpose of profit-sharing is the stimulation of interest in the company's operations and encouragement of performance to increase the earnings of the

[21] See *Compensation of Management Personnel* (Chicago: The Dartnell Corporation, 1952), Section 1.

[22] See "Executive Compensation," *Personnel Policies Survey No. 45* (Washington, D.C.: Bureau of National Affairs, December, 1957).

organization. The profit-sharing bonus already described, where individual earnings are related to company earnings, is typical of most profit-sharing plans.

Profit-sharing supplements would appear to add little to salary in the attraction of personnel apart from the implication that total compensation over a period of time will be greater than without profit-sharing. The profit-sharing supplement may influence the individual's interpretation of company philosophy, the implication being that the organization is concerned with sharing company progress with members of the management team. Profit-sharing provides little direct incentive for individual performance except at higher levels of management where the individual's performance has a direct bearing upon company performance. It does tend, however, to focus attention upon company performance and probably serves as an incentive to relate individual performance to company performance in so far as is possible. Incentives for individual performance and individual self-development are provided through reinforcement of the salary structure, since shared profits commonly are allocated in accordance with the salary structure. The influence of profit-sharing upon the retention of personnel also appears limited to this reinforcing of the basic salary structure. The relationship between compensation and company earnings is an advantage and a disadvantage at the same time. The fixed nature of compensation can be reduced through the substitution of profit-sharing for salary, a possibility which makes profit-sharing attractive to the company unable or unwilling to commit large amounts for management salaries. The extent to which profit-sharing can be substituted for salary is limited, however, by the size of total compensation provided each position; the salary commitment for each position must be sufficient to provide a guarantee of security for the incumbent. This relationship between compensation and company earnings has proved a disadvantage at times, profit-sharing losing its appeal for the individual manager during periods of reduced company earnings. Thus, again, profit-sharing must be treated as a supplement and never as a substitute for basic compensation except in a very limited sense.

Stock-option and stock-purchase supplements focus attention upon still other objectives of management compensation. The primary advantages of these supplements lie in the attention focused upon company performance and the minimizing of compensation cost to the organization. These stock-purchase supplements compensate the manager through capital gains in the value of his stock and, to a lesser extent, through dividends received on the stock. It is hoped that they provide a sense of ownership of the company and an interest in the company welfare which could not be achieved through salary compensation alone. They also tend to focus attention upon an aspect of company performance not recognized in profit-sharing and bonus plans—the capital value of the company as reflected in stock prices. Thus it is hoped that an incentive is provided to improve the long-run value of the company as well as current earnings. Much of the discussion of profit-sharing as a form of compensation applies as well to stock-purchase plans. For example, this supplement also provides a direct incentive for individual performance only at higher levels of management, where performance is closely related to company operations. Stock-purchase plans also tend to reinforce the influence of the salary structure, since opportunities for stock purchase tend to vary with the level of salary. Stock-purchase plans can be quite useful, particularly in smaller companies, in the recruitment of managerial personnel and in their retention with the company. Smaller companies which may be unable to compete salary-wise in the recruitment of managers can offer opportunities for greater income to the manager which cost the company less than an equivalent salary. These opportunities arise from the nature of income tax provisions, capital gains being taxed at a lower rate than salary income. The stock-purchase plan also may be useful in the retention of personnel, since it offers them an opportunity to build an estate—which would be more difficult to accomplish through salary compensation alone.

Some concern has been expressed about the dilution of stockholder equity through stock-option and purchase plans. One variation of stock-purchase plans has been developed and is being used to prevent dilution of stockholder equities. Under this plan, the individual manager never actually gains control of stock which he purchases; instead, he is credited with the purchase of shares held in a common pool for this purpose. He receives dividends on the shares bought and may sell the shares as he wishes, always selling them back to the company. Ownership of the shares, thus, remains with the issuing company, the manager selling his shares in the case of separation from the company.[23] It is true that such a plan restricts the dilution of stockholder equity and certainly prevents alteration of stockholder control over the company. It should be recognized, however, that such a plan tends to restrict development of a sense of ownership by the manager and also limits the contribution of this compensation to the goal of estate-building by the manager.

The forms of compensation discussed in this section tend to supplement and reinforce salary compensation, thus enlarging the influence of salary compensation. At the same time, they tend to add flexibility to the compensation program by relating compensation to some measure of performance. This relationship of compensation with performance attempts to provide incentives influencing behavior of the members of the management team. However, the specific incentives provided vary considerably from one supplement to another, as does the compensation cost of these supplements. Thus, while all of the supplements add reinforcement of the salary structure and flexibility to the program, they must be considered individually in the selection of supplements to accomplish definite objectives of the organization.

Fringe Benefits

The term "fringe benefits" has been defined at various times to include almost every form of compensation other than salary payments. This occurs because the term "fringe" implies something which is supplemental, something unnecessary in itself but which is an addition or supplement in much the same manner that frosting enhances the attractiveness of a cake. All supplements to salary compensation conceivably could be classed as fringe benefits. The great variety of supplements to salary compensation, however, requires differentiation and classification for analysis. We have already identified as salary supplements those forms of compensation most closely related in purpose and method of payment to salary compensation. We shall distinguish also between what we term *fringe benefits* and *benefits and services.* Included in the former are forms of compensation designed to provide protection and security for the manager, forms such as insurance, pensions, and deferred compensation. The latter term includes forms of compensation with

---

[23] William J. Casey, *Executive Pay Plans* (New York: Institute for Business Planning, Inc., 1956), Chapter 10.

the apparent purpose of providing elements of status and benefits which contribute to the attractiveness of the position.

Fringe benefits appear in general to attempt to provide protection for the manager's income and a measure of security unavailable through other forms of compensation. They have the purpose of freeing the individual manager from concern over family security, thus permitting him to put greater concentration on his assignment. In has been observed that the provision of this security is the only manner in which the organization can free the manager from personal concern which prevents the full utilization of his talents hired by the organization. At the same time, it must be recognized that protective compensation is an attraction in itself, and that it supplements salary compensation by providing satisfaction of personal objectives of the individual manager. Furthermore, the value of fringes tends to vary in accordance with the salary structure, thus reinforcing the salary structure in much the same manner as do salary supplements.

The most common fringe benefit employed in the compensation of managers is the pension plan. Virtually every company provides pensions for management personnel today, although only about one-half of the companies provided such pensions in 1949.[24] Because of this, pensions are considered today almost as basic an element of management compensation as salary. Just as salary levels vary among companies and among positions within a single company, so pension benefits and qualifications for pensions vary. The same considerations which figured in our analysis of salary as an element of management compensation apply equally in the analysis of pension plans. Furthermore, pension provisions tend to vary in accordance with the level of salary, thus reinforcing the influence of salary compensation, as noted above. Two important differences between pensions and salary must be noted, however. The first concerns the influence of pensions upon one of the objectives of management compensation, the retention of personnel. The pension is considered a reward for service, and pension benefits vary with the length of service of the individual. They thus serve to discourage mobility of managers to a greater extent than does salary. How-

[24] See "The Trends in Executive Compensation Plans, A Dartnell Survey," *American Business*, February 1955, pp. 9-11; and "Compensation of Top Executives," *Studies in Labor Statistics No. 17* (New York: National Industrial Conference Board, 1956).

ever, the pension should not be relied upon as the major element of compensation designed to promote long service. It is possible to design a pension plan where separation of individual managers would involve the forfeiting of such liberal benefits that they would rarely consider leaving the organization. While such a pension plan might prevent manager turnover, it certainly would not elicit complete effort and cooperation of the managers. Rather, the pension should be viewed as providing an element of protective compensation unavailable through salary, and should not be used as a tool to overcome deficiencies of salary compensation for the retention of personnel. A second major difference between the pension and salary is found in the compensation cost. Management salaries might be increased to provide the opportunity for the individual manager to purchase annuities for his own retirement income. Present income tax regulations make it much less expensive, however, for the organization to purchase this pension than to provide the manager with the income required for his purchase of annuities. It is not uncommon for the organization to provide only a portion of the payments required for pension provisions, with the manager also contributing to his own pension.[25] Such an arrangement has the value of periodically reminding the manager of current company contributions and of promoting a partnership feeling about the pension.

Deferred compensation is a somewhat less common fringe benefit but one which appears to be growing in popularity. Only 18 per cent of a group of companies surveyed in 1952 made provision for deferred compensation, while in 1955, 90 per cent of the companies listed on the New York Stock Exchange made provision for some form of deferred compensation.[26] Deferred compensation is not so common as suggested by this latter survey, however, since it is provided most frequently in large firms. It also is a restrictive form of compensation in that it commonly is provided only for highly paid positions. In general, deferred compensation provides for postponement of certain compensation payments until after retire-

[25] J. O'Brien, "Bonus and Incentive Plans for Supervisors," *Management Record,* Vol. 18, No. 1, January 1956, pp. 2-5.

[26] See R. B. Fetter and D. C. Johnson, *Compensation and Incentives for Industrial Executives* (Bloomington, Indiana: Indiana University Press, 1952); and Arch Patton, "Annual Report on Executive Compensation," *Harvard Business Review,* Vol. 35, No. 5, September 1957, pp. 125-136.

ment or other termination of employment. Compensation is postponed in an attempt to level off the individual's earning curve over his lifetime, providing relatively greater income after retirement than would otherwise be available. This deferred compensation cushions the adjustment of income following retirement or termination of employment. Deferred compensation also provides much greater total compensation over the years at the same cost to the company, since lower rates of taxation are applied to the deferred portion of compensation than would be the case if they had been paid as salary during the period of employment. This arrangement permits the manager to build up a guaranteed retirement income and an estate which it would otherwise be impossible for him to do out of current income. Payment of deferred compensation in some companies is made contingent upon the performance of advisory services for the company following termination, or else carries with it the prohibition of employment with a competitor company. Ford Motor Company, for example, provides $25,000 a year deferred compensation for ten years after termination of employment of key executives on the condition that they do not accept work with a competitor company.[27] While such requirements may be considered necessary in a highly competitive industry like the automobile industry, it is not common in smaller companies or less competitive industries. Another automobile company, General Motors, employs a variation of deferred income in the payment of earned bonuses. Although an annual bonus is declared, only one-fifth of it is payable in any one year, the remainder being paid in succeeding years. Thus, the bonus received in any one year reflects the bonuses earned during the past five years, tending to smooth out annual fluctuations and cushion any sharp decline of the bonus. Furthermore, approximately two years of earned bonuses are retained in the manager's account at any point in time—bonuses that will be paid only upon condition of continued employment or retirement.[28] Thus, the deferred bonus plan attempts to retain executives in the face of opportunities for higher salary which may be offered by other companies.

[27] "How Ford Holds Its Top Men," *Business Week*, No. 1374, December 31, 1955, p. 41.

[28] See Merle C. Hale, "The Bonus as an Incentive in Management Motivation," *Executive Compensation Policies and Practices, Financial Management Series No.* 97 (New York: American Management Association, 1951), pp. 8-11.

In a very general sense, deferred compensation is similar to pensions, providing income after termination of employment and thus subject to the same considerations as mentioned above. It is a much more specialized and versatile technique of compensating executives, however. For example, deferred compensation can be provided on a group basis or an individual basis, permitting variation to fit the individual case. It can be a very attractive alternative to current salary and bonus payments for the highly paid executive, permitting him to pay a lower rate of taxes at the time of payment. Thus, deferred compensation, either salary or bonus payments, can be used much more effectively than pensions or bonuses in the recruitment of personnel. In one sense, deferred compensation can be viewed as current compensation and thus equivalent to salary but a form of salary that is held by the company and paid out at lower rates of taxation in later years. Thus, deferred compensation can be tailored to fulfill many of the purposes of both salaries and pensions.

A third type of fringe benefit is insurance provided for the manager by the employing organization. Insurance is a form of protective compensation which can be purchased directly by the organization at lower cost than it could be purchased out of current income by the individual manager. Common forms of insurance include life insurance, sickness and disability, hospitalization, and major medical insurance, all provided by about 90 per cent of companies.[29] The major purpose of such insurance is to provide the manager with security and thus free him from concern over common risks of insecurity. As with pensions, insurance benefits tend to vary with salary levels, thus reinforcing the impact of salary upon manager behavior. It would not appear that insurances add much, however, in the recruitment of personnel, in motivation for performance and development, or in the retention of personnel. Rather, this form of compensation is intended to provide an element of security for the manager at minimum cost, thus permitting more complete utilization of his capabilities in employment. Such insurance is considered almost as much a part of basic compensation today as are salary and pension compensation.

The fringe-benefit forms of compensation considered here share

[29] See "Fringe Benefits for Supervisors," *Personnel Policies Forum Survey No. 16* (Washington, D. C.: Bureau of National Affairs, January 1953), 14 pp.; and *Fringe Benefits for Executives* (Dartnell Press, 1956).

in common their relationship to the provision of security for the manager. They all tend to protect the manager against loss of income due to retirement, death, or the necessity of medical expense. In general, they seek to influence the retention of personnel and to free managers from family concerns, thus permitting greater attention to employment. At the same time, they provide these benefits at a lower net cost than would be the case if the manager were compensated through salary and then expected to purchase his own provisions for security. As protective forms of compensation, the structure of fringe compensation can be expected to change over time as the major elements of insecurity facing managers change. For example, a relatively new type of fringe compensation provides scholarships for the education of the manager's children; these scholarships provide security against the increasing costs of college education and the growing importance of this education for children. Similarly, other fringe benefits will be introduced as managers encounter new and different needs for protection and security. The existing structure of taxation, combined with increasing incomes, also can be expected to favor the growth in importance of fringe benefits in managerial compensation.

Benefits and Services

A fourth category of management compensation practices includes the various benefits and services provided the manager directly by the organization. These benefits and services often are overlooked in discussions of management compensation, since they appear rather incidental to the other forms of management compensation. They frequently are viewed as rather irksome additions to the management compensation program which add little to the impact of the program upon the individual manager but which are required in meeting the offers of competing firms. It is true, in this regard, that each of the benefits and services forms a small element of management compensation cost, although the entire program of benefits and services may constitute a sizable element of cost. However, the influence of benefits and services upon the individual manager probably is underestimated; the diversity of benefits and services made available provides a number of different compensation approaches, any one of which may appeal to the individual manager. In this sense, the benefits and services program is a buckshot approach to compensation—one of the many benefits and services probably finds its mark with each manager.

Each form of management compensation tends to influence both the real income and the psychic income of the manager. Salary compensation, capital gains compensation, and fringes provided directly by the company all have an immediate bearing upon the real income and the standard of living provided the manager. Furthermore, the relationship between the manager's level in the scalar hierarchy of management is reflected in both the amount and the form of compensation provided him, and each element of compensation thus reflects his status in the organization and community and adds to psychic income. Compensation through benefits and services also contributes to both real and psychic income.

Benefits and services compensation is similar to fringe compensation in that the organization provides the compensation directly to the manager without incidence of income taxation. In both cases, the organization purchases the compensation item and furnishes it to the manager, thus eliminating the need for the manager to purchase it out of his income. Benefits and services differ somewhat from fringes, however, in that they are less concerned with the security of the manager. Rather, the specific purposes of various benefits and services are quite varied, the most common single purpose apparently being the addition to the manager's income of items which he might be reluctant to obtain but which are less expensive for the company to purchase than it would be for the company to compensate the manager for his purchase of them. Thus, for example, a country club membership can be provided by the company at a lower cost than would be the case if the manager's salary were raised sufficiently to permit him to secure the membership after paying income taxes. Benefits and services thus also contribute to the status and prestige of the manager by providing him with benefits which imply a much larger personal income than is the actual case.

Certain of the benefits and services provided managers of an organization are merely extensions of benefits and services provided all employees. Thus, for example, the most common benefit of management compensation is the vacation, a benefit awarded all employees whether managerial or not.[30] The distinction between

[30] "Executive Vacations: A Survey of Company Policies," *American Business*, March 1957, pp. 25-34; Elizabeth R. Floyd, "Executive Vacation Practices, Results of a Survey," *Management News*, August 1957, pp. 7-8; and *Fringe Benefits for Executives* (Dartnell Press, 1956).

vacations at various levels of the company hierarchy is the length of vacation and the flexibility in timing, managers receiving relatively longer vacations and the opportunity to schedule them in accordance with personal desires. Much the same considerations hold for personal leaves granted for sickness or other reasons, this benefit being much more common at managerial levels and much more flexible in application.[31] Vacation and sick-leave benefits are provided for several purposes. First, they are intended as a form of compensation to the individual. At the same time, however, the organization seeks a definite gain from the vacation and sick-leave benefits: it is hoped that the manager will take advantage of these benefits and that they will contribute to his personal well-being, which in turn is expected to influence his performance. Many companies are becoming quite concerned about the failure of their executives to take advantage of vacations, and, in some instances, they are considering steps to encourage or force managers to utilize vacations to rest from their tasks and acquire a new outlook upon their positions. Somewhat related to the vacation benefit is a newer and less common benefit: payment by the company for the manager's vacation either at a special resort or at vacation facilities owned by the organization. Several large companies make a practice of purchasing vacation retreats for use as vacation facilities or conference and meeting facilities; these facilities are made available to vacationing managers in an attempt to encourage vacations and as a means of supplementing the manager's real income or standard of living. Other companies make a practice of leasing vacation facilities to be made available to managers, or of encouraging the manager's family to accompany him on business trips which might be turned into vacations.

The provision of medical examinations and consultation is a related benefit for managers which is growing in popularity; again, the gains are intended for both the individual and the organization.[32] Health is a concern to most people, and the provision of free medical examinations and consultation is a supplement to the individual's real income. At the same time, managerial health is becoming an increasingly important problem to the organization, and anything

[31] See "Executive Sick Leave Policies: A Survey," *The Management Review*, Vol. 54, No. 12, December 1955, pp. 842-843.
[32] *Ibid.*

which promotes the manager's well-being is considered a direct benefit to the organization. Many companies, consequently, are turning to the provision of medical benefits to the manager, some going so far as to demand annual check-ups for key managers. A question of ethics has arisen in this regard which is still unresolved in some organizations; this concerns the release of medical information about the manager. Some organizations insist that health information about the manager is a vital concern of the organization and should be made available to the management to permit the taking of necessary action. On the other hand, the more common approach recognizes that health information, while of concern to the organization, is essentially a personal matter. Thus, medical information is made available to the organization only if the manager wishes it. The individual manager is provided the results of his examination and the doctors counsel him on health problems; the manager then is trusted to take the action necessary for his personal benefit and for the benefit of the organization.

There is a whole class of benefits which might be viewed as direct contributions to the performance and efficiency of the manager but which at the same time extend beyond the mere demands of the position. They are, in a sense, indirect compensation for the manager. As one of these forms of indirect compensation, the expense account is rather directly related to the demands of the position. Here the manager is compensated for any out-of-pocket expenses involved in the performance of his responsibilities, expenses which otherwise would be paid out of personal income or else not incurred. Thus, the expense account protects the manager's standard of living made available by his basic compensation and insures that expenses necessary for the efficient performance of responsibilities will be covered. At the same time, the expense account frequently provides compensation in the improved standard of living made available to the manager when performing business of the organization; the business luncheon, or entertainment, frequently provides a standard of living higher than that normally enjoyed by the manager. Although the expense account has encountered much criticism in recent years for this characteristic and its effects upon the individual and his family, it cannot be denied that this element of the expense account benefit does figure as an element of compensation and does contribute to the real and psychic income of the manager.[33] Many of the same considerations would apply in a discussion of similar forms of indirect compensation—organization-paid professional and social memberships, provision of a company car for business and personal use, and so forth—all less common benefits but growing in usage.

Somewhat less related to performance of the manager's responsibilities are a number of benefits and services which probably have most importance as status symbols and thus contribute to psychic income. Included in this group would be such items as separate dining facilities for managers, special parking and transportation facilities for managers, segregated washroom facilities, office size, location, and furnishings, and position titles.[34] Almost anything can become a status symbol within a single organization as long as it is associated traditionally with scalar level in the management hierarchy. For example, managers in one organization used to compete for office equipment, the prized item being one of several old, scarred roll-top desks, prized because the president used a similar old desk in his office. Noticing the significance of these old desks, the president refurnished his office and discarded the desk, eliminating the status value of the remaining old desks. This concern over status symbols is the subject of a number of business reformers who would eliminate their influence. It certainly is true that concern for such status symbols can get out of hand and result in more attention being given them than is given performance. However, this situation suggests a need for revision of the basis for awarding status symbols—not the elimination of such symbols. Status symbols can serve as true incentives, incentives which can be utilized in management compensation if they are truly related to desired performance.

In summary, benefits and services form a definite part of a complete management compensation program. If well administered, they may truly serve to attract, motivate, and retain management personnel. Extreme care is called for, however, in the selection of benefits and services to be employed in the program, since each has a special appeal for different groups of people. Furthermore, the

[33] See "Executive Expense Accounts: A Survey of Company Practices," *American Business,* January 1957, pp. 29-34; and "Luxury on the Cuff: The World of the Big Expense Account," *The Management Review,* Vol. 46, No. 4, April 1957, pp. 9-10.

[34] See "The Rising Status of Status Symbols," *The Wall Street Journal,* October 29, 1957, pp. 1-2.

administration of these benefits and services must be controlled to insure their relation to desired objectives. A shotgun approach in the provision of benefits and services is likely to prove one of the most wasteful forms of management compensation, while a selectively balanced and well-administered program of benefits and services may prove quite effective.

MANAGEMENT COMPENSATION GUIDES

In summary, it can be said that management compensation can be a powerful tool of management development. The specific compensation practices of any organization contribute to the shaping of the management team as they affect the recruitment, motivation, and retention of managerial personnel. Thus, whether intended or not, management compensation is a factor in management development, and its potential influence must be accounted for, if not utilized in, the development of the management team. Several over-all guides for the utilization of management compensation policy and practice for the development of the management team are suggested in this section.

The designing of an effective program of management compensation involves selection of specific practices from among the many varied practices available. The brief review of practices in the preceding section points up some of the diversity of practice available. The observer of management compensation practices cannot help but be impressed by the lack of over-all compensation philosophy and policy illustrated by the practices of many companies. It appears that the choice of practices in many companies is based upon a "follow the leader" concept and the attraction to new practices. Additional practices are tacked onto an already existing set of practices seemingly because they are new developments or because some respected company employs the practices. A well thought-out and considered philosophy of management compensation is necessary for an effective program which will aid the development of a strong management team. Goals of management compensation must be developed and made known for the evaluation and selection of specific practices to achieve these objectives. In short, most organizations would benefit from a thorough examination and consideration of their compensation objectives and policies. Much of the confusion and criticism of management compensation practices could be eliminated through the development of a sound philosophy of management compensation.

A closely related thought concerns the education of employees, stockholders, and the general public concerning the functions of management compensation. Much of the criticism of management compensation stemming from these groups results from the lack of a consistent philosophy of management compensation. Managements have hesitated to make public their compensation philosophy and practices and have treated such matters as confidential whenever possible. Much of our knowledge today concerning management compensation is derived from proxy statements and compensation information filed with the Securities and Exchange Commission according to law. This hesitancy to disclose compensation information is interpreted as stemming from a lack of justification for current practices. The concept of the "just wage" is still applied by the public considering the compensation of various occupations, and the relatively high rates of management compensation tend to be condemned as unjustified unless acceptable explanations are offered. Such explanations are rarely offered. There need be no hesitancy of making public the concepts and principles of management compensation if they are based upon an acceptable philosophy of compensation. Thus, development of this over-all philosophy should be followed with the presentation and explanation of management compensation. Employee, stockholder, and public groups will not criticize and restrict management compensation practices which can be justified on a sound economic basis. They will remain suspicious and attempt to restrict company practice, however, in the absence of a known and accepted philosophy of management compensation.

A third guide concerns the application of compensation policy in the development of a program of practices. The wide diversity of management compensation practices offers an excellent opportunity to shape the compensation program to achieve specific needs and objectives. The special objectives of management compensation and the discussion of the preceding section also suggest the importance of flexibility in the application of specific compensation practices. Consistency of policy is an important guide in most all management action, while flexibility in practice can contribute much to the achievement of policy objectives. For example, many of the practices discussed in the preceding section have special appeals to managers of different ages and family situations. The young manager with a number of pressing family obligations has slightly different personal objectives and needs from those of the manager with few family obligations; thus, the former manager probably will be more interested in salary income and protective fringes, whereas the latter will be more interested in salary supplements which permit him to build an estate for retirement. As another example, some people receive greater personal satisfaction from status symbols or from benefits and services which contribute directly to their manner of living, while others receive greater satisfaction from monetary income. These differences should be kept in mind in the design of a compensation program so that maximum incentive is offered each individual manager. A great deal more flexibility of compensation practices could be provided than is found at present. There is no apparent reason, for example, why the individual manager should not be permitted to express his choice of methods of compensation. Compensation scales could be specified in terms of total cost to the company, and the individual manager might be permitted to determine the particular form this compensation should take. In short, we should recognize in practice that management compensation is intended to facilitate the achievement of individual objectives through participation in the organization and should provide the flexibility of practice necessary to make the most effective use of compensation expenses.

Another guide relates back to the philosophy and policy of management compensation; this guide concerns the need for continual research and evaluation of management compensation practices. Very little is known about the actual effects of different compensation practices or the degree to which they achieve specific objectives. The evaluation of practices in the preceding section, for example, is based largely upon hunches and expectations. Research and evaluation have been prevented in many instances by a lack of clear-cut objectives; this shortcoming can be overcome with the development of a sound philosophy and policy of management compensation as recommended above. Development of an effective program of compensation to achieve stated objectives depends in large part upon the initiation of research for the evaluation of alternative practices. There probably is no other single element of management development which is in greater need of evaluation than the area of management compensation. Attempts at evaluation of other elements of management development are under way already; it is equally important that we evaluate management compensation practices.

SELECTED BIBLIOGRAPHY

Abbott, Charles C., J. D. Forbes, and Lorin A. Thompson, *The Executive Function and Its Compensation*, prepared by the Graduate School of Business Administration of the University of Virginia for General Dynamics Corporation, 1957.

Casey, William J., *Executive Pay Plans* (New York: Institute for Business Planning, Inc., 1956).

Meiklejohn, Robert P., "A Philosophy of Executive Compensation," in *Improved Techniques for Administration and Control, General Management Series No. 187* (New York: American Management Association, 1957).

Chapter SEVEN

Recruiting for Management

INTRODUCTION

Every organization faces the need to recruit candidates for the management team at one time or another. Retirements, deaths, and terminations occasion periodic needs for replacement and recruiting, and a growing organization creates continuing needs for new talent to staff expanding responsibilities. The close relationship between recruiting for management and the development and maintenance of a strong management should be obvious. The capacity and potential of personnel recruited to the management team largely determine the limits of effective team performance which can be achieved through management development. Recruiting for management is an integral part of management development and contributes most when closely coordinated with other activities for development of the management team.

Recruiting for management is viewed as the process of locating and identifying potential candidates for the management team and enlisting interested candidates. A preliminary and partial screening of candidates is included in recruiting, but final evaluation of qualifications of candidates and selection for hiring is considered a separate and distinct process. A further distinction should be drawn between the recruiting of relatively inexperienced personnel for training and development as managers and the recruiting of capable, experienced managers to contribute to immediate performance of the management team. The problems giving rise to these alternative approaches to recruiting are somewhat different and the techniques appropriate to each are different. We shall refer to these differences from time to time in our discussion of recruiting for management.

PROBLEMS OF RECRUITING

The entire recruiting process can be divided into two stages: first, the determination of recruiting needs and objectives, and second, the accomplishment of these objectives. The most basic problems of recruiting for management arise in the determination of needs and objectives, although most attention has been devoted to the techniques and approaches most useful in locating and securing candidates for the management team. Furthermore, the integration of management recruiting with other phases of management development is most critical in the determination of recruiting objectives. For example, one problem of coordination occurs in the staffing of key managerial positions. Most organizations profess an intent to staff these positions through promotion from within the organization.[1] Practical realization of this objective depends upon the recruitment of management trainees of sufficient capacity to advance to key positions. Any intended reliance upon promotion from within as a staffing policy is a key factor in determining the relationship between recruiting for management and other activities designed to develop the management team. It also should be an important influence shaping the nature of the management recruiting program.

A closely related issue concerns the orientation of management recruiting toward long-run or short-run objectives. This orientation determines the relative weight to be given to considerations of qualifications for immediate performance and to potential for development and future performance. For example, the requirements for effective performance of advanced managerial positions may appear quite different from the requirements of supervisory management positions, creating a potential conflict in recruiting objec-

[1] See Esther C. Lawton, "To What Extent Should Executive Positions Be Filled from Outside?" *Personnel Administration*, Vol. 20, No. 1, January-February 1957, pp. 46-49, for an interesting discussion of viewpoints.

tives. This conflict is illustrated in the differences between recruiting objectives established by top-management and by lower-management personnel.[2] Lower levels of management tend to stress specialized training and qualifications for immediate performance in vacant positions. Top management, on the other hand, tends to stress the need for a general background and training to qualify for more responsible positions at some future date, and so is less concerned with immediate performance. Such conflict arises from a misunderstanding of the objectives of management recruiting and their relationship to the more general objectives of management development. Coordination between objectives at the stage of planning recruiting activities is necessary for an effective over-all program of development.

The potential conflict between long-run and short-run recruiting objectives probably is seen most clearly in the delegation of recruiting responsibilities. Decentralization of recruiting responsibilities through delegation to individual operating units provides greater opportunity for variation in general recruiting objectives and makes more difficult the control of recruiting activities in accord with the objectives of other phases of management development. At the same time, however, decentralization offers many advantages which were discussed briefly in Chapter 3. Sylvania Electric Products provides an example of an organization which has effectively delegated recruiting responsibilities to the individual plants and operating units of the company.[3] The key to effective delegation of such responsibilities lies in a comparable delegation of responsibilities for other activities of management development; the coordination of recruiting, training, and promotion practices need not suffer if all are decentralized to the same extent. The major problems of coordination of management recruiting with other activities for management development arise from an ignorance of their close relationship and from barriers to communication and cooperation.

---

[2] For examples of this disagreement, see John L. McCaffrey, "Wanted: More 'Generalists,'" *Personnel Journal,* Vol. 33, No. 3, July-August 1954, pp. 86-89; Herrymon Maurer, "The Worst Shortage in Business," *Fortune,* Vol. 53, No. 4, April 1956, pp. 147-149, 200-209; "Crown Princes of Business," *Fortune,* Vol. 48, No. 4, October 1953, pp. 150-153, 258-268; "The Popular BA," *Business Week,* No. 1318, December 4, 1954, pp. 92-94.

[3] See D. W. Currier, and D. P. Whiteley, "Sylvania Electric Products, Inc.," in M. Joseph Dooher and Elizabeth Marting (editors), *Selection of Management Personnel,* Vol. II (New York: American Management Association, 1957), pp. 318-338.

Decentralization of recruiting responsibilities need create no real problems for development of the management team if coordinated with the delegation of responsibilities for other activities of management development.

THE RECRUITING PROCESS

The process of recruiting for management consists of a number of separate steps, starting with the determination of recruiting needs. Specific considerations within each of the steps will vary, but the same general process is involved in recruiting management trainees as in recruiting experienced managers.

Determination of Recruiting Needs

All recruiting activities are based upon some estimate of management manpower needs. These needs are implied in recruiting activities, and organizations which do not provide for formal estimation of needs often find the estimates determined informally by the actions of recruiters. Estimates of manpower needs are expressed in both quantitative and qualitative terms—how many and what kinds of people are needed. These estimates should take into account anticipated needs and recruit for them before these needs become apparent. The period of anticipation varies considerably from one organization to another, depending upon commitment to maintenance of the management team, size of the organization, and frequency of formal recruiting activities. Larger organizations, for example, usually attempt to predict needs from one to five years in advance, and then revise these estimates as necessary. The period of anticipation usually is longer in these organizations than it is in small organizations because of the relative difficulties of recruiting larger numbers of managerial candidates. Furthermore, frequent revision of estimates is possible, since these large organizations conduct recruiting activities fairly frequently. Smaller organizations with less regular recruiting needs tend to estimate their needs more informally and initiate recruiting activities as needed.

A survey by the National Industrial Conference Board indicates that in one or more companies responsibilities for the estimation of management manpower needs are assigned to almost every conceivable position or unit in the management organization. The most common assignment of these responsibilities lies in the personnel department or with the heads of operating units.[4] The assignment of this responsibility often influences the accuracy and relevance of estimates. For example, estimation of the number of candidates required should be based upon a knowledge of plans for growth and expansion as well as of plans for change in the organization structure. Delegation and decentralization of recruiting responsibilities beyond the area of knowledge of such plans will produce manpower estimates at variance with actual needs. Also, determination of qualitative recruiting needs can vary with the level and type of position responsible for determining qualifications. A potential conflict between staff and line views of desired qualifications of managerial candidates was pointed up in a survey by *Fortune* magazine. Two descriptions of qualifications for managerial candidates were prepared and mailed to company presidents and personnel executives who were asked to choose the description they considered most adequate in the recruitment and selection of managers. The company presidents split, 50 per cent voting for each of the descriptions, while the personnel executives voted 71 per cent in favor of the description of the "administrator" type of manager and only 29 per cent voted in favor of the "entrepreneur" type of manager.[5] This small survey illustrates the known possibility of different views toward managerial requirements, views resulting from different vantage points within the organization. The existence of such varying viewpoints indicates the need for organization analysis and the formulation of relatively objective position requirements as well as provisions for coordination between line and staff managers in the determination of recruiting needs.

Several different approaches can be taken in the determination of recruiting needs. All of these approaches involve estimation of the total managerial needs of the organization at some point in the future and a prediction of the number of managers which must be recruited to staff these requirements, taking into account present staff, retirement, and turnover. Colonel Lyndall Urwick suggests the simple rule that four times the estimated future requirements for managers should be in training at any time; one-fourth of these managers will be dead or disabled by the time they are needed,

[4] "College Recruits in Industry: Recruiting and Selecting Employees," *Studies in Personnel Policy No. 89* (New York: National Industrial Conference Board, 1954).

[5] See "Crown Princes of Business," *Fortune*, Vol. 48, No. 4, October 1953, pp. 150-153, 258-268.

and another fourth will have failed, leaving two candidates for each post when needed.[6] The general concepts expressed in this guide are worth while, although the exact requirements will vary considerably with each company's experience. Two of the more common approaches to the prediction of recruiting needs are illustrated by the approaches of Minnesota Mining and Manufacturing and Socony Vacuum. The first of these might be called the "gross" approach, and the latter the "specific" approach to determination of recruiting needs.

The "gross" approach used at Minnesota Mining is based upon extensive research and study of relationships between the size of the management organization and indexes of company activity. A close relationship was discovered between total annual sales of the parent company and the number of management positions in each of five divisions—sales, laboratory, engineering, administration, and production. The observed relationships between sales and the number of management positions are used in computing the estimated number of management positions from sales forecasts. This estimate is reduced by the number of managers now employed, the remainder indicating the number of new positions to be staffed during the year. Replacement needs are predicted by applying past turnover rates to the estimated size of the organization, and the sum of predicted replacements and new additions indicates the total needs for recruiting during the year. As suggested by the label "gross," this approach is more concerned with the quantitative needs than qualitative needs for recruiting. The only indication of skills and capabilities required of the managerial candidates is provided by the indication of the division for which the personnel are to be recruited. This approach has been used at Minnesota Mining since 1954 with errors of less than one per cent, suggesting that quite accurate predictions of number of managers required can be made, although these predictions offer little in the way of recruitment specifications.[7] Application of the approach to job families with similar requirements would be more useful in the determination of recruiting guides, but probably would involve increased error in the prediction of numbers of candidates required.

---

[6] Lyndall Urwick, *16 Questions About the Selection and Training of Managers* (London: Urwick, Orr & Partners, 1958), 35 pp.

[7] See Wendel W. Burton, "Forecasting Manpower Needs: A Tested Formula," in "Labor and Management Face the Future," *Personnel Series No. 172* (New York: American Management Association, 1957).

The approach taken at Socony Vacuum is much more specific in nature than the Minnesota Mining approach. Recruiting needs are predicted for each organization unit and summed to provide over-all guides to recruiting. The approach starts with organization analysis and planning, pointing up the positions to be added, eliminated, or changed during the coming year or five years. These organization plans indicate total future needs of the organization unit. The inventory of incumbent managers is then compared with these plans to determine specific lacks in the personnel of the unit and needs for recruitment. Age distributions are used in the prediction of retirements and deaths, and an estimate of turnover is included in determining replacements to be considered. As estimates of recruiting needs are built up for each organization unit, these are reviewed along with the total inventory of managers to identify needs which can be met through promotion and transfer among units. Remaining needs are used as guides to the recruitment of managers and managerial candidates during the year. These needs are expressed in terms of both numbers of personnel required and rather definite specifications required for performance.[8]

Both of these approaches to the determination of recruiting needs are useful, although in different respects. The "gross" approach probably is most useful in the prediction of over-all needs for a long-range estimate, say five years, and the "specific" approach probably is most useful in the encouragement of promotion from within and in the identification of specific qualifications required of candidates. There is no single best approach for every organization. Some combination or variation of these general approaches must be worked out for each company and evaluated during a trial period if the most useful estimates of recruiting needs are to be prepared.

Sources of Management Recruits

The second major step in the recruiting process concerns the investigation and selection of sources to be exploited in the recruitment of managers. Pinpointing the most likely source of each type or group of managers desired facilitates the concentration of efforts in the most efficient and appropriate manner. Two major divisions of sources can be identified—sources within the organization and

---

[8] Discussed in C. H. Stone and W. E. Kendall, *Effective Personnel Selection Procedures* (Englewood Cliffs, New Jersey: Prentice-Hall, Inc., 1956).

sources outside the organization. Such a division is appropriate both in the sense that different types of recruits are likely to be found from these sources and in the sense that different recruiting techniques are appropriate in the exploitation of these sources.

Inside the organization. Lower levels of the organization constitute a prime source of potential candidates for positions at higher levels. It is difficult to evaluate the practical importance of these sources of candidates throughout industry because there is little evidence indicating the actual extent of promotion from within for staffing managerial positions. Practices undoubtedly vary considerably from one organization to another because of differences in policy and differences in the degree to which less responsible positions provide opportunities to develop the skills and abilities needed for higher management responsibilities. Furthermore, the extent to which recruits are drawn from lower levels in the organization varies with the level of the position being filled. For example, many companies today will consider non-managerial personnel as candidates for supervisory positions, while advancement beyond the supervisory level is effectively restricted to management trainees and others recruited directly into the management organization. Professional and staff employees provide a source of candidates for more responsible management positions in many of these companies.[9] More commonly, the practical significance of sources of candidates within the organization is unknown because of inadequate facilities for the review and consideration of present employees in recruiting for the management team. This review and consideration of present employees can be facilitated by the identification of job families throughout the organization and by the differentiation among job types as sources of potential candidates. Job families, as described in an earlier chapter, are groupings of positions with similar skill and ability requirements. This grouping of positions in different parts of the organization helps to spotlight sources of candidates for any single position and to focus attention upon personnel performing related tasks in other positions.

Various methods are used by different organizations to encourage recruitment or promotion from within. Several companies recruit

[9] See George S. Odiorne, "Finding Managers Among Technical Personnel," in *Selection of Management Personnel,* Vol. I, edited by M. Joseph Dooher and Elizabeth Marting (New York: American Management Association, 1957), pp. 418-426.

supervisors by inviting non-supervisory employees to apply and nominate themselves for consideration.[10] Both Armstrong Cork and Detroit Edison invite these self-nominations as a supplement to the review and nomination of candidates by members of the management staff. Such self-nomination insures the opportunity for consideration to each employee and probably serves to check the adequacy of the review and nominations of the management. Furthermore, self-nomination can serve as a screening device in recruitment for supervision. Self-nomination in the long run will work, however, only in an atmosphere of trust and confidence. It should not be attempted in an organization where self-nominations will not be given careful consideration and where there is a refusal to explain and discuss the final selection of personnel.

A much more common method for recruitment from within involves use of the management inventory and/or skill inventory of non-managerial employees. A complete inventory of personnel and their experiences, their education, their skills, and their performance appraisals is maintained for review in the staffing of positions. Such an inventory is particularly necessary in a large organization where the manager responsible for filling a vacancy will not be familiar with the complete background and interests of every potential candidate within the organization. Large organizations such as General Electric and General Mills have developed punch-card methods of recording inventory information which facilitate this review. Given the specifications for a particular position, these cards can be reviewed mechanically and the available candidates with the required specifications selected for more intensive review and consideration. Other methods for facilitation of this review involve the flagging of personnel files with special-colored tabs and similar visual indicators.

It is one thing, however, to maintain an inventory and quite another to utilize this information in management staffing. Use of this information must be made easy and advantageous to the management staff. A common approach to this problem is to assign responsibility for maintenance and utilization of the inventory to a single position and to require managers to consult the inventory before submitting a request for outside recruiting. For example, position

---

[10] See "Armstrong Cork Company" discussion and George U. Callens, "Detroit Edison Company," in Dooher and Marting, *op. cit.*, Vol. II, pp. 36-58, 120-134.

specifications could be submitted to a coordinator who reviews the inventory of managers and selects the several most-qualified candidates. The recruiting manager would review the qualifications of these candidates and select from among them or decide that none was qualified. Sylvania Electric Products maintains a cross-indexed personnel inventory of both personal information and appraisal information on all employees earning at least $6,000 a year. This inventory is consulted in staffing all positions paying $7,000 or more a year. Company officials estimate that 85 per cent of such openings are staffed by promotion from within as a result of using this inventory.[11] Maintenance of a management inventory can be an aid to recruitment from within, but it is only an aid. The inventory must be accurate, up to date, and easy to consult and use if sources of management talent within the organization are to be fully exploited in recruitment for the management team.

Outside the organization. Candidates for the management team must be recruited from outside the organization at some point regardless of the effectiveness of development and promotion from within. Most of those recruited from outside the organization probably will be candidates for entry-level managerial positions, although experienced managers are sought from time to time as candidates for middle and upper levels of management. Experienced managers are recruited from outside the organization much less frequently than are management trainees, most of the higher management positions being filled by promotion from within. An American Management Association survey indicates that almost 60 per cent of companies fill 10 per cent or less of their executive openings with personnel recruited from outside the organization.[12] The recruitment of experienced managers into the organization, although infrequent, has a far greater individual impact upon the organization than the recruitment of management trainees because of the responsibility of the positions involved. The sources of experienced managers and the methods for exploiting these sources are quite different from those appropriate in the recruitment of management trainees. Both the sources and the procedures for recruiting execu-

---

[11] Don G. Mitchell, "The 'Pace-Setter' Organization," *The Management Review,* Vol. 46, No. 7, July 1957, pp. 71-79.

[12] See Lydia Strong, "Recruiting at Middle and Upper Executive Levels," in Dooher and Marting, *op. cit.,* Vol. I, pp. 404-417; and "Recruiting Executives from Outside Your Firm," *Management Methods,* February 1956, pp. 28-31.

tives are much less formal and organized than is the case in recruiting managerial trainees. For example, the most commonly reported source of candidates for executive positions lies in business contacts where executives are recruited from competing organizations.[13] Personal recommendations, advertising, and executive recruiting agencies follow in order of frequency of use. On the other hand, college and university recruiting and unsolicited applications provide the majority of management trainees recruited.

The recruiting of experienced managers from among business contacts and through personal recommendation is widely employed for several reasons. Managers located with related organizations—suppliers, customers, and competitors—are more likely to be familiar with the problems and the operations of the industry and the recruiting organization than are managers recruited from unrelated organizations. Further, managers recruited in this manner are known by someone familiar with the organization and its needs, and thus are more likely to prove satisfactory. Also, relatively more information often is available about the manager's abilities and experience in this case.

Direct advertising is not a widely used approach to managerial recruiting. Most organizations prefer to be more selective in recruiting experienced managers, exploring market sources carefully before making direct appeals for applicants. Thus, direct advertising is most likely to be used in the recruitment of managers for relatively specialized responsibilities; sources of candidates for these responsibilities often can be more specifically identified and contacted through professional publications than is the case in recruiting candidates for general managerial responsibilities. A major difficulty in the use of advertising lies in the reluctance of the organization to identify itself in advertising, with the consequent need to use blind ads. Blind ads normally do not attract the interest that identified advertisements do, and generally they are much less effective.

Management consultants are becoming increasingly active in the recruitment of experienced managers for responsible managerial and executive positions. Relatively little is known about the activities of professional recruiters because of an admitted reluctance to publicize their activities. However, estimates suggest that recruiting consultants are retained by approximately 40 to 50 per cent of

---

[13] See Lydia Strong, "Executives Wanted: The Managerial Manhunt," *The Management Review*, Vol. 46, No. 2, February 1957, pp. 53-68.

larger organizations.[14] Many of these consultants began recruiting activities as a sideline arising out of their consulting contacts and hesitate to specialize in recruiting because of the fluctuation in calls for recruiting activities, the consultants being contacted for recruiting only when the executive market becomes tight. Organizations tend to turn to executive recruiters when the organizations' recruiting proves unsuccessful. The consultant recruiter takes over and attempts to locate a satisfactory candidate among contacts in other organizations. While the charge of pirating is often leveled against the activities of consultant recruiters, these consultants argue that they never recruit from client companies and that they perform a service by recruiting only from organizations where adequate backstops are available already. In almost all instances, the consultant seeks the individual for the open position, rather than vice versa; relatively few of these consultants accept applications from executives seeking positions. Estimates of time required to locate acceptable candidates vary around an average of from 10 to 12 weeks, with approximately 85 per cent success. Fees are always paid by the recruiting company, the average fee being about 20 per cent of the first year's salary plus recruiting expenses or $2,500, whichever is larger, if an acceptable candidate is located, and $150 a day for recruiting if a candidate is not located. An examination of these fees indicates why most organizations are reluctant to turn to consultant recruiting until all other activities have failed, and to use consultant recruiters only for executive recruiting. The recruiting consultant does offer a last resort, however, in executive recruiting, a resort which will be used increasingly as the executive market becomes increasingly tight. It is unlikely that consultant recruiting will continue to grow or to retain its importance in executive recruiting if the executive job market eases in coming years.

Unsolicited applications provide a source of candidates for the management team particularly in the recruiting of inexperienced managers for training and development. Competition in the recruiting of competent experienced managers since World War II has been such that unsolicited applications for responsible managerial positions would be viewed with suspicion and play only an insignificant part in the recruitment of experienced managers. Sylvania

[14] See discussions of S. Habbe, "What About Executive Recruiters?" *op. cit.;* L. Strong, "Executives Wanted: The Managerial Manhunt," *op. cit.;* and "How Professionals Find Managers," *op. cit.*

Electric Products and Consolidated Edison Company of New York are two organizations which still rely heavily upon unsolicited applications in recruiting management trainees, although most organizations place little reliance upon this source.[15] Consolidated Edison, for example, conducted almost no special recruiting activities until 1956, and it still relies upon unsolicited applications for a large proportion of managerial recruits. Only companies with comparable reputations can rely upon this source of candidates, however. The majority of organizations must actively seek out candidates for the management team if they are to obtain the quality and number of recruits desired.

Colleges and universities form the most important single source of managerial candidates. Many organizations already have committed themselves to primary reliance upon this source in the future by requiring college graduation as a qualification for managerial candidates. Recognizing the implications of this commitment, a number of business organizations already are developing closer ties with educational institutions through which they can contribute to the improved development of managerial talent in the schools. Increasing cooperation can be expected in future years with the further realization of the importance of this pre-employment development of candidates for the management team. The campus market for managerial candidates is relatively diverse, and recruiting organizations should attempt to identify and pinpoint specific sources within this market. For example, differences in admissions requirements and educational standards have a direct influence upon the potential of graduates. Furthermore, the size of the graduating class and the expected success of recruiting from the class influence the net cost of recruiting managerial candidates. Future years should bring about considerably more evaluation of alternative college sources. There should be increased efforts by business organizations to improve the quality of graduating candidates because of the growing importance of school training in the development of a strong management team.

The choice of sources to be exploited in attempts to recruit managers is a major determinant of recruiting costs and success. In a very real sense, the selection of sources can be compared with the

[15] See case studies of "Sylvania Electric Products, Inc." and "Consolidated Edison Company of New York" in Dooher and Marting, *op. cit.*, Vol. II, pp. 318-338, 272-279; and Strong, *op. cit.*, pp. 404-417.

selection of candidates, since only candidates from the chosen sources are considered as potential recruits. There are a number of available measures which can be employed in the evaluation of sources of managerial recruits, particularly within companies which recruit relatively large numbers of managerial candidates. Certain of these measures are discussed in a later section of this chapter.

RECRUITING PRACTICES

A host of specific managerial recruiting techniques have been developed.[16] Many of these are specific to particular needs and situations. We shall not examine all of these specific recruiting practices here. Instead, we shall look at several more general considerations which arise in the evaluation and selection of specific practices to be employed in recruiting. In general, candidates are attracted to an organization because they perceive an opportunity to achieve personal goals through association with the organization. The most effective recruiting techniques in any specific situation are likely to be those which display an understanding of the individual's objectives and which point up the advantages of the organization in terms of those objectives. Thus, practices which are effective in recruiting experienced managers may be of little value in campus recruiting. Consideration of the personal goals and objectives of managerial recruits apparently plays a minor role at present in the evaluation of recruiting practices, for we know relatively little about these goals and objectives. A few studies of job preferences of management recruits have been conducted with inconclusive results. In general, these studies suggest that college recruits are most interested in the type of work performed in the organization, opportunities for development and advancement, starting salary, and location of the organization. They are least influenced by the hours of work, fringe benefits, and working conditions.[17] Even less is known about the factors important in

[16] For a review of these practices, see C. H. Stone and W. E. Kendall, *Effective Personnel Selection Procedures* (Englewood Cliffs, New Jersey: Prentice-Hall, Inc., 1956).

[17] For examples, see R. E. Barmeier and R. J. Kellar, "How College Graduates Evaluate Job Factors," *Personnel*, Vol. 33, No. 5, March 1957, pp. 490-494; Douglas T. Jaeger, "Campus Recruiting: What's Your 'S-Appeal'?" *Personnel*, Vol. 31, No. 4, January 1955, pp. 361-364; "Attracting Future Executives: What Bait Are You Using?" *Dun's Review and Modern Industry*, Vol. 70, No. 3, September 1957, pp. 51-53; and "What You Should Know About Your College Recruit," *Management Methods*, Vol. 12, No. 2, May 1957, pp. 36-40 ff.

recruiting experienced managers, although many of the same factors probably are relevant. Organizational relationships of positions probably are more relevant in recruiting experienced managers and programs for training and development considerably less important.[18] The information available concerning the factors which influence recruiting decisions is far from satisfactory, however, and further study of these factors would be fruitful in the improvement of managerial recruiting and development of the management team.

A number of varied practices are found in campus recruiting programs.[19] One general problem concerns the selection of recruiters to visit the college campuses. A relatively common practice involves the selection of recent graduates as recruiters—often, graduates of the college visited. This practice is based upon an assumption that the young recruiter will be familiar with the hopes and fears of graduating seniors and will be better able to talk to the graduating senior. Furthermore, the young recruiter presents proof of the opportunities that exist for college graduates in the recruiting organization. This practice has been criticized by college seniors because they have found that the recruiter is unable to answer their questions about the organization owing to his lack of experience in the organization.[20] The selection of young managers as recruiters also contributes to the divergence noted earlier between stated demands of top management for highly qualified generalists and the practice of recruiters to prefer technically trained graduates. The recruiter who knows relatively little about the organization and its jobs other than the personnel specifications provided him will tend to rely upon proof of technical competence rather than personal judgments of capacity

[18] See Robert Hershey, "The Executive Changes His Job," *Personnel Journal,* Vol. 36, No. 8, January 1958, pp. 295-297.

[19] See the following for extensive discussions of college recruiting: Allen, *op. cit.;* S. Habbe, "College Recruitment in 1958," *Management Record,* Vol. 20, No. 1, January 1958, pp. 6-8; C. S. Fernow, "Personalized Placement Pays Off in College Recruitment," *Personnel,* Vol. 34, No. 4, January-February 1958, pp. 77-80; George M. Zabka, "Getting Better Results from College Recruitment," *Personnel,* Vol. 31, No. 4, January 1955, pp. 364-371; "A Guide to College Recruitment," *Pamphlet No. 12* (Washington, D.C.: Society for Personnel Administration, 1956); "How to Recruit College Graduates," *Management Methods,* Vol. 2, No. 5, February 1957, pp. 12-23 ff.; *Recruiting and Placing College Graduates in Business* (New York: Metropolitan Life Insurance Company, Policyholders' Service Bureau, 1950); "College Graduates in Industry: Recruiting and Placing Employees," *op. cit.;* "Recruiting College Graduates," *Personnel Policies Forum Survey No. 5* (Washington, D.C.: Bureau of National Affairs, July 1951).

[20] Edward M. Krech, Jr., "What Students Think of Campus Recruiters," *Personnel,* Vol. 35, No. 2, September-October 1958, pp. 72-76.

to develop as a general manager. At the other extreme, managers supervising the positions to be filled have been selected as recruiters. These managers are familiar with the position requirements and are in a position to explain the organization and position fully to interested candidates. Furthermore, they are in a position to recruit personally for their vacancies rather than rely upon the judgments of others. However, these managers also often tend to emphasize qualifications for immediate performance rather than potential for advancement, and they will be less likely to understand and sympathize with the students interviewed. As a consequence, a few organizations now use recruiting teams composed of staff personnel and line managers in campus recruiting.[21] Many of the problems of campus recruiting could be reduced with the use of teams such as these to combine the understanding of recent graduates with the experience of older line managers and the technical skill of the staff personnel representative.

EVALUATION OF RECRUITING PRACTICES

Periodic evaluation is important to the long-run success of every management program. Periodic evaluation is necessary to provide controls for portions of the program and to suggest needs and methods for revision and improvement of the program. It is particularly important in a program for management recruiting. The needs for management recruiting, sources of candidates, and qualifications of candidates are constantly changing, and recruiting practices and techniques should be changed and adapted to the changed situation. A periodic evaluation of the results of the recruiting program is necessary to point up the need for change and to suggest the necessary changes.

A periodic evaluation of management recruiting is most helpful if directed toward specific practices rather than toward the entire program. The over-all evaluation provides a summary measure of recruiting success but does not point up specific areas of failure or faulty practices. One partial evaluation which is particularly important in adaptation of the recruiting program is an evaluation of various sources of candidates. Recruiting success for each source contacted should be computed annually to identify changes and

[21] "Techniques of College Recruiting" (Washington, D.C.: Bureau of National Affairs, 1951).

trends useful in planning recruiting activities for the following year. The final or ultimate evaluation of particular practices or sources is possible only after a number of years, when recruits have had a chance to prove themselves in development within the organization. The use of less conclusive but more readily available measures in evaluation permits constant evaluation, which is most useful in adapting the program to short-run changes of situations.

One of the most commonly used measures in the evaluation of management recruiting is some sort of "acceptance rate." As a general rule, this rate expresses the percentage of interviewed candidates who were finally recruited into the organization and thus provides a measure of the efficiency of recruiting. This rate might be used in the evaluation of various sources of candidates, for example, the source with the largest acceptance rate providing the most fruitful pool of candidates. This acceptance rate will vary with changed situations in the market for managerial candidates, the rate tending to drop with increased competition for candidates. As an example, Sears Roebuck reports that an average of 100 interviews of college seniors was necessary in 1956 to locate 15 prospective candidates, half of whom would accept company offers—an acceptance rate of seven per cent.[22] A similar measure for evaluation is the cost per recruit or the cost of filling an opening. Strong estimates from a survey of the American Management Association that the median cost of filling executive positions is $1,600, not including any training or orientation for the position or the salary paid.[23] This cost obviously will vary for the type of candidate sought and the position to be filled. It would be useful, however, in comparing various sources of candidates for managerial training.

A less immediate evaluation measure might concern the performance of recruits after hiring. Performance evaluations of recruits obtained from different sources or recruited by various methods might be compared for differences useful in designing future recruiting activities. Or, turnover of recruits after hiring might be compared. As examples of these measures, Strong estimates, from the same AMA survey, that 80 per cent of the candidates recruited by companies during 1956 were judged successful, and the American Bankers Association reports turnover measures of 25 per cent and 50 per cent among college graduates recruited by member

[22] See Barmeier and Kellar, *op. cit.*
[23] See Strong, "Executives Wanted: The Managerial Manhunt," *op. cit.*

banks.[24] Again, these measures will vary among companies and with the nature of the managerial job market. They are useful for evaluation within a single company, however.

A somewhat more intensive evaluation of specific recruiting elements is reported by Barmeier, of Sears Roebuck.[25] Sears noticed a definite lack of interest in company offers among college seniors recruited in a recent year. To check upon the adequacy of their offers and their approach to recruitment, Sears sent an anonymous questionnaire to 600 candidates, some of whom had rejected offers of employment and others who were hired by Sears. Candidates were asked to indicate the job factors they considered most important in the selection of a company and the factors they considered least important. Results pointed up those factors which should be discussed and considered in college recruiting—factors to be emphasized in recruiting brochures and interviews. This type of evaluation, where acceptable candidates who decided not to join the organization are polled as well as those who joined the organization, can provide useful comparisons for the improvement of recruiting practices.

The examples of recruiting-evaluation measures mentioned here are not common. The most usual practice involves informal evaluation by the company management—evaluation of the over-all recruiting program. For example, a significant increase in trainee turnover is noticed immediately, or a series of mistakes in selection is noted. It is not the intensive or specific evaluation which is most useful in adapting the program. The specific evaluations discussed here will become more important as competition for managerial recruits grows; the most successful organization will be the one that uses evaluation to adapt and improve its recruiting efforts.

SELECTED BIBLIOGRAPHY

Dooher, M. Joseph, and Elizabeth Marting (editors), *Selection of Management Personnel* (New York: American Management Association, 1957).

---

[24] See *Executive Development in Banking* (New York: American Bankers Association, 1955), 99 pp.

[25] See R. E. Barmeier and R. J. Kellar, "How College Graduates Evaluate Job Factors," *Personnel*, Vol. 33, No. 5, March 1957, pp. 490-494.

Stone, C. Harold, and William E. Kendall, *Effective Personnel Selection Procedures* (Englewood Cliffs, New Jersey: Prentice-Hall, Inc., 1956).

Techniques of College Recruiting (Washington, D. C.: Bureau of National Affairs, 1951).

Chapter EIGHT

Identification of Management Potential

INTRODUCTION

Decisions made in the selection and assignment of management personnel are critical to the success of the enterprise. These decisions largely determine both the immediate and the long-run performance of the management team and thus determine the performance of the entire organization. Training and development activities may influence and improve the performance of managers, but the effects of these activities are limited by the latent potential of individual members of the management team. Assignment decisions determine performance of the management team as they affect the utilization of management skills and abilities and as they influence individual development through experience. All in all, management selection and assignment activities are vital determinants of the development and performance of the management team and probably should be given more consideration as elements of management development than they now receive.

A distinction frequently is made between the concepts of selection and job assignment. Selection is viewed as a negative process in which candidates are rejected from consideration, and assignment is viewed as a positive process in which the individual's skills and abilities are matched with job requirements which will provide maximum utilization of his abilities. This distinction is not important to our discussion of management selection and assignment. Regardless of the concept employed in these decisions, the objective is the identification of the candidate who will most effectively accomplish the objectives of the staffing situation. The same general problem is faced in all management staffing situations, and the same general concepts and principles are applicable to their solution. Decisions concerning selection, assignment, transfer, and promotion are all concerned with the identification of the candidate or candidates most likely to prove effective in the pending assignment.

Managerial staffing decisions must be based upon predictions of managerial effectiveness. Decisions made on the basis of these predictions are gambles in the same manner that a decision to back a given horse in a race is a gamble. Management staffing decisions can be quite expensive gambles, since the impact of a single decision can affect the entire organization. A wrong decision in managerial staffing affects the performance of the position staffed and the performance of subordinates to this position and of other members of the management team, and it may affect over-all performance of the management team through its impact upon the morale and spirit of the team. The risk involved in such decisions varies with the accuracy of predictions of managerial effectiveness and the relative importance of the staffing decisions; anything which improves predictions reduces the risk involved and contributes to over-all performance and development of the management team. We shall discuss the nature of the managerial staffing process and methods for the prediction of managerial effectiveness in this chapter. We start with the objectives of staffing decisions and then consider the general nature of staffing prediction and decision-making and methods for developing systems for prediction of managerial effectiveness, and finally, we review current thinking and research concerning predictors.

MANAGERIAL STAFFING OBJECTIVES

The general objective of managerial staffing decisions is improved performance of the management team in the immediate and long-run future through improved development and utilization of managerial talents. This is to be accomplished through the recruitment and selection of high-potential candidates and the utilization of skills and abilities through assignments for maximum effectiveness of the entire management team. All of these decisions involve predictions of individual potential and probable effectiveness of performance. A necessary first step in making reliable and accurate predictions of potential and effectiveness lies in the operational definition of staffing objectives. Staffing predictions concern management potential and effectiveness—relatively vague and general objectives. We must ask "potential for what?" and "effectiveness of what?" in defining staffing objectives that are useful in making the necessary predictions for managerial staffing decisions.

Managerial staffing objectives vary from one situation to another with differences in jobs, companies, and even time periods. The specific objectives of each staffing situation are unique to that situation. There are certain elements common to the objectives of all staffing situations or to groups of situations, however, which permit us to generalize. Experiences in these related situations also permit us to generalize somewhat in the establishment of principles and guides for staffing. It has been pointed out earlier that the organization guide and position descriptions set forth certain organization needs, needs which may be viewed as the objectives of staffing decisions.[1] The performance outlined in the description of a single management position or any group of positions outlines the performance objectives of staffing decisions for these positions. These descriptions are not sufficient for all staffing decisions, however. They merely describe the organization of responsibilities as it exists at a given time and in this manner reflect the problems faced by the organization at that time. These problems will change over time, calling for a different organization of responsibilities and, possibly, for new responsibilities. Thus, the effective performance sought in staffing decisions cannot be stated precisely for all time, and it will include both required present performance and unforeseen changes which will be called for. Effective performance today and effective performance in the future may be defined quite differently for a single position. Expectations and objectives concerning management potential become important at this point; selection of an individual with potential for change and development to meet future performance requirements becomes an objective in staffing. This consideration is particularly true when the position is viewed as a train-

[1] See Chapter 3.

ing ground or steppingstone to other, more responsible positions, and in the selection of candidates for management training and development. Effective performance in these situations is of less importance than effective performance in an often undefined future.

Effective performance is the ultimate objective of managerial staffing. Definition of the effective performance desired is an aid in the prediction of probable performance, since it narrows and focuses the area of speculation. However, effective performance is almost impossible to define in many situations, and the identification of individuals with potential for development becomes a more operational objective. Wherever possible, the definition of potential and the effective performance sought should be made specific as an aid to prediction. Every attempt should be made to define the specific potential and performance sought, since the effort expended here can result in vastly improved predictions of effectiveness and reduce the gamble in managerial staffing.

PREDICTING MANAGERIAL EFFECTIVENESS

Predictions of the future are based upon past observations of factors believed to be closely associated with future developments. Thus, we make predictions about future managerial effectiveness on the basis of observations of personal characteristics and behavior selected as particularly indicative of managerial effectiveness. The reliability and accuracy of predictions depend upon two major factors—the degree of relationship between predictors and the predicted which exists in fact, and the reliability and accuracy of measures employed in predictions. For example, predictions of managerial effectiveness based upon estimates of intelligence may be inaccurate because there exists no actual relationship between intelligence and effectiveness. On the other hand, an actual relationship may exist and predictions still be inaccurate merely because we are unable to measure either intelligence or effectiveness with any degree of accuracy; in short, we are unable to discover and demonstrate the relationship. The term "predictor" in this example refers to the concept of personal characteristics believed to influence effectiveness, and "measures of predictors" refer to the operational definitions of these characteristics provided in specific measures such as psychological tests. It is the relationship between measures of predictors and managerial effectiveness which is of practical interest and concern in making predictions, not the relationship between concepts of personal characteristics and effectiveness. However, the relationships between the concepts assumed to underlie the relationships between measures of the concepts are of interest and concern in directing attention toward the choice of measures to be developed and investigated. Predictions of effectiveness can be improved both by focusing attention upon more relevant relationships and by developing improved measures of predictors and effectiveness.

Validation of Predictors

Predictors of managerial effectiveness or management potential usually are suggested on the basis of hunch and deduction. Predictors may be suggested through deductive analysis of staffing objectives and definitions of effective managerial performance, through an analysis of the characteristics of successful managers, or through a comparison of the careers of successful managers with the careers of their less successful contemporaries. Examples of the hunches obtained in this manner are common in the numerous listings of "what it takes to be a good manager." [2] An immediately apparent shortcoming of this approach to the selection of predictors appears in the widespread disagreement over factors considered relevant. A *Fortune* magazine survey of executives indicates the lack of agreement upon predictors of effectiveness; much of the meager agreement concerning predictors also disappears with the finding that the executives surveyed couldn't agree upon the definition of one predictor considered important by all.[3] The process of hunch and deduction in the selection of predictors of managerial effectiveness provides suggestions of predictors, but these suggestions can hardly be employed

[2] For examples, see Chris Argyris, "Some Characteristics of Successful Executives," *Personnel Journal,* Vol. 32, No. 2, June 1953, pp. 50-55; Eli Ginzberg (editor), *What Makes an Executive?* (New York: Columbia University Press, 1955); Joseph M. Dodge, "Some Special Characteristics of Successful Management," *Advanced Management,* Vol. 20, No. 4, April 1955, pp. 5-8; John M. Fox, "What It Takes to Be a Manager," *Advanced Management,* Vol. 22, No. 6, June 1957, pp. 18-21; Robert W. Heffner, "What Makes a Good Executive?" *Advanced Management,* Vol. 19, No. 12, December 1954, pp. 21-23; James H. Rand, Walter Wheeler, Jr., and Robert Morse, Jr., "What Makes a Good President?" *Dun's Review and Modern Industry,* Vol. 65, No. 2321, January 1955, pp. 43 ff.; "How 500 Presidents Set Off on Their Long Climb," *Business Week,* No. 1397, June 9, 1956, pp. 110-116; "The Nine Hundred," *Fortune,* November 1952, Vol. 46, No. 5, pp. 132-135 ff.

[3] See Perrin Stryker, "On the Meaning of Executive Qualities," *Fortune,* Vol. 57, No. 6, June 1958, pp. 116-119, 186 ff.; and "What Makes an 'Emotionally Stable' Executive?" *Fortune,* Vol. 58, No. 1, July 1958, pp. 116-117, 166-168.

in the prediction of effectiveness until they are demonstrated to be reliable and accurate in prediction. Unfortunately, too much reliance is placed upon these hunches in management staffing decisions, and too little effort is given to improvement of staffing predictions.

Procedures for the development and validation of predictors of job performance are fairly well developed and standardized.[4] These procedures are employed quite commonly in the development of selection and staffing procedures for non-managerial positions but are much less common in the staffing of managerial positions. Part of this lag in the application of techniques to managerial staffing results from a natural reluctance on the part of managers to submit to the more formalized prediction techniques, and part from some very real obstacles encountered when dealing with managerial positions. Managerial positions, for example, are relatively less standardized than non-managerial positions and, in many organizations, have not been formally established. Furthermore, the development of reliable predictors requires the analysis of larger numbers of managers and/or managerial staffing decisions than can be found in many small organizations. Several large organizations have carried out the research necessary for validation of predictors of managerial effectiveness, and several large research projects have been initiated to pool the experiences of cooperating companies. Results of these studies should contribute to the development and validation of predictors which can be adapted easily for application in other situations.

One of the major problems in the validation of predictors of managerial effectiveness stems from the lack of adequate criteria of managerial effectiveness. It is relatively easy to identify and measure effective performance in the majority of non-managerial positions, but we lack any generally acceptable definition or measure of managerial effectiveness.[5] Obviously, it is rather difficult to develop valid predictors of an unknown quantity. Various measures of effectiveness have been employed in studies of management potential, but few of these possess the reliability and validity desired of criteria. One of these involves the ranking of managers in terms of a

[4] See C. Harold Stone and William E. Kendall, *Effective Personnel Selection Procedures* (Englewood Cliffs, N. J.: Prentice-Hall, Inc., 1956), especially Chapters 9-11.

[5] See S. Rains Wallace, "Contributions to Business and Industry," in *Planning for Progress* (Pittsburgh: American Institute for Research), March 22, 1956, pp. 13-19; and *Assessing Managerial Potential* (Ann Arbor, Michigan: Foundation for Research on Human Behavior, 1958), Chapter 3, for discussions of the problem of criterion development.

relatively undefined concept of general managerial effectiveness, and has provided reliable rankings in many studies.[6] Apparently, raters performing this ranking employ an identical criterion of effectiveness, although efforts to determine what this criterion is have not proven very successful. While reliable predictors of managerial effectiveness measured by these various research criteria can be developed, they will prove to be relatively useless unless these criteria are valid and relevant measures of effectiveness. Considerable study and research are necessary in the development of adequate criteria if the maximum possible efficiency of staffing decisions is to be attained.

The validation of predictors of managerial effectiveness begins with the application of effectiveness criteria to present managers, identifying the most effective and the least effective managers. Possible predictors are then evaluated in terms of their efficiency in differentiating the highly successful managers from their less effective colleagues and from the general population. Various measures can be tested as predictors, either measures of predictors suggested through hunches or any other measures available, regardless of the logic of their hypothesized relationship to effectiveness. Those measures which are found to differentiate between the highly effective and the less effective managers are then checked out again with another group of managers to insure their value in prediction. Those measures which are useful in both tests can be accepted for application in staffing predictions. The validity of predictors should never be assumed for any situation, for what works in one situation may be of no value in another situation; and even what works at one time may not work as conditions change with time. Thus, predictors of effectiveness validated in studies of a given situation should be checked periodically over time to insure their continued efficiency in prediction of managerial effectiveness.

Predictors of Managerial Effectiveness

The search for predictors of managerial effectiveness usually begins with an attempt to define and measure management potential. It is assumed that many factors influence and determine the future effectiveness of individual managers, and that management staffing decisions concern only potential for development and effective performance. Development of this potential and motivation for perform-

[6] See *Assessing Managerial Potential,* pp. 23-27.

ance must be accomplished through means other than selection for assignments.

Two different approaches to the definition of effectiveness and the potential for achieving this effectiveness can be observed. Many students of management view managing as a general process common to all positions of leadership and management, implying that there are general measures of managerial effectiveness and that management potential can be viewed as a single phenomenon. This approach seeks the identification of predictors of effectiveness which can be employed in all managerial staffing situations. The second approach views managerial effectiveness as specific to the situation. It is argued that different situations require different management performance to be considered effective performance, and that each situation must be considered unique. Thus, a number of varying potentialities must be considered in the prediction of effectiveness. Stogdill, for example, concluded from an examination of leadership studies that the characteristics of successful leadership in nonbusiness situations vary considerably from one situation to another, implying that potential for managerial effectiveness is highly specific.[7] There is no need, however, to choose between these two approaches to the definition of managerial effectiveness and management potential; both are relevant. Certainly management and leadership situations do vary, and the most efficient predictors would be those related to the exact situation. The studies of management jobs and predictors of managerial effectiveness suggest that there are characteristics or elements of effective performance and measures of potential which are common to a number of staffing situations. We probably should expect certain common predictors of managerial effectiveness which can be used for gross predictions in a number of situations, and other more specific predictors which improve the efficiency of prediction for any single situation. The apparent conflict between these two approaches is not likely to be solved through discussion and speculation; further research and study of management potential are necessary.

Definitions of management potential and predictors of managerial effectiveness are found in company practices in the selection and appraisal of managers as well as in suggested programs for the identification of management potential. Some of these predictors are

[7] Ralph M. Stogdill, "Personal Factors Associated with Leadership: A Survey of the Literature," *Journal of Psychology*, 1948, Vol. 25, pp. 35-71.

based upon hunches and others have been discovered and validated in specific research studies. Practically every suggested predictor is used in the prediction of effectiveness in one or another situation, regardless of the demonstrated validity of the predictor. Certain of the differences among suggested predictors stem from the vague and inadequate definitions of effectiveness applied both in logical deduction and in validation studies. Other differences stem from the generality and vagueness of the concepts of predictors which are suggested. Consequently, there is a great deal of overlap, duplication, and conflict among the numerous lists of suggested predictors of managerial effectiveness. A review of the thinking and research concerning predictors can be useful in developing a firmer concept of management potential and in suggesting leads for further study and research. Certain rather general recommendations also can be drawn from this review.

No generally satisfactory system for the classification of personal characteristics and traits exists at present. The lack of precision in many of the concepts and definitions of characteristics makes it possible to classify each characteristic under any of a number of different groupings. The classification employed here includes four general classifications: physical characteristics, abilities and skills, interests, and personality characteristics. However, certain characteristics are difficult to classify even with this broad, general system, and characteristics are rather arbitrarily grouped in some instances.

Physical characteristics. Various physical characteristics have been suggested repeatedly as qualifications for effective managerial performance and as indicators of management potential. Poor health usually is recognized as a deterrent to managerial performance, but few of the suggested physical characteristics have been found positively related to effectiveness. Build and physique sometimes are suggested as indicators of management potential, although studies indicate little if any relationship between them and effectiveness.[8] One study in 1918 revealed that executives in industry and government tended to be slightly taller and heavier than non-executives, and studies of leadership characteristics in non-business situations report a consistently low positive relationship between leadership and height and weight.[9] More recent studies comparing managers of varying

[8] See Glen U. Cleeton and Charles W. Mason, *Executive Ability* (Yellow Springs, Ohio: The Antioch Press, 1946); and Stogdill, *op. cit.*, p. 37.
[9] Stogdill, *op. cit.*, p. 37.

degrees of effectiveness report no consistent relationship between managerial effectiveness and these physical characteristics, however.[10]

The most frequently mentioned physical characteristics of leaders in business and government concern vitality, energy, and physical endurance.[11] Vitality and energy of the leader are suggested as aids to leadership because they inspire confidence and motivate subordinates. The energetic leader sets an example of work and performance that stimulates subordinates to like efforts. Physical endurance is suggested as necessary to permit the work and effort required in acquiring the knowledge and experience necessary for management, as well as the extraordinary physical demands of prolonged periods of work and effort. There are certain critical periods when the presence of the leader is required, and absence at this time can destroy the manager's ability to lead. Health characteristics of effective management have received increased attention in recent years with the recognition of the physical demands of the job of the manager and with several studies indicating obesity, nervous tension, and heart trouble prevalent among executives.[12] However, more recent studies suggest that fears of special health hazards associated with management jobs probably are exaggerated. In summary, health and physical factors probably are important in so far as they may restrict the extraordinary attention and efforts required in management. Reasonably good health is demanded, but this probably is more a result of preventive medicine than of unusual qualifications.

Abilities and skills. Various abilities and skills have been suggested as predictors of managerial effectiveness, and measures of a number of abilities and skills are included in management selection and placement programs. Probably the abilities most frequently mentioned as comprising management potential are intellectual and mental abilities. Numerous studies have indicated a positive relationship between measures of intellectual factors and managerial effective-

---

[10] Thomas A. Mahoney, Thomas H. Jerdee, and Allan N. Nash, "Predicting Managerial Effectiveness," *Personnel Psychology*, Summer 1960.

[11] Chester I. Barnard, *The Functions of the Executive* (Cambridge, Massachusetts: Harvard University Press, 1947), pp. 275-280; and Eli Ginzberg, *op. cit.*, Chapter 2.

[12] See Jack Kirk, "R.I.P.: The Overworked Executive," *Journal of Commerce*, December 30, 1953, p. 1; "Executive Health Problems: Fact or Fancy?" *Advertising Age*, October 4, 1954; *Industrial Relations News*, Vol. 6, No. 14, April 7, 1956; and Life Extension Foundation, "Job Stress and the Executive: 6,000 Managers Report Their Experience," *The Management Review*, Vol. 47, May, 1958, pp. 13-22.

ness, and it is generally accepted that managerial candidates should possess above-average intelligence. While above-average intelligence appears important to managerial effectiveness, there is some doubt about the relationship of highly superior intelligence to effectiveness. Stogdill reports from his review of research that the intelligence of a leader should be above that of his subordinates or followers, but that a marked difference of intelligence appears just as destructive of managerial effectiveness as does lowered intelligence.[13] The exact nature of the relationship is not known, however, and further study is required to determine the relationship between markedly superior intelligence and managerial effectiveness.

Intelligence is a rather complex characteristic with many different facets which may be related in varying degrees to managerial effectiveness. Abstract reasoning ability is one facet of intelligence usually included in discussions of managerial potential; the manager is expected to be able to summarize information, to generalize with abstract concepts, and to view relationships within the organization as abstract concepts. At least one measure of abstract reasoning ability has been found predictive of managerial effectiveness, suggesting the usefulness of this concept as a predictor in managerial staffing.[14] Mental flexibility is another such facet of intelligence, the effective manager being expected to accept new ideas and concepts readily and fit them into his total body of knowledge. Judgment also is an intellectual factor frequently cited as an element of management potential. Although the concept of judgment is difficult to define precisely, it appears to be the ability to consider alternative courses of action, draw the proper implications from each, and assign the proper weight to each consideration in making a choice. Several measures of judgment have been employed in studies of predictors of managerial effectiveness with positive results.[15] General ability to

[13] Stogdill, *op. cit.*, pp. 44-45.

[14] See Milton M. Mandell, "Research Findings in the Field of Supervision and Executive Selection," *Personnel,* Vol. 27, No. 3, November 1950, pp. 215-216.

[15] See S. G. Dulsky and M. H. Krout, "Predicting Promotional Potential on the Basis of Psychological Tests," *Personnel Psychology,* Vol. 3, No. 3, Autumn 1950, pp. 345-351, for a report on the Cardall Test of Practical Judgment; Milton M. Mandell and Dorothy C. Adkins, "The Validity of Written Tests for the Selection of Administrative Personnel," *Educational and Psychological Measurement,* Vol. 6, No. 3, Autumn 1946, pp. 293-312; and Milton M. Mandell, "Selecting Trainees for Management," *Personnel Administration,* Vol. 19, No. 3, May-June 1956, pp. 44-46, for reports on the Administrative Judgment Test.

learn and problem-solving abilities are additional facets of intelligence considered as predictors of managerial effectiveness. Various measures of general intelligence, which supposedly measure these facets, have been developed and tested in studies of management potential. Results of these studies indicate that above-average intelligence is a directly contributing factor in managerial effectiveness. Intelligence is a factor in other measures found related to managerial effectiveness, measures which also reflect influences other than intelligence. For example, level of education, grades earned in school, and age of graduation have all been found related to managerial effectiveness.[16] In summary, intelligence appears to be a general predictor of managerial effectiveness, although the implications of markedly superior intelligence are not yet known. The measure of intelligence most useful in predicting effectiveness probably will vary with the situation, but some measure of intelligence should be included in most attempts to predict managerial effectiveness.

Empathic ability—the ability to predict and understand the reactions of others to various ideas and situations—is mentioned frequently in theories of management potential. It is argued that the successful leader must know and understand the feelings and attitudes of his followers, and must use this knowledge in shaping programs and directives to enlist the support of followers. In short, this ability enables the leader or manager to better secure the willing cooperation of subordinates and to motivate them to improved performance. Various attempts have been made to measure empathy and to measure the relationship between these measures and managerial effectiveness.[17] Thus far, these attempts have had little success, either because the measures developed are not truly measuring empathic ability, or because empathy is not important in the prediction of managerial effectiveness.

---

[16] See Donald S. Bridgman, "Success in College and Business," *Personnel Journal,* Vol. 9, No. 1, 1930-1931, pp. 1-9; and Milton M. Mandell, "The Selection of Executives," in M. Joseph Dooher and Elizabeth Marting (editors), *Selection of Management Personnel,* Vol. I (New York: American Management Association, 1957), pp. 270-272.

[17] See, for example, G. B. Bell and R. Stolper, "An Attempt at Validation of the Empathy Test," *Journal of Applied Psychology,* Vol. 39, No. 6, December 1955, pp. 442-443; Rosalind Dymond, "A Preliminary Investigation of the Relation of Insight and Empathy," *Journal of Consulting Psychology,* Vol. 12, 1948, pp. 228-233; R. Dymond, "A Scale for the Measurement of Empathic Ability," *Journal of Consulting Psychology,* Vol. 3, 1949, pp. 127-133; and Wendell M. Patton, Jr., "A Study of Supervisory Empathy in the Textile Industry," *Journal of Applied Psychology,* Vol. 38, No. 5, October 1954, pp. 285-288.

Verbal ability is another ability mentioned frequently in theories of management and leadership. Verbal ability is considered involved in the ability to speak persuasively, the ability to write clearly and convincingly, and the ability to read—all specific abilities mentioned as important for managerial effectiveness. The manager accomplishes the objectives of his position through the direction and coordination of the efforts of others, a task which calls for communication. Thus, verbal ability, as seen in both receiving and transmitting information and communications, is listed as an element of management potential. Relatively little research has been reported concerning the relationship between verbal ability and managerial effectiveness. Various vocabulary measures—measures of one aspect of verbal ability—have been investigated and found related to effectiveness in specific situations.

Certain other abilities and skills are included in the concept of management potential for specific situations. For example, mechanical aptitude has been found related to managerial effectiveness in a number of situations requiring this aptitude. Specific knowledges also are related to effectiveness, again in situations where these knowledges are specific requirements of the position(s) being staffed. The majority of these additional abilities and skills appear to be useful in the prediction of managerial effectiveness only in those specific situations, however, and are not generally predictive of effectiveness.

Interests. Measures of aptitudes, abilities, and skills are indications of what an individual "can do," while measures of interests are designed to indicate what the individual "will do." Interests and values are considered important in the motivation of an individual and, thus, important in the prediction of effectiveness. Both ability and motivation or interests are thought to be related to performance in a somewhat compensatory manner—strong interests may compensate for certain lacks in aptitude if the individual is motivated to exert more effort. The motivation required for effectiveness is expected where the individual's interests coincide with job requirements. Thus, we might expect to identify general interest patterns related to over-all managerial effectiveness and rather more specific interest patterns associated with effectiveness in specific job situations.

Interests and values might be considered part of the concept of personality, since they probably are related to various personality aspects, such as motivation, social adjustment, and initiative. We shall treat them as separate from personality in this discussion, since they are somewhat easier to define and measure than are other aspects of personality.

Various patterns of interests and values have been found related to managerial effectiveness in studies of management potential. In general, the effective manager appears to possess broad interests with particular interest in practical matters and in literary and persuasive activities and a lack of interest in mechanical, technical, and social service activities. The University of Minnesota studies of management potential indicate that interests of effective managers in general are similar to the interests of managers of sales, purchasing agents, and manufacturing company presidents; they are dissimilar to the interests of men engaged in the biological sciences and in technical crafts.[18] Another study, this one within a large retail organization, indicates that effective managers tend to have high economic and political interests and relatively low aesthetic interests.[19] Important differences in interests of effective managers in different types of work also were indicated in this study. By comparison, effective managers within government appear to have high theoretical and social values and relatively low economic values. Several studies have indicated that effective managers in various job situations tend to have relatively broad interests, reflected either in hobbies or in extracurricular activities during high school and college.[20] In summary, interests and values of the individual appear to be an important element in the prediction of managerial effectiveness in general or in specific job situations. Interests found specifically related to the performance desired should be investigated and employed wherever possible, although the Minnesota study suggests that interest measures can be used with value in the prediction of general managerial effectiveness.

Personality. Personality is a complicated, vague, and ill-defined concept of certain personal characteristics. It commonly is viewed as the complex of attitudes, values, and traits which underlie individual behavior. There is no single integrated concept of personality, and most discussions of personality focus upon various characteristics considered as elements of personality. Certain of these character-

---

[18] Mahoney *et al., op. cit.*
[19] Cited in Mandell, "The Selection of Executives," *op. cit.*, p. 267.
[20] See Mandell, *ibid.*, pp. 270-272.

istics refer to observable behavior while others refer to rather fixed traits assumed to be influences of behavior. Almost every conceivable aspect of behavior has been classed as an element of personality by one or another author; some 3,000 to 5,000 characteristics have been counted in various discussions of personality. Discussions of personality lack precision, as do attempts to measure personality characteristics. Part of this difficulty stems from conceptual and semantic problems. Many of the characteristics mentioned in various discussions undoubtedly refer to the same general characteristics, the disagreement stemming from the interpretation of terminology or from the fact that these listed characteristics refer to different dimensions of the same general characteristic or trait. For example, what one observer calls "aggressiveness" another observer might call "perseverance." A somewhat more basic problem in the examination of personality stems from the apparent inconsistency of personality characteristics; people do not display the same behavioral tendencies in all situations. Thus, a person described as generous and kind in one situation might appear stingy and mean in another situation. In short, we are not sure what personality is or exactly how to describe it. Nevertheless, there is a widespread conviction that personality characteristics play an important role in determining the effectiveness of a manager; certain characteristics are required for effective performance while others hinder it. Thus, personality usually is considered in assessing management potential and in predicting managerial effectiveness. We shall consider a number of personality characteristics commonly suggested as predictors of managerial effectiveness, recognizing that few of them have been tested and proven useful in this prediction. This lack of demonstrated relationship probably stems from our present lack of reliable and valid measures of personality, although it may result from a lack of anything stable which we can class as personality and which is related to managerial effectiveness in fact. The personality concepts discussed here are generalizations based upon the many discussions of personality and managerial effectiveness. These generalizations are intended to provide a framework for our discussion and are not intended as a definitive classification of personality characteristics.

One grouping of personality characteristics, suggested as predictors of managerial effectiveness, includes the concepts of ambition, motivation, and drive-to-achieve. The potentially effective manager is described as possessing a high level of aspiration and a real desire for achievement; it is this which furnishes the motivation to undergo the necessary development and to withstand the pressures encountered by the manager. Several studies report the relationship between effectiveness and some measure of ambition or drive, although no generally satisfactory measure has been discovered.[21] Indications of this drive may be sought in experiences, such as work during the individual's education and other early work experiences. It is difficult to suggest any single best motivation for managers, whether it be social prestige, money, family security, authority, power, or merely the thrill of achievement. In fact, the studies of values reported earlier suggest that the motivations will vary for managers in different fields of endeavor. It seems reasonable, however, that there should be some motivating factor which provides a real desire to succeed and which goads the manager to seek successful performance.

Another set of closely related concepts refers to the energy, drive, and activity of the manager. The effective manager has been described as an individual who works long and hard and who drives himself. These concepts also are closely related to the concept of vitality discussed earlier as a physical characteristic. Again, there is no commonly accepted measure of this group of characteristics, and little research which does more than suggest the predictive value of possible measures.

A third set of concepts may be described as including the concepts of self-confidence and social poise, freedom from inferiority, emotional or personal adjustment, and maturity. In general, these concepts point up the need for a realistic understanding of one's abilities and shortcomings and an acceptance of them. Several studies employing measures purporting to measure self-confidence and emotional maturity have found a positive relationship between these measures and managerial effectiveness, suggesting that measures of these concepts may be predictive of effectiveness, although, again,

[21] See Mabel B. Cohen and R. A. Cohen, "Personality as a Factor in Administrative Decision," *Psychiatry*, Vol. 14, 1951, pp. 47-53; E. E. Ghiselli and R. Barthol, "Role Perceptions of Successful and Unsuccessful Supervisors," *Journal of Applied Psychology*, Vol. 40, No. 4, August 1956, pp. 241-244; Joan S. Guilford, "Temperament Traits of Executives and Supervisors Measured by the Guilford Personality Inventories," *Journal of Applied Psychology*, Vol. 36, 1952, pp. 228-233; D. Starch, "An Analysis of the Careers of 150 Executives," *Psychology Bulletin*, Vol. 39, No. 7, July 1942, p. 435; Robert M. Wald and Roy A. Doty, "The Top Executive—A Firsthand Profile," *Harvard Business Review*, Vol. 32, No. 4, July-August 1954, pp. 45-54.

there is no generally acceptable measure of these concepts, and any measure employed should be validated carefully.[22]

Closely correlated with the characteristics of confidence and adjustment are the concepts of courage and decisiveness. In fact, these characteristics might be included with the previous group. It is argued that the effective manager must be a leader and must inspire confidence in others, and that courage and decisiveness are necessary for this. The effective manager is expected to make decisions, even unpopular decisions, and then to stick by his convictions. Despite the appeal of this argument, there are no conclusive studies indicating a positive relationship between courage and effectiveness. These concepts certainly would be difficult to measure and may already have been measured in the measures of self-confidence.

The successful manager also is expected to possess a sense of dominance. This is interpreted to mean that the effective manager must desire to lead and to direct, and that he takes the initiative in his relationships with others. He is not expected to dictate, but to dominate through leadership. Several studies have employed measures of dominance and report a positive relationship with effectiveness.[23] Further study is necessary to determine the extent of relationship, however. It is entirely possible that extreme dominance, like extreme intelligence, may be detrimental to effectiveness as a manager.

The concepts of agreeableness, cooperativeness, and sociability comprise another set of characteristics suggested as predictive of managerial effectiveness. In short, the effective manager is described as a "likable" person. Perhaps it is this set of characteristics which tempers the characteristic of dominance. Measures of these characteristics are far from reliable, and studies of their relationship with effectiveness are only suggestive of relationships.

A final group of characteristics refers to characteristics usually mentioned as most important in the determination of managerial effectiveness. These concern the integrity, character, and ethical standards of the individual. The effective manager is described as possessing a real respect for individuals and as conducting himself in accordance with this respect. He is expected to possess relatively high ethical standards in his dealings with others and in his relation-

[22] See Guilford, *op. cit.*, pp. 228-233.

[23] See William J. Saunders, Jr., "Armco Steel Corporation," in Dooher and Marting, *op. cit.*, Vol. II, pp. 256-271; and Nelson G. Hanawalt and Helen M. Richardson, "Leadership as Related to the Bernreuter Personality Measures," *Journal of Applied Psychology*, Vol. 29, No. 5, 1944, pp. 397-411.

ships to gain and hold the respect of subordinates and colleagues. Although difficult to measure with any precision, this group of characteristics is accepted generally as a prerequisite for effective management. Probably the best measures of them are obtained through observations of behavior and experience, deviations from the required standards being easier to note than the exact degree of the standards possessed.

In summary, personality characteristics generally are included in any attempt to assess management potential. Few of these characteristics are defined with any precision, and they are quite difficult to estimate or measure. Research results to date are far from conclusive in the discovery of relationships between presently available measures of personality and effectiveness. This is not to imply that further research will not result in improved measures of personality or reliable predictors of managerial effectiveness. Rather, it should suggest that all assessments of personality characteristics be viewed with skepticism, and that little reliance be placed on predictions of effectiveness based upon these assessments. All use of personality measures in the prediction of managerial effectiveness should be carefully validated in the specific situation where they will be used.

Measuring Personal Characteristics

Attempts to predict managerial effectiveness from measures or estimates of various personal characteristics depend upon two conditions for success. First, there must be an actual relationship between the personal characteristic measured and managerial effectiveness. Second, the measures of personal characteristics employed in these predictions must provide reliable and accurate measures of these characteristics. A number of personal characteristics were suggested in the preceding section as predictors of managerial effectiveness. The validity of predictions made on the basis of estimates of these characteristics has been demonstrated in relatively few instances. This does not mean that measures of the remaining characteristics might not be useful in the prediction of managerial effectiveness. Rather, it means that further research and study are necessary to evaluate measures of each of these characteristics as a predictor of effectiveness.

The general techniques for validation of a set of predictors have already been described. The first step in this process involves selection of those characteristics to be investigated as possible predictors.

Personal characteristics such as those included in the preceding section are reviewed and considered as determinants of effective managerial performance. Those factors or characteristics considered most essential for effective performance are then selected for study. The second step involves the selection or development of measures of these characteristics. There are a number of alternative methods for measurement of personal characteristics, and those measures which provide the most reliable and valid measures should be selected for investigation in the validation process.

The ideal measure of any characteristic is objective, yields the same results regardless of user or number of applications, is practical to administer, and actually measures the intended characteristic. Figure 11 illustrates the degree to which different measures approach the ideal and the type of measure usually associated with different types of personal characteristics. The degree to which the ideal measure is approached varies considerably with the type of characteristic measured. Relatively objective measures are available for physical characteristics such as height and weight, for example. These characteristics are very clearly defined and can be measured in terms of a single dimension. Presently available measures of more complicated characteristics such as personality fall far short of the ideal largely because of the complex nature of these characteristics and the lack of any generally accepted definitions. This doesn't mean that measures of these more complicated characteristics can't be developed. Rather, it suggests that much more research and study should be devoted to development of measures for them. In the meantime, available measures of these characteristics should be studied carefully in the selection of measures for use in the prediction of managerial effectiveness.

Biographical information. Biographical information available in the form of application blanks and personnel records is a commonly used measure of personal characteristics for the prediction of managerial effectiveness. These biographical or experience measures are relatively reliable, objective, and valid. Their relevance in the prediction of effectiveness is recognized most readily in the case of assuring competence in areas of knowledge and experience requirements. It should be recognized, however, that biographical information also reflects the interests, motivation, and personality of the individual and frequently may be used as an indirect measure of these less specific characteristics. The attainment of a college

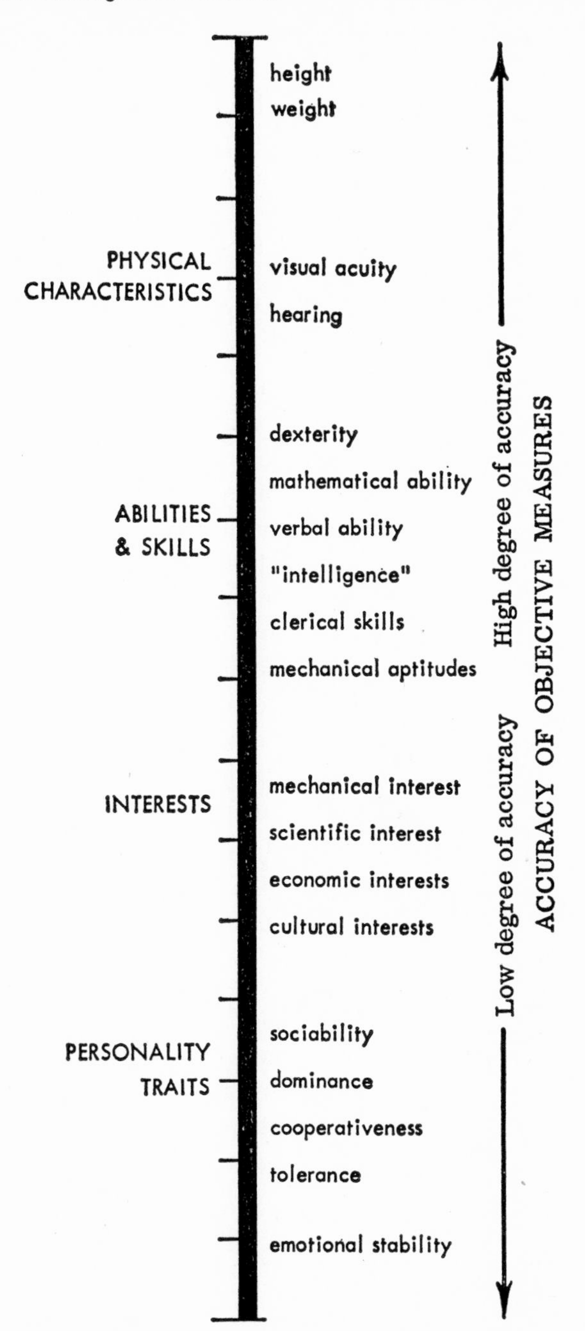

Fig. 11. Measures of Human Characteristics. From Herbert H. Meyer and J. M. Bertotti, "Uses and Misuses of Tests in Selecting Key Personnel," *Personnel,* Vol. 33, No. 3, p. 280, published by the American Management Association, Inc.

degree in engineering, for example, may be viewed as evidence of specific knowledge and ability and also as indicative of the individual's ability to learn, as well as his interests and his persistence in the pursuit of goals. Certain biographical items may be selected for investigation as predictors of managerial effectiveness on the basis of an assumed relationship between the biographical data and a characteristic thought necessary for managerial effectiveness. However, other biographical information may be equally predictive of managerial effectiveness, although there is no apparent relationship of that information to a desired personal characteristic. For example, automobile preferences may be predictive of managerial effectiveness, although it would be difficult to construct a rationale for consideration of this item. The important relationship is that which exists between the specific biographic information and managerial effectiveness, not the relationship between that information and some selected personal characteristic.

The relevance of biographical information in the prediction of managerial effectiveness varies from situation to situation, some items predicting effectiveness in one situation and other items predicting effectiveness in another. Despite the relative reliability of biographical measures, indiscriminate interpretation and application of these measures in the prediction of effectiveness may produce highly unreliable and irrelevant predictions. Relatively simple techniques exist for the evaluation of biographical information as predictors of managerial effectiveness and for the development of weights to be used in making such predictions.[24] These techniques can be applied in the development of weights for the prediction of some rather general criterion of over-all effectiveness or of a criterion of effectiveness within a specific job situation; they can be applied with information available in application blanks or maintained in personnel records. This information is consulted invariably in making selection, placement, and promotion decisions and is evaluated subjectively in making the decision. The reliability and accuracy of predictions made from this information can be improved considerably with the application of these techniques for constructing a weighted application blank.

Certain of the biographical items found predictive of various

[24] See Josephine Welch, C. Harold Stone, and Donald G. Paterson, *How to Develop a Weighted Application Blank,* Research and Technical Report 11, Industrial Relations Center, University of Minnesota (Dubuque, Iowa: William C. Brown Co., 1952).

criteria of managerial effectiveness in different studies were mentioned in the preceding section. Since the measures predicted in these studies varied considerably from one study to another, none of these biographical items should be accepted as predictive of managerial effectiveness in a new situation without investigation of their validity in the new situation. Items which have been found useful in prediction in various situations include high school study habits, age of high school graduation, organizations and offices held, leisure-time activities, extra-curricular activities during school, high school and college grades, college curriculum, and extent of self-support during school. The study of management potential at the University of Minnesota has identified several items predictive of effectiveness in a large group of company and job situations.[25] These items include memberships in high school organizations, number of sports and hobbies as a young man, number of offices held in organizations, highest grade completed in school by the individual and by his wife, and length of employment of the individual's wife after marriage.

In summary, biographical measures of experience provide a potentially useful source of measures predictive of managerial effectiveness. These measures are indirect measures of various personal characteristics and tend to be more reliable than many of the attempts to measure personal characteristics more directly through various tests. Behavior in school, on past jobs, and in personal activities reflects personal characteristics, just as does behavior in the completion of specially constructed tests, and in most instances is more reliable and practical to administer as a measure. The relatively simple techniques which exist for the validation of biographical predictors of effectiveness suggest that such measures should be exploited more than they are in the making of accurate predictions of effectiveness.

Psychological tests. Psychological testing in the measurement of personal characteristics is similar in many respects to the use of biographical information in the prediction of managerial effectiveness. In both instances, recorded or observed behavior is used to predict future behavior. Personal characteristics are defined in terms of observable behavior. Individual behavior of this type is predicted

[25] See Thomas A. Mahoney, Thomas H. Jerdee, and Allan N. Nash, *The Identification of Management Potential* (Dubuque, Iowa: William C. Brown Company, 1960).

from behavior observed in the past situation on the basis of known relationships between these two sets of behavior. Thus, performance in the solution of problems in a paper-and-pencil test may be predictive of problem-solving behavior in other situations. A valid test is one which predicts accurately some specifically defined behavior, such as school performance, job performance, or social behavior. However, a valid test need not be a valid predictor of managerial effectiveness, as when a test accurately predicts some behavior which is unrelated to managerial effectiveness. Thus, validity of the test as a predictor of effectiveness should be established before it is used in the making of such predictions, just as validity should be established in the use of biographical information. Psychological tests do possess certain advantages not found in biographical information, however. Psychological tests involve the standardization of testing conditions and of interpretations of test performance. For example, differences in high school grade averages of two people may exist merely because the people took different courses, or because different grading standards were applied. Two people taking the same psychological tests are subjected to the same conditions, and their behavior under these conditions is measured and interpreted in the same manner.

Psychological tests have been developed in attempts to measure a number of different concepts of personal characteristics. Not all of these characteristics are relevant in the prediction of managerial effectiveness. Our earlier discussion suggested that several of these characteristics would be relevant; their exact relevance must be established in each situation where predictions of effectiveness are to be made. The validity of the test as a measure of the intended personal characteristic is a factor to be considered in the selection of tests for validation as predictors of effectiveness. Presently available psychological tests are much more accurate and reliable in the measurement of specific characteristics, such as knowledge and aptitude, than they are in the measurement of complicated concepts of personality, for reasons mentioned earlier. Just as a valid measure of a personal characteristic may be irrelevant as a predictor of managerial effectiveness, a relatively inaccurate measure of some personal characteristic may turn out to be highly valid in the prediction of effectiveness. Therefore, no test need be discarded from study as a predictor of effectiveness because it fails to measure some known personal characteristic.

(1) Ability and aptitude tests. Tests of ability and aptitude are among the most commonly used psychological tests. These tests attempt to measure an individual's ability or aptitude for learning a particular type of behavior. For example, intelligence tests frequently attempt to measure an individual's ability to learn material presented in formal schooling. Many of these tests are among the most reliable and valid psychological measures now available, largely because development of these tests has received more attention than has the development of other tests, and because many of them are validated against quite specific operational definitions of abilities. This has been particularly true in the development of measures of physical and mechanical aptitudes. It has been somewhat more difficult to develop measures of managerial abilities and aptitudes.

Probably the most widely used ability test is the intelligence test designed in general to measure ability to learn. As indicated earlier, measures of intelligence have been found predictive of managerial effectiveness in a number of situations. The most frequently mentioned tests of intelligence in this connection include the *Wonderlic Personnel Test,* the *Otis Self-Administering Test, American Council of Education Psychological Examination,* and the *California Test of Mental Maturity.* In addition to these tests of general problem-solving ability, there are a number of specialized intelligence tests. For example, there are several tests which attempt to measure judgment, abstract reasoning, intellectual flexibility, and memory.

Several tests of different abilities have been found predictive of managerial effectiveness. These particular abilities, however, would appear to be peculiar to certain situations and not so generally predictive as the tests of intelligence. One such test is the *Michigan Vocabulary Test,* which measures interests as well as verbal ability. Another frequently used test is the *Bennet Test of Mechanical Comprehension,* testing an ability which probably is predictive of effectiveness only in certain situations. Empathic ability—the ability to predict others' feelings and reactions—frequently is hypothesized as an element of management potential. There are several tests which attempt to measure empathy, but none of them have appeared predictive of effectiveness in reported studies. Any number of additional tests of ability and aptitude might be mentioned as possible predictors of managerial effectiveness in situations requiring special abilities. Only the more commonly investigated abilities and the tests appearing as predictive in reported studies have been included here.

(2) Interest and value tests. Interests and values were discussed earlier as indications of an individual's motivations. Several psychological measures of interests and values are used widely in occupational and vocational counseling and in selection and placement of employees because of the relationships found between interests, values, and job success. Repeated studies of management potential suggest the value of such tests in predicting managerial effectiveness.

The two most widely used tests of interests are the *Kuder Preference Record* and the *Strong Vocational Interest Blank*. Both of these tests attempt to measure an individual's interests through his expressed likes and dislikes, including preferences concerning occupation, hobbies, and leisure activities. *Kuder* scores express interests in terms of several general dimensions of interests—scientific, mechanical, persuasive, literary, and artistic. *Strong* scores, on the other hand, compare the individual's expressed interests directly with the interests expressed by persons successfully engaged in various occupations. No comparison is made in the *Strong* scores between an individual's interests and interests of managers in general, although interests are compared with those of production managers, sales managers, and presidents of manufacturing concerns. Studies of management potential at the University of Minnesota have found patterns of scores on the *Strong* test predictive of managerial effectiveness in a wide variety of situations, and studies within individual companies have identified score patterns predictive of effectiveness within specific company situations.[26] The *Kuder* test has been employed in a number of other studies of management potential, and scores on this test have been identified as predictive of effectiveness within specific company situations.[27]

---

[26] See Deryck Adamson, "Shawinigan Water and Power Company" in Dooher and Marting (editors), *Selection of Management Personnel,* Vol. II (New York: American Management Association, 1958), pp. 85-106; Mahoney *et al., op. cit.;* and Edward K. Strong, Jr., "Interests of the Public Administrators," *Public Personnel Review,* Vol. 6, 1945, pp. 166-173.

[27] See S. G. Dulsky and M. H. Krout, "Predicting Promotional Potential on the Basis of Psychological Tests," *Personnel Psychology,* Vol. 3, No. 3, Autumn, 1950, pp. 345-351; C. E. Thompson, "Selecting Executives by Psychological Tests," *Educational and Psychological Measurement,* Vol. 7, 1947, pp. 773-778; Robert M. Wald and Roy A. Doty, *op. cit.;* and James C. Worthy, "Planned Executive Development: The Experience of Sears, Roebuck and Company," *Personnel Series No. 137* (New York: American Management Association, 1951), pp. 3-26.

The *Allport-Vernon Study of Values* test is used somewhat less widely than the above interest measures, although it also has been reported to be predictive of managerial effectiveness in specific organizational situations.[28] This test attempts to measure six dimensions of value orientation—theoretical, economic, aesthetic, political, social, and religious. The dimension scores predictive of managerial effectiveness appear to vary considerably from one situation to another; high theoretical and social values with low economic values are reported predictive of effectiveness in government service, and high economic and political values with low aesthetic values are reported predictive of success in industry. These results suggest that this measure of values can be useful in predicting management effectiveness, but that there is no general requirement for all managerial positions; rather, the test must be validated specifically for each situation in which it will be used.

(3) Personality tests. Progress in the validation of personality tests as predictors of managerial effectiveness lags behind the validation of other measures. Personality characteristics almost always are included among predictor suggestions, but relatively few personality measures have been demonstrated to be useful predictors. The difficulty here may lie in the lack of reliability and validity of these measures as indicators of personality, in the lack of relationship between personality characteristics and effectiveness, or in the nature of the measured personality characteristics.

The development of useful personality measures, as indicated earlier, has been hampered by a lack of specific concepts and definitions of personality characteristics. As a result, many of the personality tests are scored on the basis of judgment and clinical interpretation of the meaning of various test answers. Certain of the tests are scored on an empirical basis, the answers being interpreted in terms of the way that known personality types answer the same questions. As a result, such tests have been developed and validated for abnormal personality characteristics. The *Minnesota Multiphasic Personality Inventory*, for example, is one of the best-constructed personality measures, but its value lies primarily in the identification of abnormal characteristics. Available personality measures range from the paper-and-pencil inventory, such as the *MMPI*, to projective techniques which require a clinical interpretation.

---

[28] See Mandell, *op. cit.*, pp. 267-268.

The general lack of demonstrated relationships between personality measures and effectiveness may stem also from a lack of any real relationship between the suggested personality characteristics and effectiveness. It is entirely possible that any number of personality patterns may result in equal effectiveness in managerial positions—that there is no identifiable personality required. Furthermore, personality characteristics measured in one situation are not always consistent with measures obtained in another situation. Thus, personality measures obtained at the time of employment may be of relatively little value in the prediction of personality six months after employment. Certainly some of this inconsistency of measures results from the transparency of various personality tests and the ease of faking answers to provide the desired results. A number of personality tests have been severely criticized because of their "apparent" answers and the ease of faking.[29] These tests may be useful in the clinical situation, where a patient has an incentive to be honest, and fail in the industrial situation where the candidate for selection has an incentive to supply the answers he thinks desired.

In summary, personality measures have not yet proven so useful in the prediction of managerial effectiveness as might be expected from the attention given personality characteristics in theoretical examinations of the requirements of managers. It is difficult to interpret this lack of relationship in view of our present inadequate knowledge of personality components. It is quite likely that continued study and research concerning personality will permit the development of useful measures of personality and the assessment of personality requirements of managers. In the meantime, however, the use of personality predictors of managerial effectiveness should be viewed with caution and skepticism.

Appraisals. Another source of information about candidates for managerial assignments is found in appraisals of performance and/or potential where the candidates already are members of the organization. Consideration of these appraisal results can be particularly valuable in making assignments of present managers and in promotions from within the organization. The appraisal provides a possibility for much more accurate assessment of personal characteristics and the prediction of future behavior, since predictions are

[29] See William H. Whyte, Jr., "The Fallacies of Personality Testing," *Fortune*, Vol. 50, No. 3, September 1954, pp. 117-121, 204-210.

based upon longer and more varied observations of past behavior. Furthermore, the observed behavior is job behavior rather than non-job and psychological test behavior. Appraisals generally have not proven so valuable in the prediction of effectiveness as might be expected, however. Probably the primary reason for this is found in the shortcomings of the usual appraisal as a measure. First, it is difficult to select those elements of past or present performance which are most relevant in the prediction of future behavior and to abstract from these for useful predictions. Second, less effort has been devoted to the development of reliable and accurate measures of performance. The shortcomings of the majority of current management appraisal programs and suggestions for their improvement were discussed in an earlier chapter. Management appraisals offer possibly the best opportunity for prediction of managerial effectiveness because of the relevance of observations of behavior and because of the length of observation. Further research and development of reliable and useful appraisal measures should improve predictions in the placement and promotion of managers.

Guide to Developing a Prediction System

Studies of predictors of managerial effectiveness conducted at the University of Minnesota provide an illustration of a fruitful approach to the development of guides for predicting managerial effectiveness.[30] These studies have sought predictors of a general criterion of managerial effectiveness rather than predictors of effectiveness peculiar to an individual company or job situation. Results of the studies consequently have a much wider application than do the results of more specific approaches. Thirteen companies employing a total of 1,175 managers cooperated in these studies and pooled their resources to make the studies possible. Companies ranged in size from 100 employees to approximately 4,000 employees, the number of managers employed ranging from 24 to over 350. Industries represented by the cooperating companies included heavy and light manufacturing, finance, wholesale distribution, insurance, public utilities, and agricultural products. A total of 468 managerial assignments in cooperating companies were selected for

---

[30] For complete details of these studies and guides to the application of their findings, see Thomas A. Mahoney, Thomas H. Jerdee, and Allan N. Nash, *The Identification of Management Potential* (Dubuque, Iowa: William C. Brown Company, 1960).

consideration in the studies. These assignments represented all levels of the management organizations and all major types of work in the cooperating companies. Examples of specific assignments included production foreman, export sales manager, controller, company president, factory manager, director of purchasing, and personnel director. Personal characteristics and managerial effectiveness of managers in the sampled assignments were measured simultaneously. Managers participating in the studies were divided into two groups matched on the basis of industry, company, type of work, and organization level of assignment. Relationships between measures of personal characteristics and managerial effectiveness found in the analysis of one group of managers were used in the construction of a prediction system which then was validated in application to the second group of managers.

Ninety-eight specific measures of personal characteristics were obtained in these studies. These included measures of intelligence, empathic ability, personality characteristics, and personal biographical information. An alternation ranking of general managerial effectiveness of the managers was obtained in each company and used to divide the managers into three criterion groups: (1) the top-ranked one-third of the managers in each company, (2) the middle-ranked one-third of the managers, and (3) the lowest-ranked one-third of the managers. Measures of personal characteristics of the top-ranked and low-ranked managers were compared to identify those measures which successfully differentiated between managers in these criterion groups. Eighteen of the measures of personal characteristics were found to be individually related to managerial effectiveness. These measures were grouped for prediction purposes as follows:

Group A. Comparison of vocational interests with those of men in biological sciences and technical crafts.
Group B. Comparison of interests with those of men in business occupations.
Group C. Intelligence.
Group D. Personality characteristics.
Group E. Educational background.
Group F. Activity in sports, hobbies, and organizations.

In words, the more effective manager tends to be more intelligent than the less effective manager; his vocational interests are more similar to those of sales managers, purchasing agents, and manufacturing company presidents, and less similar to the interests of men in the biological sciences and technical crafts such as dentistry, veterinary medicine, printing, carpentry, and farming; he tends to be more aggressive, persuasive, and self-reliant; he has had more educational training and was more active in sports and hobbies as a young man; and his wife has had more educational training and worked a shorter time after marriage. A prediction system based upon these measures successfully predicted the effectiveness ranking of 63 per cent of the top-ranked managers and 77 per cent of the lowest-ranked managers; 37 per cent of the top-ranked managers and 23 per cent of the lowest-ranked managers were misclassified using the prediction system.

This prediction system then was applied to the second sample of managers as an independent test of its validity. Results in the second sample were almost identical with results in the first sample: 62 per cent of the top-ranked managers and 71 per cent of the lowest-ranked managers were classified correctly using the prediction system. In general, a predictive efficiency of better than 60 per cent was obtained when the system was altered to provide various over-all selection ratios. Application of the prediction system within each of the participating companies resulted in correct predictions ranging from 50 per cent to 100 per cent of the managers in each company with an average of 69 per cent over all of the companies.

The significance of these studies appears first in the identification of predictors of managerial effectiveness which are valid in a wide variety of situations. This finding suggests that there is a phenomenon of general managerial effectiveness which can be identified and predicted regardless of the specific assignment of a manager. Findings of these and similar studies are applicable in predicting managerial effectiveness in varied companies and industries. Furthermore, findings of these studies are available for immediate application within individual organizations. The prediction system developed in the Minnesota studies can be applied directly by small organizations unable to develop prediction systems specific to their organizations, and larger organizations with the necessary resources and facilities can use these results as a basis for refinement and development of an improved system specific to their situations. Further studies of this type and continued refinement of prediction systems specific to individual situations should considerably improve our ability to identify management potential and to utilize it most effectively in development of the management team.

SUMMARY

The problem of identification of management potential and the prediction of managerial effectiveness underlies all attempts at management development. No single approach to the prediction of managerial effectiveness is likely to prove equally effective in all managerial staffing situations. Rather, generally useful guides and approaches must be tailored and refined to fit the individual situation. Measures of management potential which have been found useful in one or more situations have been reviewed in this chapter, as well as techniques for the validation of management selection techniques. An over-all guide to the prediction of managerial effectiveness has been outlined. Improved identification of management potential will result from the refinement of this and similar guides to take account of individual organizations and their needs.

SELECTED BIBLIOGRAPHY

Dooher, M. Joseph, and Elizabeth Marting (editors), *Selection of Management Personnel* (New York: American Management Association, 1957).

Ginzberg, Eli (editor), *What Makes an Executive?* (New York: Columbia University Press, 1955).

Stone, C. Harold, and William E. Kendall, *Effective Personnel Selection Procedures* (Englewood Cliffs, N. J.: Prentice-Hall, Inc., 1956).

Assessing Managerial Potential (Ann Arbor, Michigan: Foundation for Research on Human Behavior, 1958).

Chapter NINE

Individual Training and Development

INTRODUCTION

The training and development of individual managers form an important element, although only a single element, of a comprehensive program for management development. The concept of management development employed in this book concerns development of the management team for improved performance in both the present and the future. This development is sought through an improved utilization of the potential and the abilities of individual members of the management team. A comprehensive program for development of the management team was outlined in an earlier chapter, and individual training and development were discussed there in relation to other elements of management development. More effort probably has been given to manager training and development within organizations than to other elements of management development. This concentration of emphasis is unfortunate, not because individual training and development are unimportant, but because such concentration tends to confuse individual development with the larger concept of management development. The training and development of individual managers certainly contribute to improved performance of the management team, but so also do other activities which improve the coordination of team members, their motivation, and the effective assignment of managers to specific positions. Activities for the training and development of managers contribute most to the improved performance of the management team if these activities are integrated with the other elements of management development.

Various techniques for the training and development of managers are discussed and examined in this chapter. This examination is based upon several general concepts which should be stated at the outset.

First, the training and development of individual managers is recognized as a responsibility of the organization. Just as it is the responsibility of the organization to provide for improved and continued performance of the management team, so is this single element of management development its responsibility. As one observer has put it, management development involves the development of managers, by management, for management purposes.[1]

Second, the term "development" refers to growth and advancement of latent abilities. This growth occurs as the individual encounters new experiences which are interpreted and integrated into the individual's background of knowledge. Individual development thus varies with the nature of information and experience encountered, the background brought to these encounters, and the individual's ability to interpret and integrate these experiences into his background. This suggests that all development is individual in the sense that results of identical training experiences will vary among the individuals trained. Whether such training experiences are presented individually or in groups, the accomplishments of training will vary with the individual. Consequently, the most effective training is likely to be training which is prescribed on an individual basis, taking into account the individual's need for training, his background of experiences, and his ability to profit from training.

A related concept concerns the nature of development and training experiences. In a very real sense, all learning and development occur through experience, and the sum of an individual's experiences contributes to the shaping of his knowledge and behavior. These experiences may include reading, classroom instruction, observation, and similar experiences in addition to job performance,

[1] William Oncken, Jr., "Experience Isn't Enough," *Advanced Management*, Vol. 23, No. 2, February 1958, pp. 13-14.

and they will vary in terms of effectiveness in changing behavior. Job performance will constitute a large element of any manager's experience, and this day-to-day work experience will shape the individual's development. Special training experiences can be used as supplements to this work experience, but they cannot substitute for it. Recent studies have indicated that the value of supplementary training also is influenced largely by the work climate where the individual is expected to apply the knowledge secured by this training. An individual manager's behavior is directed by his superior and motivation is provided by his superior. The manager will learn and apply only what is consistent with the reward system of his superior. It is important that we recognize the role of work experience in individual development and the role played by each superior manager in guiding and directing the development and performance of subordinates.

Finally, we should recognize that all development is self-development in the long run. While the organization must assume responsibility for the development of individuals and the management team, individual development is individual growth and cannot be forced. The most that the organization can do in the development of individuals is to provide opportunities for self-development and create a climate which encourages and stimulates the development required for improved performance of the management team. Individuals selected for management should be capable of development and interested in personal development. Guidance in development and opportunities for development must then be provided by the organization. The use to which these opportunities are put and the results will depend largely upon the individual. Too frequently organizations tend to stifle this personal self-development through the emphasis placed upon organized experiences for development and through creation of a belief that the organization alone is responsible for development. An adjunct of this is the opinion that the individual shares no responsibility for his own development. The formal techniques of training too frequently shift attention from daily self-development to company-sponsored development.[2]

---

[2] For a discussion of general problems of individual development, see Chris Argyris, "Executive Development Programs: Some Unresolved Problems," *Personnel*, July 1956, pp. 33-41; Lincoln Atkiss, "Executive Personnel Development," *Office Executive*, August 1956, pp. 36-38; Julius E. Eitington, "Do It Yourself—The Key to Leadership Training," *Personnel Administration*,

Effective development of the management team requires that individual training and development be fitted into an over-all scheme for development, and that techniques for individual development be applied carefully to achieve maximum benefits for the management team. In short, effective training and development of individuals must be carefully planned and integrated into a master plan for development of the management team. The proliferation of special training courses and gimmicks, without such integration, achieves desired results only by accident.

IDENTIFYING NEEDS FOR DEVELOPMENT

The obvious first step in individual training and development involves the determination of training needs. A diagnosis of specific training needs is necessary for the prescription of training and development activities most apt to prove beneficial to development of the management team. Obvious as this step may appear, it is overlooked too frequently in actual practice, or a nonexistent need is assumed in justification of training activities. Sloppy diagnosis and prescription of development activities are inefficient and also may prove dangerous to any attempt at long-run management development. Development activities conducted without any clear purpose, or where there is no specific need, can create a resentment against such activities and an attitude that management development is a luxury rather than a necessary element of good management.

Training needs can be viewed from the standpoint of the individual manager or of the management organization.[3] This distinction can be important where conflicting programs of action are called for in accomplishing development, and where a choice must

Vol. 19, No. 5, September-October 1956, pp. 34-41; Myles L. Mace, *The Growth and Development of Executives* (Boston: The Graduate School of Business Administration, Harvard University, 1950), 200 pp.; Earl G. Planty and J. Thomas Freeston, *Developing Management Ability* (New York: Ronald Press, 1954), 447 pp.; John W. Riegel, *Executive Development* (Ann Arbor: University of Michigan Press, 1952), 332 pp.; Robert K. Stolz, "Getting Back to Fundamentals in Executive Development," *Personnel,* Vol. 30, No. 6, May 1954, pp. 434-444; Perrin Stryker, "The Growing Pains of Executive Development," *Advanced Management,* Vol. 19, No. 8, August 1954, pp. 14-16; and Lyndall F. Urwick, "How to Improve Executive Training," *Nation's Business,* Vol. 46, No. 7, July 1958, pp. 32 ff.

[3] See Chris Argyris, "Top Management Dilemma: Company Needs vs. Individual Development," *Personnel,* Vol. 32, No. 2, September 1955, pp. 123-134.

be made in determining the relative emphasis to be given each set of training needs. Development needs as viewed from the standpoint of the management team usually will be more inclusive than those viewed from the standpoint of the individual manager and will tend to include these individual needs. For example, development needs of the management team may call for the recruitment of managers from outside the organization as well as the development of individuals within the organization. It is useful to analyze development needs from both standpoints, recognizing that our primary concern lies with the over-all performance and development of the management team. These needs ultimately are stated in terms of individual needs and will reflect the needs of both the organization and the individual managers.

A distinction can also be made between shortcomings of the individual manager in meeting performance objectives of his present position and shortcomings in qualification for more responsible positions. Both of these measures of need for development are relevant in development of the management team, one in the short run and the other in the long run. Conflict between these two statements of need or shortcomings is more apparent than real, since development of an individual for improved performance normally will also contribute to his development for promotion. However, consideration of the needs for qualification for promotion may be useful in the selection of specific needs for improved performance which should be given the most attention; those shortcomings in current performance which are most closely related to promotion considerations may be given priorities in the statement of development needs.

The general process of determining needs for development has been described briefly in earlier chapters.[4] This process involves the measurement of "gaps" between an existing situation and specified goals and objectives. These goals and objectives are stated in the organization plans and position descriptions, and measures of present performance of individual managers and their ability to meet organization plans are obtained in the appraisal and inventory of managerial personnel. Individual manager appraisals point up weaknesses in present manager performance and shortcomings in qualification for promotion, and the management inventory should point up weaknesses of the organization and probable staffing problems which will arise in the future. Additional indications of

[4] See Chapters 3 and 5.

organizational weaknesses are provided in the comparison of organizational performance with objectives—indexes of production, costs, sales, turnover, morale, and so forth. Any gap between actual performance and desired performance on the part of the individual or of the management team points up weaknesses or needs for development activities to correct the situation. Following the procedure outlined earlier in our discussion of management appraisal and inventory, each manager is responsible for the appraisal and analysis of weaknesses of individual performance and of organizational strength in those units under his supervision. These analyses and statements of weaknesses are coordinated and grouped at each successive level in the management hierarchy to provide an over-all appraisal of the management organization and its members.[5]

We are concerned here with the training and development of individual managers in accord with an over-all plan for development of the management team, so we shall concentrate upon the analysis of individual needs and weaknesses and the prescription of development activities to correct these. A complete appraisal of individual managers should involve the measurement of current performance and qualification for advancement, indicating the gaps in performance and qualifications of the individual. However, a mere identification of weaknesses is insufficient; the appraisal should also involve an analysis of reasons for any gaps noted and recommendations for aiding the individual to overcome these weaknesses. The individual or committee responsible for the appraisal presumably is in the best position to note the individual's performance and qualifications, and thus also to analyze his needs for development. Furthermore, certain of the appraisers will be responsible for carrying out suggested development activities and should be involved in their prescription. By the same token, the individual manager being appraised should be encouraged to contribute his own analysis of needs and prescription of solutions; advantages of this participation and suggestions for its encouragement were discussed in an earlier chapter.

---

[5] For example, see the descriptions of company programs given in E. L. Baab, "Management Training: Organizing the 'Communications Flow'," *Personnel,* Vol. 33, No. 5, March 1957, pp. 457-460; John E. Ehrmantraut, "Development at the Executive Level," *The Journal of the American Society of Training Directors,* Vol. 11, No. 6, November-December 1957, pp. 18-19; and Richard J. Frost and Preston P. LeBreton, "An Effective Management Development Program," *University of Washington Business Review,* Vol. 17, No. 5, February 1958, pp. 14-28.

Specific weaknesses and needs for development will vary considerably from one manager to another. A careful analysis of needs will involve consideration of much more than present performance. Many companies, for example, provide for the appraiser or appraisers to review the individual's personal history and qualifications as well as his present performance in an attempt to better analyze his weaknesses.[6] This personal history is of little relevance in the evaluation of present performance but can be a real aid in the analysis of reasons for shortcomings in performance. In general, we can identify four broad types of weaknesses or needs for development, recognizing the many variations within each type.

(1) The need for increased knowledge and ability to perform specific duties of the individual's present position or a more responsible position.
(2) The need for increased knowledge and ability within the general field of the individual's work.
(3) The need for broadened over-all knowledge and understanding not restricted to any one field of endeavor.
(4) The need for desirable personal characteristics and attitudes.

This classification of general types of development needs is suggested only as a general guide for the analysis of needs and the prescription of development activities, since certain activities are more appropriate than others in development to overcome weaknesses. The appraiser or appraisers responsible for analyzing an individual manager's weaknesses should attempt to be as specific as possible, thus providing more useful guidance for the appraised manager.

PROVIDING DEVELOPMENT OPPORTUNITIES

Development of individual managers involves filling in the gaps in individual qualifications suggested for improved performance or for qualification for promotion. These gaps in experience, knowledge, ability, and personal characteristics will

[6] For example, see L. A. Russ, "Case 9: Westinghouse Electric Company," Chapter 39 in M. Joseph Dooher and Vivienne Marquis (editors), *The Development of Executive Talent* (New York: American Management Association, 1952), pp. 419-445.

vary from one individual to another depending upon the individual's background. Certain of these gaps may be common to more than one individual, in which case identical or group opportunities for development can be prescribed. These prescriptions of common development activities should proceed from the analysis of individual needs, however, rather than from an assumption that certain activities are beneficial for all managers.

We mentioned earlier that all development ultimately is self-development. The management organization can provide opportunities for development and can seek to encourage and stimulate individual managers to profit from these opportunities, but the result of development experiences will depend almost entirely upon the individual. A first step in such self-development is recognition by the individual manager of his needs for development. Participation of the individual manager in the analysis of his own needs and in the suggestion of development experiences to help him in overcoming his deficiencies should contribute a great deal to the encouragement of self-development.

Opportunities for self-development abound in every organization, and many opportunities are available outside the organization through universities and professional management associations. The use that can be made of these opportunities will depend upon the size of the organization, the available resources and facilities, and the imagination of those responsible for prescribing individual programs of development. We shall review here only the most commonly used opportunities; an imaginative management can adapt many of these and fashion other opportunities to fit special needs of individual managers.

Opportunities Within the Organization

The most readily usable opportunities for development are those already available within the organization. These also are the opportunities most commonly overlooked in considering management development, since they usually involve job performance of one type or another and have received less attention as purely development opportunities. They probably are most practical, since they provide for development through performance, and since they tend to involve less expense than do opportunities outside the organization. Furthermore, they can be more specific to needs of development of the management team, since they involve development within the context of organization operations and philosophy. These opportunities available within the organization probably should be viewed as the core of development opportunities to be utilized at all times, while opportunities available outside the organization should be viewed as supplements available for specific needs which cannot be met within the organization.

Delegation. The most commonly available and probably least effectively utilized opportunity for individual development lies in the progressive delegation of responsibilities by superior managers. This opportunity for development of subordinate managers is available in every boss-subordinate relationship and should be utilized by individual managers regardless of the extent of additional formal opportunities for development within the organization. Furthermore, delegation can be a particularly effective method for development of individual subordinates, since it involves work experience. Individuals learn by doing, and the assignment of additional responsibilities through delegation can provide numerous opportunities for such learning. Few opportunities provide the challenge for development which are provided by the assignment of new responsibilities. The subordinate manager is encouraged in his development by the confidence shown in delegation and by the challenge of a work assignment, as compared with a more artificial training assignment. Delegation of responsibilities also is a very flexible technique in the sense that responsibilities for delegation can be selected on the basis of the subordinate's needs and adjusted to his present capabilities. Opportunities for development through delegation can be tailor-made for the individual need and situation.[7]

Delegation of responsibilities should not be viewed as a separate and unique technique for individual development. Rather, it is involved in most opportunities for development within the organization. We have considered it separately here because of its importance in all individual development, and because this aspect of individual development is overlooked too frequently in the consideration of management development. Delegation of responsibilities is recognized by most managers as both a desirable management practice and a useful tool in the development of subordinates.

---

[7] See John H. Gorsuch, "Good Management Men Delegate Authority," *Advanced Management,* Vol. 24, No. 9, September 1954, pp. 5-8; Donald A. Laird, "Executive Development by Delegation," *Management Methods,* July 1957, pp. 52-53; and Mace, *op. cit.,* Chapter VI.

But too few managers actually carry through in delegating to subordinates. While there undoubtedly are many factors which contribute to the failure to delegate, several of them deserve mention here. Many managers apparently fail to delegate as effectively as possible because of a fear or hesitancy that subordinates will not perform as desired. This fear may reflect a lack of confidence in the potential of subordinates to react to the challenge of new responsibilities, an unwillingness to permit the mistakes necessary in individual learning, or a lack of effective controls permitting the superior manager to keep track of performance and to take steps to insure adequate performance. Many managers fail to recognize the importance of work performance in the development of subordinates and hesitate to delegate until the subordinate is competent to perform additional responsibilities without difficulty. At this point, delegation has little impact upon the individual's development and serves little purpose. Rather, the individual should be challenged by new responsibilities which provide learning opportunities. Furthermore, managers often fail to recognize that responsibilities can be performed in various ways and be equally effective. They tend to underrate the subordinate's ability to perform the responsibility as it has been performed, and forget that he might develop an alternative, but equally effective, method of performance. Delegation too frequently is viewed by managers as the relinquishment of authority, and they fear the consequences of delegation unless they can adequately insure the expected performance of subordinates. Such a fear stems in part from a failure to recognize the importance of controls which permit the superior manager to check upon performance of delegated responsibilities and take the action necessary to insure desired performance. The design and exercise of such controls may require more time and attention than would performance of the responsibility by the superior manager, and they may appear inefficient as a way of performing the work of the organization. However, the attention given to controls which permit delegation is repaid in the development of subordinates. Real self-control on the part of the delegating manager is required for effective delegation, self-control to refrain from the old ways of operation and to permit the subordinate manager to learn by doing. Delegation may involve inefficient performance for the organization for a short period of time, but its return in the development of subordinates and the long-run efficiency are well worth the short-run cost.

A realization of the importance of delegation in individual development and of the techniques contributing to effective delegation is necessary for most management development. Opportunities for self-development of the manager within the organization usually involve work performance that is assigned through delegation.

Coaching. Most surveys of management-development practices of organizations indicate that job experience and coaching of subordinates are among the most common methods of individual development.[8] As a matter of fact, job experience and coaching should be considered inseparable; either without the other is of little value in development. "Coaching" refers to the daily guidance and help given by a manager in the development of subordinates. It involves all of the many forms of help and assistance which the superior manager provides a subordinate in helping the subordinate to improve his performance. Coaching refers to development of the subordinate's knowledge and abilities as they relate to his current responsibilities. These knowledges and abilities usually will be relevant in the qualification of the subordinate for advanced responsibilities, but they are chosen for coaching as they bear upon the individual's performance of present responsibilities.[9]

There is no single best technique for coaching. Effective techniques will vary with the position and the relationship between the superior and the subordinate. As a general rule, however, coaching is viewed as guidance in helping the subordinate find solutions and answers rather than as teaching or telling the subordinate the solutions sought. This work can be tackled in several ways. For example, coaching is performed when the superior manager requires subordinates to bring suggested solutions each time they discuss problems, or when the superior helps the subordinate by listening to and reviewing ideas rather than providing ideas. In short, coach-

---

[8] See Bureau of National Affairs, "The Executive," *Survey No. 37 of Personnel Policies Forum* (Washington, D. C., July 1956), 14 pp.; Joseph M. Trickett, "A Survey of Management Development," *Management Education for Itself and Its Employees: Part II* (New York: American Management Association, 1954), 61 pp.

[9] See Mace, *op. cit.*, Chapters VI and VII; Riegel, *op. cit.*, Chapter XII; Earl G. Planty and Freeston, *op. cit.;* William A. Vernon, "Coaching in Middle and Lower Management," *The Journal of the American Society of Training Directors,* Vol. 12, No. 5, May 1958, pp. 46-50; and "Executive Coaching Catches On," *Business Week,* No. 1436, March 9, 1957, pp. 61-72.

ing requires the superior manager to supervise less by direction and more by the guidance provided through asking questions and challenging the subordinate. Viewed in this sense, coaching is an everyday part of the superior's job, not a once-a-year task. Many companies relate coaching to the management appraisal and to the appraisal interview, requiring the appraising manager to outline plans for coaching at the time of appraisal and suggesting that this coaching be started at the time of the appraisal interview. Certainly the appraisal should be used as the basis for outlining the points to be developed through coaching and the specific steps to be taken. However, coaching should not be limited to the appraisal interview. Just as with delegation, coaching requires constant self-control and guidance. The coach should be easily available to subordinates, but should force them to analyze and develop their own solutions to problems; he should guide but refrain from directing.

Effective coaching is difficult. It can be very time-consuming and frustrating to the manager trying to achieve performance results. It has been suggested in a number of instances that the coaching be performed by a staff adviser on management development, someone skilled in counseling and guidance. It is felt generally, however, that such staff coaching is of much less value than less skilled coaching by the manager's immediate superior. The subordinate manager tends to be more receptive to the guidance of his superior, since it relates directly to his performance and his potential on the job. Also, the mere fact that his superior takes time to consult with and aid him in overcoming problems adds to his confidence and his willingness to continue work. Very little is known about effective techniques of coaching subordinates, although almost every organization can identify one or more managers who have been quite effective in guiding and stimulating the development of subordinates. Suggestions for improved coaching throughout the organization could be drawn from observation of the techniques used by these managers and from determination of their methods. Certainly, effective coaching should be rewarded wherever it occurs in the organization. The recognition of effective coaching and its accompanying reward would tend to emphasize its importance to the organization and remove some of the pressure for results of performance which tends to restrict the attention and time that managers give to coaching. Coaching, as delegation, is almost as much a frame of mind and an outlook as it is a technique of behavior. Managers should accept the concepts of coaching and recognize the desirability of coaching if the techniques used are to be of value. In fact, the effectiveness of techniques probably is related quite closely to the manner in which they are applied.

Counseling. Counseling for individual development often is confused with coaching and, in fact, is somewhat similar to coaching. Counseling for development is reported to be almost as common a technique as coaching, and probably is confused with coaching by many reporting companies. However, a distinction has been made between coaching and counseling, a distinction that is useful in consideration of the two forms of development, although of little value in actual practice.[10] The term "counseling" in our discussion refers to guidance provided the subordinate manager for improvement of his performance and for qualification for advancement. "Counseling" usually refers to behavior noted in job performance, as does coaching, but counseling is applied when the source of shortcomings lies outside the framework of the job. For example, where coaching might be provided in teaching a subordinate to be more thorough in his analysis of problems, counseling would be appropriate in attempting to bring about a change of attitudes or general outlook. Coaching is used primarily in the change and development of manager work skills and abilities, whereas counseling is used in the development of personal characteristics which influence job performance. This distinction between coaching and counseling is practical only in the sense that it focuses attention upon these two major areas of individual development—skills and characteristics. It also tends to point up the difference in approach necessary to bring about change in these two areas. The manager's superior is in the appropriate position to serve as coach, whereas trained counselors may perform most usefully in counseling for development.

The tendency toward development and application of performance standards to replace standards of personal characteristics for management appraisal illustrates the difference between coaching and counseling, particularly with respect to the requirements of the coach or counselor. The appraised manager's superior fre-

[10] For further discussion of the distinction between coaching and counseling, see Myles L. Mace, *op. cit.*, Chapter VI; and John W. Riegel, *op. cit.*, Chapter XII.

quently feels incapable of counseling and, in fact, may hinder development of the subordinate through improper counseling. On the other hand, coaching can be properly performed by no one other than the superior, regardless of the manager's skill as a coach. This difficulty has been noted already in an earlier chapter. However, the difficulties experienced in counseling by managers are not sufficient to warrant ignoring the development of personal characteristics of the individual manager. Instead, many companies today are turning to professional counselors to work with individual managers in the appraisal and development of personal characteristics. One approach utilizes a full-time counselor within the organization who is available to counsel and work with individual managers in improving their personal qualifications for performance and advancement. An alternative approach makes available the services of a consulting counselor who meets with individual managers to assist them in a self-appraisal of their abilities and shortcomings and to aid them in personal development.[11] Regardless of the individual who performs the counseling, both appraisal by the manager's superior and by the manager himself should form the basis for counseling and development. The counselor can only assist the manager and his superior; he cannot perform their responsibilities for appraisal.

Coaching and counseling, then, are two general techniques which are similar in many respects. The primary distinction lies in the fact that one concerns performance shortcomings related to a lack of skills, knowledge, and abilities, while the other concerns shortcomings stemming from more pervasive sources, such as the individual's outlook toward life. In actual practice, the distinction will be made only where the functions of counselor and coach are separated. Where the individual manager's superior is capable and comfortable functioning in both capacities, coaching and counseling will be merged into the same process.

Guided experience. Guided experience is the general term given to a host of approaches to individual development. It ranges from one extreme of informal consideration of the individual manager's potential and abilities in planning changes in assignment to another extreme of highly formalized job rotation, where the individual moves among jobs and departments on a very formal

[11] See Riegel, *op. cit.*, pp. 218-220, for a discussion of these approaches.

schedule. In general terms, all organizations guide the experience of individual managers in their development. The differences lie in the amount of consideration given the individual's development as compared with the immediate staffing needs of the organization and the degree of formality associated with this guided experience. Other terms given to specific types of guided experience include "planned progression," "flying squadrons," "job rotation," and "work experience." [12]

Programs of guided experience usually emphasize the importance of work experience in development and provide for specific types of experience in the development of the individual manager. Certain of these programs, however, merely provide for observation rather than work experience, although the general principles of the programs are similar. Programs of guided experience when combined with coaching are intended to develop certain knowledge and information as well as specific skills. These programs tend to be based upon the assumption that the competent manager should have a varied background, a background that should include specific experiences and knowledges. It is interesting to speculate upon the types of experience deemed important to managerial success in any endeavor; unfortunately, too many of these programs are based upon such speculations rather than upon careful study of the manager's job. The Armed Forces appear to have been particularly successful over the years in determining the desired experiences for development of their executive officers. Their career programs are specified in enough detail to provide real guidance to the assigning officers, yet general enough to provide flexibility to account for individual differences among officers and needs of the services. Few civilian organizations have worked out as careful programs for career development as have the services, and they might well profit from adaptation of the concept of career programming to fit their situations. Certainly, the general idea of career programming underlies many of the plans made for guiding the experiences of individual managers, although there may be no general guides available for all managers. Some organizations shy away from the

[12] See Mace, *op. cit.*, Chapter V; Earl G. Planty and Carlos Efferson, "The Guided Experience Method," in Dooher and Marquis, *op. cit.;* Dwight S. Sargent, "The Job Rotation Method," in Dooher and Marquis, *op. cit.;* and James Morris, *Job Rotation: A Study and Program, Occasional Papers in Management–Organization–Industrial Relations,* No. 11, September 1957 (Chicago: Industrial Relations Center, University of Chicago), 16 pp.

idea of career planning for individual managers, because such plans might become known to the individual, who would then be disillusioned if each step in the plan were not realized. Furthermore, there is a certain fear that, once such plans have been made for an individual manager, he will be subjected to less critical appraisal and scrutiny in the making of future assignments. In short, he may become a "fair-haired boy" or "jet job," as management trainees are known in some companies. In general, it would appear desirable to identify experiences useful in the development of managers for various jobs and levels of the management hierarchy, and to use these as a general guide in planning assignments of all managers. Such plans should be general enough to serve for guidance in making most managerial assignments and yet specific enough to provide valuable individual assistance. As general guides, they would not become identified with any individual manager or group of trainees. A necessary first task in the development of such plans will involve the study of managers' jobs and the comparison of careers of successful and unsuccessful managers. Critical experiences identified in this manner should be considered seriously in the structuring of such guides.

Somewhat more formal programs of guided experience are found in the various plans for job rotation.[13] Certain of these are intended primarily to familiarize the management trainee with various aspects of the organization and its work. Here the trainee is routed through a number of different departments and positions, primarily as an observer. He may be required to write his impressions of the activities observed or to carry out special investigations in connection with his observations, but the primary purpose is to insure observation and study of the organization, rather than to develop specific managerial skills. In short, this flying squadron or trainee-rotation type of guided experience is intended to familiarize the trainee with the organization and to teach him the general structure of activities conducted within the organization. A program for training new college graduates and selected employees for management in the Ford Motor Company of Canada provides an example of this approach to job rotation.[14] Job rotation is used in this program largely for orientation. Management trainees begin with a

---

[13] See Morris, *op. cit.*

[14] See "Training New College Graduates," *Management Record,* Vol. 16, No. 8, August, 1954, p. 296.

TO CO-MANAGER ASSIGNMENT

TRAINING PHASE	WEEKS		ON-THE-JOB DEVELOPMENT	YOUR REPORTS
CO-MANAGER	12	4	MANAGEMENT PERFORMANCE	
		8	CO-MANAGER TRAINING	
DIVISION OFFICE	8	4	PRODUCE MERCHANDISING DEPARTMENT	
		4	GROCERY MERCHANDISING DEPARTMENT	
FRONT-END	8	2	MANAGEMENT PERFORMANCE	DEPARTMENT OPERATION REPORT (At end of this step.)
		3	HEAD CHECKER DUTIES	ACTIVITY REPORT (Each 2 weeks)
		3	BASIC CHECKER DUTIES	
MEAT	8	4	HEAD MEAT CUTTER DUTIES	
		4	BASIC MEAT DUTIES	
PRODUCE	16	8	MANAGEMENT PERFORMANCE	DEPARTMENT OPERATION REPORT (At end of this step.)
		6	HEAD CLERK DUTIES	ACTIVITY REPORT (Each 2 weeks)
		2	BASIC DUTIES	
DAIRY	4	2	HEAD CLERK DUTIES	
		2	BASIC DUTIES	
GROCERY	18	8	MANAGEMENT PERFORMANCE	DEPARTMENT OPERATION REPORT (At end of this step.)
		6	HEAD CLERK DUTIES	ACTIVITY REPORT (Each 2 weeks)
		4	BASIC DUTIES	
ORIENTATION	4	2	TRAINING STORE	
		2	DIVISION OFFICE	

MANAGEMENT TRAINEE

Fig. 12. Job Rotation Schedule. From "Management Development Plan, Schedule B for Grocery and Produce Management Trainees," Kroger Company.

three-month tour of all operating divisions of the company, followed with three assignments of three months each within a single division. Trainees then are assigned to the division as regular managerial employees following this year of rotation and orientation. Management trainees at Consolidated Edison Company undergo a somewhat similar program of job rotation, although training assignments are considerably longer and attempt to develop skills as well as to provide an orientation to the management operations.[15] This is a five-year program consisting of five one-year assignments in various divisions of the company. Also notice the job-rotation schedule of the Kroger Company in Figure 12.

A somewhat different pattern of guided experience is found

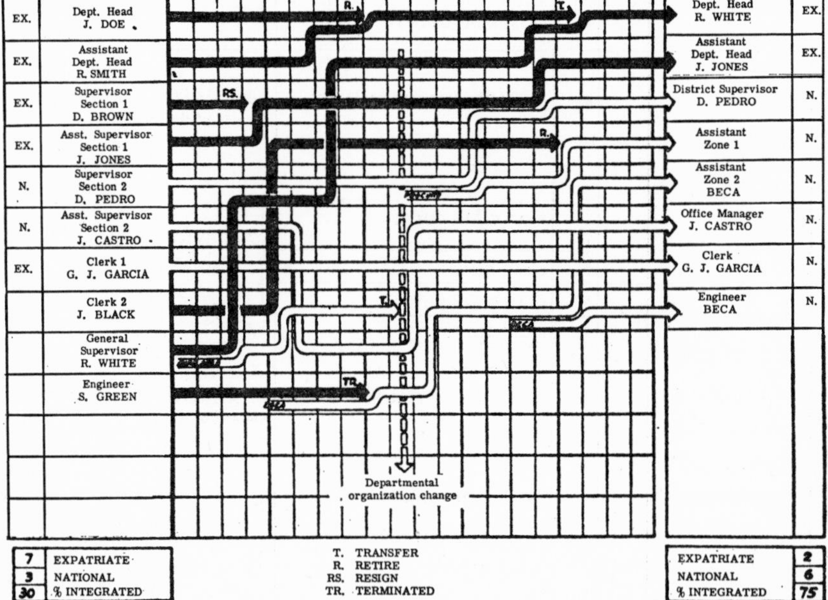

Fig. 13. Personnel Development Flow Sheet. From George B. Corless, "Programming for Executive Development," *Proceedings of the 1951 Annual Fall Conference of Society for the Advancement of Management, Inc.*

[15] See Dwight S. Sargent, "A Ten-Year Evaluation of a Job Rotation Program," in Dooher and Marquis (editors), *op. cit.*, pp. 263-270.

among organizations which provide for job rotation only as the manager advances in the organization. (See Figure 13.) Here the individual manager starts his career in a specialized type of work and advances within that specialty. Rotation of assignments to insure a rounded background of experience is provided the manager just prior to advancement to a position involving supervision of functions with which he has had little if any experience. For example, a manager in retailing might advance through the merchandising line or the store service line, and he would be given the opportunity to gain experience in the other of the two lines just prior to promotion to a position involving supervision of both functions. This type of guided experience is much more a work-experience than the induction type of rotation provided the management trainee; the intent is to broaden the manager's knowledge of the business of the organization through actual experience rather than to familiarize him with operations through observation. Tours of service typically are longer in this type of guided experience than in the trainee-rotation program.

Guided experience in one form or another is found in every organization where individual manager assignments are made with the intent of devoloping the individual manager as well as of meeting existing staffing needs of the organization. In its broadest sense, guided experience merely involves the selection of assignments with a view to developing managers for responsibilities beyond the immediate assignment. Little formal consideration is likely to be given to guided experience, however, unless there is a conscious effort made to plan the ideal background of position incumbents, and to adhere to this pattern of experiences in advancing and developing managers for these positions. The development and application of career programming within industry would appear to benefit both the organization and the individual manager. It should be noted that guided experience alone will contribute little to the individual manager's development, however; it must be coupled with appraisal, coaching, and delegation for most effective usage.

Understudy positions. Recognition of the importance of experience in learning and development has led in recent years to the creation of special positions for providing development opportunities through experience. These positions provide an opportunity for the manager to understudy a particular position or a particular manager from whom he should gain added insights and knowledge of management.[16] These positions generally attempt to provide experience without the exercise of authority, although certain variations do permit the exercise of limited authority under the supervision of a superior manager. Two types of understudy positions commonly are found: the line assistant or the "assistant," and the staff assistant, known as the "assistant to." The organizational considerations of such positions already have been discussed; here we shall be concerned only with their usage in the development of managers.

The line assistant bears a secondary responsibility for the same functions as his superior, serving as manager in the superior's absence and assisting the superior manager when he is present. The actual division of responsibilities will vary with the function and the abilities and interests of the two men. However, the superior manager may use his assistant as a leg man to aid him in some specialized functions or as the manager through which subordinates report. Functioning as an assistant, the individual manager has an opportunity to observe and learn the functions of his boss's position, an opportunity to observe the techniques employed by his superior in managing the unit, and an opportunity to exercise limited authority. Viewed as a position for manager development, the understudy position can be created and destroyed at will, providing opportunities for experience and observation when desirable for individual development and canceled when no longer necessary. It is true, however, that there is something artificial about positions created merely for development, and if not required from an organizational standpoint, they may not provide the desired experience.

Somewhat less artificial understudy experiences can be provided where the subordinate manager substitutes for a superior who is on vacation or absent from the job for other reasons. These experiences provide less direct coaching and counseling, since the superior manager is absent, but the experience and an appraisal of results by the superior can be quite beneficial in the development of the subordinate. One further advantage of such positions lies in the fact that they permit relatively inexpensive development—inexpensive in the sense that the incumbent manager receives experience at a lower salary than would be the case if he encountered the experiences of the position only when qualified for the superior man-

[16] See "Training Understudies," Chapter VII in Dooher and Marquis, *op. cit.*

ager's position. Various disadvantages of such positions from the organizational standpoint already have been noted in an earlier chapter. From a development standpoint, these understudy positions have been criticized as lacking in any real responsibility, with the lack of responsibility resulting in a lack of challenge for the incumbent. Be that as it may, such positions can provide limited experience for the developing manager and should be recognized for the opportunities they can provide. They may provide opportunities for development of less experienced managers, and they should be used for this value.

The staff assistant, or "assistant to," position is another form of understudy position providing slightly different opportunities for experience.[17] The incumbent of this position aids and serves the superior manager but does not share his responsibility or authority. The opportunity to learn the responsibilities of management is provided through the special study undertaken by the "assistant to" and by the possibility of observing the superior manager, but not through exercise of line responsibility. In general, the "assistant to" position would appear to be of most value to relatively inexperienced managers who would profit more from observation and study than from actual exercise of line responsibility. Again, the advantages and disadvantages of such positions from the organizational standpoint have been discussed earlier. From the development standpoint, these positions can provide definite opportunities for learning and development.

Special assignments. Any number of special assignments are available within every organization to provide individualized opportunities for development. Many of these will be assignments with a particular unit and under the control of the manager's superior; others will be organizational assignments which must be coordinated with those of other managers. Certain of these will involve responsibility for tasks necessary in the work of the organization; others can be designed largely for the development opportunities involved. In short, special assignments provide a very flexible approach in the prescription of experiences for the development of individual managers. Possible assignments are so varied that the assignment most

---

[17] See Louis Allen, "The Uses of Assistants," *Management Record,* Vol. 17, No. 5, May 1955, pp. 174-177, 201-205; and *Management Development at the Executive Level* (Washington, D. C.: National Security Agency, 1954), 71 pp.

useful to the individual can be identified or designed to fit a particular need.[18]

Special assignments may be used to provide the individual manager with opportunities for study and observation as well as for the exercise of authority. Examples of assignments might include the referral of problems for study and recommendation to the manager's superior, assignment to special temporary task forces or *ad hoc* committees, assignments where the manager works on special problems with customers or consultants, special tours or inspection assignments among units of the organization or among other organizations, assignment to standing committees, such as a salary administration committee, temporary replacement assignments in positions of line authority, and assignments to assist and observe a superior in specific functions. In short, almost every conceivable experience can be provided the manager in temporary, special assignments. Assignments may be selected to provide the opportunity for observation and study, for experience in the exercise of authority, and for experience in the coordination of activities and individuals; they may be selected to provide opportunities for the development of highly specialized skills and knowledges or of quite general knowledge and ability.

Special assignments may call for somewhat more coaching and guidance than other types of development opportunities, particularly where the assignment has been designed for the individual manager. The manager is bound to question the purpose of the assignment and may interpret it as an indication of failure unless he is aware of the real purpose. The manager who views these special assignments as sheer drudgery that must be performed by someone, or as an indication of personal failure, is unlikely to benefit much from the assignment. On the other hand, he will know what to expect and how to benefit most from these assignments if he is aware of their purposes. Because special assignments provide such a flexible approach to individual development, they are likely to be used rather frequently, and it is important to plan them for maximum benefit.

Multiple management. The technique of multiple management has received a great deal of attention as a method of providing management-development opportunities within McCormick and Com-

[18] See Riegel, *op. cit.*, Chapters XIII and XIV, for a discussion of special assignments for individual development.

pany. As applied in that company and in others which have followed their example, multiple management takes the form of "junior boards of directors."[19] The principles of multiple management need not be restricted in application to the junior-board approach, however. Carrier Corporation, Bridgeport Brass Company, and Lehn and Fink Products Corporation provide examples of specific adaptations of the multiple-management approach employing somewhat different organizational frameworks.[20] We consider multiple management here in its more general form, regardless of whether or not the junior-board approach is used.

Multiple management is an attempt to provide managers with opportunities to study, observe, and experience the responsibilities of more advanced levels of the management organization. In one sense, it is a variation upon the understudy technique. It is more than this, however, as it provides simultaneous opportunities for a group of managers to understudy a broader expanse of responsibilities than is found in a single position. The multiple-management technique provides opportunities for broadening the manager's knowledge of the work and functions of the organization at the same time that opportunities to understudy and experience more critical responsibilities are provided. The various programs for "junior boards of directors" illustrate this. Here a number of promising subordinate managers are appointed or elected to a board of directors which is junior to the directors of the organization. Members of the junior board function in much the same manner as the senior board. They are given reports of operations and conditions throughout the organization, as well as special problems for consideration and resolution. In this manner, members of the junior board become familiar with the nature of the operations of the entire organization. Working as members of specialized study committees of the junior board, they also experience the problems encountered in more responsible positions. It is true that the junior board does not exercise the same responsibility and authority as

---

[19] See Frederick J. Bell, "Highlights of Multiple Management," in Dooher and Marquis, *op. cit.*, Chapter XI; John R. Craf, *Junior Boards of Directors* (New York: Harper and Brothers, 1958), 146 pp.; Robert C. Hood, "Group Management—The Ansul Plan," in Dooher and Marquis, *op. cit.*, Chapter XIII; and J. S. Nichols, "An Adventure in Multiple Management," in Dooher and Marquis, *op. cit.*, Chapter 12.

[20] See Edward Plaut, "Home-Grown Executives," *Dun's Review and Modern Industry*, July, 1954, pp. 29, 42-45; and "Making Specialists into Managers," *The Management Review*, April 1955, pp. 212-213.

the senior board, but the junior board may serve as assistant to the senior board and thus feel that it bears a part of this responsibility.

The concepts and principles of multiple management applied in the technique of "junior boards" can also be applied at various levels of the organization. Thus, for example, subordinate managers may serve as assistants to committees of managers in more responsible positions or may participate directly in staff meetings with their superiors. Individual managers within a given unit of the organization can attempt to provide similar opportunities for development in staff meetings of subordinates where managerial problems which are beyond the scope of responsibilities of subordinates are brought to meetings. In short, the concepts of multiple management can be applied at every level of management. They involve a sharing of responsibilities by the superior manager with subordinates as a group. Multiple management is a form of delegation where the subordinate manager is challenged with the opportunity for study and resolution of managerial issues beyond his present responsibilities.

Assigned study and reading. The individual manager can be aided in his development through assigned study and reading programs. The manager's superior can recommend or assign subjects or references for study to fill a gap in the manager's knowledge. Articles and books can be found that are helpful in the study of almost every subject, making this a very flexible technique. It also is relatively inexpensive and can be used alone or as a supplement to other aids for individual development. Coaching and guidance in the suggestion of a reading program are quite important to its success. The individual manager should be aware of the purpose of his reading and of what he is seeking.

An increasing number of companies are maintaining libraries for the use of managers, as well as subscribing to journals and magazines for managerial readership. Books and magazines can be routed among managers to encourage their reading of them. While desirable as an encouragement to individual reading and study, the routing of materials for reading as an aid to management development should be carefully controlled and checked. It is not uncommon for route lists to become matters of prestige, with the result that individuals may receive more than they can read and profit from, merely because they wish to be included in any routing of materials. Judicious routing of such materials and the recommendation of selected reading to fit the needs of subordinates would be much more effective in their development.

Training courses. Both the number and type of special training courses for managers offered within company organizations have grown at a tremendous clip during the past 15 years.[21] One company listed, in a recent catalog of courses provided within the organization, some twenty-eight different courses.[22] The number of potential subjects of courses is legion, and the variations of teaching techniques seem to grow without limitation. It is not difficult to note several reasons for the rapid growth in these courses apart from the need for management development. For one thing, such courses demonstrate the organization's concern for management development in perhaps the most obvious form. As such, and as observed by the potential management recruit or other outside observer, these courses testify to the progressive nature of the organization's personnel policies. A second basic reason for the rapid development of courses lies in the seemingly apparent value of many courses. A company president who learned to make public speeches through experience can see an apparent value in speech courses, and rapid reading courses also possess an obvious value in view of the many memos and reports which must be read as a part of the manager's job today. And, finally, the establishment of company courses to which subordinates may be sent is much easier in many respects for the manager than is the coaching, delegation, and counseling necessary for development. Thus, courses have multiplied as obvious needs have appeared and as superior managers have taken advantage of these courses to prescribe for their subordinates' needs. In fact, the development of company courses for managers is harmful in so far as it lulls the management into thinking that the individual manager need concern himself only with the identification of his subordinates' needs and the prescription of courses for them. Management training courses have a definite place in the development of individual managers, but they cannot perform the entire task. Rather, they should be viewed as supplements to the coaching, guidance, and aid given the subordinate by his superior.

Management training courses provide obvious opportunities for individual development. The effectiveness of these opportunities varies with the particular teaching techniques employed and the ap-

---

[21] See the report of Trickett, *op. cit.*

[22] See the Training Catalog of Johnson and Johnson Company.

plication of the individual enrolled in the course. Merely enrolling individual managers in a course does not insure individual development. The individual should possess a need to which the course is directed, should understand the purpose and objective of the course, and should be motivated to take advantage of the opportunities for development offered by the course. Perhaps the most important of these considerations is that of individual need; it is difficult for a manager to take an interest in a course if he is aware of no need for development. Many manager-training courses fail to achieve their potential effectiveness because of a shortcoming in this respect. Training courses often are prescribed because the superior manager recognizes the value such a course would have had for him and orders it for his subordinates regardless of their individual backgrounds. Or enrollment in a particular course may become an element of prestige, and managers enroll because of this factor rather than because of some individual need. Training courses are most effective when directed to specific needs of groups of individuals. In this respect, company training courses for managers are most appropriate in large organizations where it is possible that a large group of individuals will possess similar needs. It is highly unlikely that a large proportion of managers in a small organization will possess similar needs which can be met with a training course.

All training courses, whether offered within the organization or outside it, encounter difficulties with the transfer of learning from the training situation to the work situation. This problem is illustrated in a recent study of supervisory training within the International Harvester Company.[23] Follow-up evaluations of this company training course found little relationship between performance within the training situation and later performance on the job. A number of possible reasons for the lack of transfer of learning in such situations have been offered—probably the most plausible being those that concern the relationship between the subordinate and his boss. It was found in the International Harvester experiment that, following the course, supervisors trained in principles of human relations reverted back to their earlier methods of supervision, methods which were patterned largely after the methods employed and expected by their

---

[23] See Edwin A. Fleishman, Edwin F. Harris, and Harold E. Burtt, *Leadership and Supervision in Industry* (Columbus, Ohio: The Ohio State University, 1955); also see James N. Mosel, "Why Training Programs Fail to Carry Over," *Personnel*, Vol. 34, No. 3, November-December 1957, pp. 56-64.

superiors. In short, a primary determinant of a manager's job behavior is the direction and guidance received from his superior. Training courses which attempt to change this behavior are not likely to succeed unless they are first offered to the superior managers and result in changed behavior at that level. Wherever possible, manager-training courses should be given to superior managers prior to training their subordinates. The superior managers should at least be familiar with the content of the course and approve of it before their subordinates are trained. It is true that this procedure will not insure the acceptance of changed behavior of subordinates on the job, but it should tend to reduce manager resistance to any changed behavior. The lessons drawn from experiences similar to those of International Harvester have led many to conclude that all change in an organization must begin at the top and work down. Certainly, management training courses will effect little changed behavior unless these changes are endorsed and practiced by superior managers. This endorsement and acceptance of changed behavior will not insure transfer of learning from the training situation, but it will tend to reduce one of the major barriers to transfer.

Other practical considerations which arise in the organization of management training courses concern the location of facilities, the release of students from work responsibilities, and the selection and training of instructors. There do not appear to be any generally valid guides for decisions on these points; there has been insufficient study of the effects of differences upon the outcomes of the training. Furthermore, it would appear that answers probably vary considerably, depending upon the particular situation and the nature of the course. For example, a hotel location might be quite appropriate for a week-long conference concerning the functions of management and inappropriate for a 17-hour course in efficient reading. One general guide concerns the selection and training of instructors. Wherever possible, it is desirable to select instructors from among the company management. Such instructors may not possess the initial prestige of outside "experts," but they will be more familiar with the backgrounds of students and should be able to relate the training more directly to the work situations of the students. A major benefit of selecting managers as instructors also concerns the development of those chosen for instructors; the training received as instructor serves to develop the abilities and potential of the instructor far more than participation in the course as a student would. Several companies following this guide have developed extensive training programs staffed largely with personnel from within the organization. Formal schools or institutes for management personnel are maintained by General Electric, Allis Chalmers, Goodyear Tire and Rubber, General Motors, Ford Motor Company, and other such organizations.[24] The vast system of courses and institutes offered through the American Telephone and Telegraph Company is staffed largely by company personnel. The use of company personnel as instructors is not limited to large organizations, however. The Northwestern National Life Insurance Company staffs its management training courses almost entirely with management personnel to the benefit of the entire management organization. The development opportunities provided instructors of management training courses are considerable and should not be overlooked in the organization of such courses.

There appears to be no limit to the possible subjects of management training courses. The Johnson and Johnson training catalog mentioned earlier refers to courses in public speaking, fundamentals of management, effective interviewing, and business economics. This is not to imply that every conceivable subject can or should be taught in a special training course. Rather, training courses should be considered supplements to the work experience and daily coaching of superiors, and the subject matter of courses should be limited to this role.

There are a number of alternative training approaches and techniques, each with its advocates and critics.[25] There is no need to view these approaches as competing, since each can be employed where most appropriate. Each has advantages and disadvantages which should be taken into account in the selection of the approach most appropriate for a particular course. Guides for the selection of approaches are limited by the lack of research in the evaluation of these approaches. The guides suggested here are based upon general observations and should be tested with specific evaluations of their effectiveness.

(1) *Lecture.* The lecture is one of the oldest methods of teaching and, in many respects, the easiest for the instructor. The lecture

---

[24] See discussion of these programs in Dale Yoder *et al.*, *Handbook of Personnel Management and Labor Relations* (New York: McGraw-Hill Book Company, 1958), pp. 10.28-10.29.

[25] See Planty and Freeston, *op. cit.*, for general discussions of advantages and disadvantages of each of these approaches.

is best employed in the communication of information and known principles. It is frequently criticized as a technique for the education and development of adults, since it need involve little practice and thinking on the part of the students. Rather, it is an attempt on the part of the instructor to present the ideas and conclusions reached by more advanced students of the subject. The lecture alone is relatively inappropriate in the teaching of skills, and for this reason usually is combined with one or another approach when used for this purpose.[26]

(2) *Case study.* The case-study approach directs the attention of students to specific cases rather than to general principles, and attempts to encourage the development of general principles from these cases. At the same time, the case-study approach emphasizes that each specific case is different and that general principles cannot be applied without regard for the differences among specific cases. This approach has been criticized as an inefficient "bootstrap" method of training, since it forces all students to undergo the identical process of development of principles, a process which might be shortcut with lectures outlining these principles.[27] This criticism merely suggests that the case method is more appropriate for certain subjects than others, as is the case with all training approaches. We would hardly consider the case approach for teaching the multiplication tables, but it can be quite appropriate for teaching guides to effective human relations, where there is no single principle to be taught and it is the application of general principles to highly different situations that is important. The case approach also is used frequently in the training of skills of analysis, where the emphasis is placed upon methods of case analysis rather than upon solutions.[28]

(3) *Conference and discussion.* The conference-and-discussion approach to training is intended to overcome certain of the criticisms of the lecture. Students are involved more directly in the learning process and participate in the development and application of principles. The conference-and-discussion approach can be quite chal-

---

[26] Willard E. Bennett, "The Lecture as a Management Training Technique," *Personnel*, Vol. 32, No. 6, May 1956, pp. 497-507.

[27] Alvin Brown, "The Case (Or Bootstrap) Method," *Advanced Management*, Vol. 21, No. 7, July 1956, pp. 11-12.

[28] See Wilbur M. McFeely and William F. Mussmann, "The Case Method," in Dooher and Marquis, *op. cit.*, Chapter XV; Planty and Freeston, *op. cit.*, Chapter 10; and Joseph W. Towle and Carl A. Dauten, "Living Cases for Management Education," *Advanced Management*, Vol. 22, No. 5, May 1957, pp. 24-26.

lenging for participants, forcing them to think through and justify their concepts concerning the subject. As with the case method, however, it can be relatively inefficient for teaching relatively formalized subjects, and probably it is best used in the development of skills and in the practice application of principles.[29]

(4) *Incident process.* The incident process is a variation upon the case approach where the main concern lies with the method of analysis and solution of cases. An incomplete case is presented to students and they are required to determine what additional information would be relevant to solution of the case. The approach probably is most appropriate in training skills of analysis rather than principles of management.[30]

(5) *Role-playing.* Role-playing is intended to bring about an awareness of interpersonal relationships and the factors bearing upon these relationships. It is intended primarily as a technique for training in human relations and is relatively inappropriate for other subjects. In one sense, it is another variation upon the case study as applied to problems of human relations. Students are assigned roles of participants in the case and are asked to perform these roles. It is hoped that this participation will develop a greater awareness of factors in human relations and skill in the handling of such relationships.[31]

(6) *Business games.* The business games approach to management training represents an attempt to apply the concepts of vestibule training to management.[32] An artificial business enterprise is created and a set of hypothetical relationships among operational variables is programmed for a computer. Managers playing the game take the role of company executives responsible for various decisions. Their decisions concerning operations problems of the enter-

---

[29] See Louis A. Allen, "The Problem Solving Conference," in Dooher and Marquis, *op. cit.*, Chapter XIV; Howard P. Mold, "Management Builds Itself," in Dooher and Marquis, *op. cit.*, Chapter XVII; and Planty and Freeston, *op. cit.*, Chapter 6.

[30] "New Teaching Trick for Business," *Business Week*, May 14, 1955, pp. 76-78; and Paul and Faith Pigors, *Director's Manual: The Incident Process; Case Studies in Management Development* (Washington, D. C.: Bureau of National Affairs, 1955), looseleaf.

[31] See Leland P. Bradford and Ronald Lippitt, "Role-Playing in Management Training," in Dooher and Marquis, *op. cit.*, Chapter XX; and Norman R. F. Maier, *Supervisory and Executive Development: A Manual for Role Playing* (New York: John Wiley and Sons, 1957), 330 pp.

[32] G. R. Andlinger, "Business Games—Play One!" *Harvard Business Review*, Vol. 36, No. 2, March-April 1958, pp. 115-125.

prise are relayed to the computer, and the results of this decision upon the business are then determined. Managers practice decision-making as they play the game and evaluate their decisions on the basis of the results obtained. Students are provided with a larger variety and number of decision-making opportunities in this manner than would be provided in an equal amount of time at work. The business-game situation is somewhat unreal, however; and, although popular, the efficiency of transfer of learning from the game situation to the work situation has not been determined.

(7) *Group dynamics.* Several relatively similar approaches to training are included under the general label of "group dynamics."[33] In general, these approaches are employed in the training of managers in problems of human relations. Relatively unstructured group meetings or discussions are conducted with the objective of developing an awareness of factors affecting interpersonal relationships on the part of students. These approaches are similar to the case approach in the sense that participants are expected to analyze and develop their own conclusions; they differ from the case approach in the sense that group attention is directed toward relationships of group members rather than toward some case arising outside the group. The limitations of this approach for teaching formal, structured subjects are obvious.

The training approaches listed here by no means include all approaches in use. Rather, this listing is intended to point up certain of the major variations among training approaches. Each of these approaches has been developed for specific training purposes and is most appropriate in those situations. They should be viewed as supplementary approaches, each useful for specific purposes and not as mutually exclusive approaches.

Opportunities Outside the Organization

A number of varied opportunities for individual development exist outside the organization and can be utilized in an over-all program

---

[33] See Verne J. Kallejian, Irving R. Weschler, and Robert Tannenbaum, "Managers in Transition," *Harvard Business Review*, Vol. 33, No. 4, July-August 1955, pp. 55-64; Robert Tannenbaum, Verne Kallejian, and Irving R. Weschler, "Training Managers for Leadership," *Personnel*, Vol. 30, No. 4, January 1954, pp. 254-260; and Leland P. Bradford, "A Look at Management Growth and Development," *Journal of the American Society of Training Directors*, Vol. 12, No. 7, July 1958, pp. 3-10.

of management development. These opportunities tend to supplement those available within the organization and extend the range of experiences available for development. Experiences outside the organization cannot serve as adequate substitutes for the work experience and coaching available within the organization, although they may serve as substitutes for certain specific development experiences which may not be available within the organization. For example, these alternative opportunities may be useful for the smaller organization, where there are relatively few managers with the same needs for development. They will usually supplement the opportunities within the organization and provide specific opportunities not available within the organization.

Experiences outside the organization can be particularly useful in broadening the outlook of the individual manager and in providing a stimulation for development which cannot be found in the organization. The individual manager participating in these experiences encounters other managers with outlooks, problems, and philosophies which differ from his own. He is encouraged to question his previous ideas and concepts, and to develop a broader outlook on his job and responsibilities. The same characteristics of these outside opportunities which provide advantages for development also raise certain problems. Outside experiences, for example, increase the problems of transfer of learning because of their enlarged orientation and lack of close connection with the individual manager's job. They also may present problems of adjustment to the individual and the organization as the individual manager moves from the relatively restricted area of job concern to a broader area of concern and then back to the job and organizational framework. The individual faces problems of adjustment here, and, if maximum utilization of the individual's experiences is to be made, the organization faces similar problems of adjustment to the development of the manager. Opportunities for development outside the organization are almost as varied as those within the organization, and specific experiences can be selected to meet individual needs with a minimum of expense and adjustment for the individual and the organization.

University programs. College and university programs for management development have grown at a rapid rate during the past 15 years. The available learning experiences range from short institutes and single courses offered for part-time students to full-time programs of study lasting for several months.[34] They cover a range of subjects extensive enough to meet most individual needs. These university programs foster an attitude conducive to learning, since they remove the manager from his pressures of work and surround him with the academic setting; the full-time program obviously is more extreme in this regard than the part-time program, where the individual attends courses in addition to performing his work responsibilities. University programs also assemble students from varying backgrounds, organizations, and types of work, providing a greater diversity of individual and organizational approaches than can be found in company programs for development. A number of students and instructors of these university programs attribute much of the learning which occurs to the exchange of ideas and experiences among the students of the program.

More consideration and attention on the part of the organization is required for full-time university training of managers than is required for part-time training. In fact, the usual approach to part-time training involves encouragement and occasional guidance in the selection of programs but very little direction and nomination of individuals for training. Organizations commonly publicize part-time university offerings and provide for some sort of tuition refund or payment to encourage individual development. The decision to apply for these offerings usually is made by the individual manager, although his superior may guide him in this decision. Full-time programs of study are somewhat more complicated from the standpoint of the organization, however, and require more attention and consideration. For one thing, these programs typically are much more expensive, since the individual usually is continued on the payroll although absent from work. Largely because of these costs and the problems of adjusting to the individual's absence from work, extreme care should be exercised to insure that the potential benefits warrant the expense. Furthermore, the problems of adjustment already referred to can be particularly acute and should be considered carefully in the selection of individuals for such training. Individual managers chosen for participation in these programs should be prepared for their experiences with an explanation of the reasons for their selection, some indication of the plans for their assignment

[34] See "Executive Development Courses in Universities," *Studies in Personnel Policy, No. 160* (New York: National Industrial Conference Board, 1957), for a review of the various university programs.

upon completion of the training, and an explanation of what they can expect in the training. Such preparation should serve to eliminate many of the managers' doubts about their progress within the organization and to prepare them mentally to take full advantage of the opportunity for development. Careful plans should be made for the integration of the individual into the organization following his absence to prevent the development of a "crown prince" reaction and to provide the opportunity for application of the individual's learning.

There are a number of unanswered questions relevant to the utilization of full-time university programs for management development. One of these concerns the subject of training. Certain of these programs concern topics directly relevant to the responsibilities of management, while others concentrate upon the humanities and liberal arts without any direct reference to the managing of an enterprise. Both types of program are intended to stimulate the manager to examine and consider beliefs and behavior outside his scope of experience—the humanities approach ranging far outside the traditional interests and concerns of management. The relative effectiveness of these alternative approaches is a matter of opinion at present. Some organizations, such as the Bell Telephone system, are experimenting with both approaches, and evaluation of their experiences should provide guides for comparison of the approaches in the near future.[35]

Another question concerns the timing of university training in relation to other factors in the individual's career. For example, would individual managers profit most from such training early in their careers or when promoted to top management? This question is not so relevant when part-time training is being considered, since the individual manager can participate in these opportunities at all stages of his career, and specific experiences can be obtained as specific needs appear. However, most full-time university programs for management development prescribe certain broad experience and responsibility requirements for participation. The most common approach provides for such opportunities midway in the individual's

[35] See Melvin Anshen, "Executive Development: In-Company versus University Programs," *Harvard Business Review*, Vol. 32, No. 5, September-October 1954, pp. 83-91; and Morris S. Viteles, " 'Human Relations' and the 'Humanities' in the Education of Business Leaders: Evaluation of a Program of Humanistic Studies for Executives," *Personnel Psychology*, Vol. 12, No. 1, Spring, 1959, pp. 1-28.

career. It is felt that he will benefit most from the opportunity to examine new and different approaches to management only after he has had considerable experience in managing and as he is preparing for more advanced responsibilities where a broader outlook is required. Again, however, this practice is based largely upon opinion. Somewhat more valid guides could be obtained through study of the careers of individual managers and the results of training at different career stages. Experience in the sponsorship of management development is such that comparisons of results could be made at this time. Research similar to that suggested in the development of programs of guided experience could contribute to the identification of guides to university training.[36]

University programs for management development vary considerably in terms of cost, length, subject matter, method of teaching, and qualifications for eligibility. Several catalogs of programs are published periodically to assist the comparison of these programs in the selection of opportunities for management development.[37] There has been relatively little evaluation of these programs or the effects of their differences. The few attempts at evaluation which have been made are based largely upon subjective opinions rather than measured experiences. The number of organizations and managers which have had experience with these programs is large enough to provide a wealth of experience for evaluation, however. Selection of programs for individuals within the organization should be based upon the available evaluations as well as upon consideration of the characteristics of the programs. Most important in this consideration is recognition of the specific need of the manager concerned. University programs should be considered when an individual has a particular need which cannot be met within the organization. Any decision to participate in university training followed by the selection of individual managers to participate ignores this primary consideration. Opportunities outside the organization as well as within the organization should be selected to fit the individual's needs, rather than the reverse.

---

[36] For discussion of several of these problems, see Allison V. MacCullough, "Critical Views of Advanced Management Courses," *Advanced Management*, January 1957; and "University Courses for Executives," *Management Record*, Vol. 29, No. 5, May 1957, pp. 169-171.

[37] See *Guide to Intensive Courses and Seminars for Executives* (New York: American Management Association, 1958), 60 pp.; and National Industrial Conference Board, *Studies in Personnel Policy*, No. 160.

Associations. One of the major functions of professional and industrial associations is the stimulation of development and the provision of opportunities for development of individuals. By their nature, these associations attempt to stimulate interest in a particular profession or industry. Certain of them, such as the American Management Association and the Society for Advancement of Management, embrace all specialties of management and all industries; while others, such as the Controller's Institute and the American Banking Association, are concerned with specific functions of management and/or specific industries.

Opportunities for development provided by professional and industrial associations range from the exchange of ideas at membership meetings and through publications to courses, conferences, and educational degree programs. Most of the development opportunities offered by these associations are relatively more work-oriented and supplementary to work experience than are university-training opportunities. Membership meetings, professional literature, and periodic conferences tend to concern subjects with obvious relationship to the individual's work and professional development, and they do not require lengthy absence from the organization. Membership and participation in the activities of these associations provide readily available supplements to the individual's experiences within the organization.

The relative value of membership and participation in professional and industrial associations is difficult to determine. The benefit usually is assumed to be greater than the relatively moderate cost of membership. However, memberships should be scrutinized as carefully as are other development opportunities to insure the selection of opportunities required for individual needs. Certain associations, for example, emphasize specific functions of management and are of most value in the early stages of an individual's career. Other associations which bring together different functions of management would tend to be more valuable in later stages, where a broadening of outlook and approach is desired. Increased benefits of association memberships probably could be obtained through closer examination of the objectives and activities of associations and the needs of the individual manager. All in all, participation in professional and industrial associations can provide very useful and flexible supplements to other experiences in management development if they are carefully chosen and integrated with the over-all program for the individual.

Other opportunities. A number of other opportunities for development can be found in any community. Examples of such opportunities are provided through participation in the Junior Chamber of Commerce, Toastmasters, Great Books discussions, Junior Achievement activities, and civic groups such as the Parent Teachers Association and civic improvement associations. All of these organizations provide opportunities for experiencing leadership responsibilities, and many of them relate to specific skills such as public speaking and discussion leadership. By and large, the opportunities provided through these organizations are available to individuals without any participation of the company. These opportunities truly are opportunities for self-development. This should not imply, however, that participation in these opportunities be left entirely to the individual. Rather, he should be encouraged and guided in his participation by his superior. Superior managers should take advantage of these opportunities for development of their subordinates just as they encourage participation in other opportunities for self-development.

In summary, opportunities outside the organization are numerous and varied. They range from formal university attendance to participation in social and civic organizations. In many instances, these opportunities resemble and even overlap opportunities available within the organization; in other cases, they provide quite dissimilar opportunities. In most instances, these opportunities encourage and provide for broadening the outlook and experience of the individual merely because they exist apart from the organization and bring together individuals of varied backgrounds and experiences. These opportunities should be examined in exactly the same manner as are experiences within the organization in the guidance of individual development; any suggestion for participation in these outside experiences should proceed from an analysis of the individual manager's needs.

FOLLOW-UP AND EVALUATION

The efficient utilization of opportunities for individual development requires careful follow-up and evaluation of the results of development experiences. This follow-up and evaluation serves as a control of individual activities for development, as a guide for improvement of these opportunities, and as an incentive for efficient utilization of them.

Any evaluation of the efficiency of alternative opportunities for individual development involves some measurement of the achievement of objectives. This evaluation is made difficult by the failure to specify clear and distinct objectives for each development opportunity, by the fact that the objectives frequently concern performance in the distant future, and by problems in the design and application of measures. Some attempts are being made to evaluate the results of specific development experiences. Many of these, however, can be improved considerably with more careful consideration and design of experiments for evaluation.

One approach to evaluation and follow-up of individual-development activities already has been discussed in our consideration of the management appraisal. This approach involves the follow-up and evaluation of individual progress in development. We have already discussed the individual manager's responsibility for development of his subordinates and the desirability of outlining a plan for development as the last step in the management appraisal. This program for action should be quite specific in outlining the steps to be taken in meeting the needs for development identified in the appraisal; each statement of need should be accompanid by a specific proposal for action to overcome this need. Each succeeding appraisal should evaluate specifically the progress of the individual manager in achieving the goals outlined in his previous appraisal. Thus, action taken for individual development can be controlled, an incentive is provided for the manager to utilize this action, and results of such action can be taken into account in the prescription of following programs for the manager's development. Furthermore, the accumulation of such evaluations among the entire management team will facilitate the over-all evaluation of commonly prescribed development action and the identification of situations in which each type of action is most fruitful. In the same manner, each superior manager should be held responsible for the development of individual managers under his direction and appraised on the basis of the progress of these subordinates. This appraisal serves as a control and an incentive for action on his part in the same manner as the appraisal of individual progress.

A second approach to evaluation focuses attention directly upon the particular development opportunity or activity rather than upon individual progress. Here, for example, the results of a particular development experience, such as a training course, are measured directly in terms of development of those experiencing the course, rather than as a side-effect of measures of progress of the individuals which occurs in the appraisal. This second approach provides results most readily usable in the comparison and evaluation of alternative activities for development. Both approaches are useful, however. The first serves as a control and incentive for individual development; the second, as a comparative evaluation of training and development techniques.

Criteria for the evaluation of any developmental activity should be based upon the specific objectives of that activity and should measure their achievement as precisely as possible. The difficulties encountered in the design of useful criteria from development objectives probably cause the most trouble in evaluation. The ultimate objectives of development concern the improved performance of the entire organization. Criteria of long-run organizational performance are rather impractical in the evaluation of specific training and development activities, however; training results may not be reflected in organizational performance until five years or more after the training, and it is virtually impossible to isolate the results of training from results of many other changes which have occurred during this period. As a result, many managements accept the conclusion that evaluation is impossible. Others accept more immediate criteria of effectiveness—criteria which they believe relate to the ultimate objective of long-run performance. Four general types of more immediate criteria usually are employed. Ranged in order of immediate relationship to the specific development or training, they are attitudes and opinions changed by the training, knowledge gained, performance of the manager, and performance of the manager's subordinates.[38] Changes in these four types of criteria are accepted as less conclusive but more readily available measures of the effects of training. The gap between changes in attitudes and organizational

[38] See Daniel M. Goodacre, "Experimental Evaluation of Training," *Journal of Personnel Administration and Industrial Relations,* Vol. 2, 1955, pp. 143-149; D. L. Kirkpatrick, "How to Start an Objective Evaluation of Your Training Program," *Journal of American Society of Training Directors,* May-June 1956, pp. 18-22; and A. C. MacKinney, "Progressive Levels in the Evaluation of Training Programs," *Personnel,* Vol. 34, No. 3, November-December 1957, pp. 72-77.

performance is recognized, and the attitude measure is accepted only as a substitute criterion for evaluation. The specific attitudes, knowledges, and performances which the training is designed to promote shape the various criteria employed in the evaluation.

Measures of the criteria of effectiveness range from subjective estimates of the criteria to highly objective measures. Examples of attitude scales, knowledge tests, and objective performance measures can be found in reported training evaluations, but the collection of subjective opinions is far more common. In general, the use of objective measures can be expected to grow as more attention and emphasis are given to evaluation, although certain students have argued that the subjective opinions and attitudes form a far more meaningful evaluation.[39]

Development of objective criteria for measurement of trainee attitudes, knowledge, and performance is not sufficient to insure conclusive evaluations. The design of the evaluation study largely determines the conclusions which can be drawn from the measures obtained. For example, three general designs are noted in reported studies of evaluation. The first and simplest involves the collection of measures of trainees following the development experience.[40] These measures may indicate the level of knowledge or performance found after the experience, but they tell nothing of the change which occurred with the experience. It is entirely possible that measures obtained prior to the training experience might have been higher. A second approach involves the collection of measures preceding and following the training.[41] Comparison of these measures indicates the

[39] See Kenneth R. Andrews, "Is Management Training Effective?" *Harvard Business Review,* Vol. 35, No. 1, January-February 1957, pp. 85-94; and Vol. 35, No. 2, March-April 1957, pp. 63-72.

[40] See Paul C. Buchanan, "Evaluating the Results of Supervisory Training," *Personnel,* Vol. 33, No. 4, January 1957, pp. 362-370; Morris A. Savitt, "Is Management Training Worthwhile?" *Personnel,* September-October 1957, pp. 79-82; and David S. Vogels, Jr., "An Evaluation of a Management Training Course," *Journal of American Society of Training Directors,* Vol. 12, No. 1, January 1958, pp. 44-51, for examples.

[41] See Richard P. Barthol and Martin Zeigler, "Evaluation of a Supervisory Training Program," *Journal of Applied Psychology,* Vol. 40, No. 6, 1956, pp. 403-405; Paul C. Buchanan, "Factors Making for Effective Supervisory Training," *Personnel,* Vol. 34, No. 5, March-April 1958, pp. 46-53; Edwin A. Fleishman, Edwin F. Harris, and Harold E. Burtt, *Leadership and Supervision in Industry: An Evaluation of a Supervisor Training Program* (Columbus, Ohio: Ohio State University, Bureau of Educational Research, 1955), 110 pp.; Theodore Lindbom, *Supervisory Training and Employee Attitudes* (unpublished Ph.D. dissertation), University of Minnesota; and Niles Soik, "Evaluation of a Human Relations Training Program," *Journal of American Society of Training Directors,* Vol. 12, No. 3, March 1958, pp. 34-39, for examples.

amount and direction of change associated with the training. We cannot attribute all of this change to the particular training or development activity, however. Trainees were affected by many coincident experiences which may have influenced the change in knowledge or performance. The third approach is that of the controlled experiment.[42] Here measures are obtained preceding and following the experience, and similar measures are obtained from a control group similar to the experimental group in every way except that they are exempted from the training experience. Comparisons of the change occurring in the control and experimental groups of managers indicate the particular changes associated with the training experience. Examples of the controlled experiment are rare, in part because of the mechanical difficulties involved and partly because of a reluctance to exempt managers from a training experience thought desirable. The controlled experiment provides the most conclusive evaluations, however, and is reported more and more frequently.

Follow-up and evaluation of individual development is essential and critical to the effectiveness of development activities. The demand for evaluation is growing and can be expected to grow in the future. Realization of the importance of objective measures and controlled experiments also is growing, and managements can be expected to become more demanding of improved evaluations. Present attempts at individual development must be recognized as experimental in nature, with a need for careful evaluation, if we are to progress in the experiment.

SELECTED BIBLIOGRAPHY

Dooher, M. Joseph, and Vivienne Marquis (editors), *The Development of Executive Talent* (New York: American Management Association, 1952).

---

[42] See Brent Baxter, Andrew A. Taaffe, and Joseph F. Hughes, "A Training Evaluation Study," *Personnel Psychology,* Vol. 6, No. 4, 1953, pp. 403-417; R. R. Cantor, Jr., "A Human Relations Training Program," *Journal of Applied Psychology,* Vol. 35, No. 1, 1951, pp. 38-45; Daniel M. Goodacre, "The Experimental Evaluation of Management Training," *Personnel,* Vol. 33, No. 6, May 1957, pp. 534-538; William McGeehee and J. E. Gardner, "Supervisory Training and Attitude Change," *Personnel Psychology,* Winter 1955, pp. 449-460; and James N. Mosel and Harry J. Tsacnaris, "Evaluating the Supervisor Training Program," *Journal of Personnel Administration and Industrial Relations,* Vol. 1, No. 2, 1954, pp. 99-104.

Mace, Myles L., *The Growth and Development of Executives* (Boston: The Graduate School of Business Administration, Harvard University, 1950).

Planty, Earl G., and J. Thomas Freeston, *Developing Management Ability* (New York: Ronald Press, 1954).

Riegel, John W., *Executive Development* (Ann Arbor, Michigan: University of Michigan Press, 1952).

Chapter TEN

Management Development Research and Evaluation

MANAGEMENT DEVELOPMENT RESEARCH

Management development exists as a problem area and not as a fully developed field of knowledge. The major problem of individual and team development for improved performance encompasses a host of smaller, more specific problems. Our knowledge of management development will grow only through the solution of these problems and the questions which they raise. This knowledge is obtained through careful research and study, and not through debate and the clash of opinions. There are numerous opinions concerning the solution of the problems of management development, but we know relatively little about the worth and validity of these opinions. For example, the basic questions, "What is an executive?" and "What constitutes effective executive action?", are as yet unanswered. It is unlikely that we shall progress far in the solution of problems of management development without answers to these and other similar questions.

The problems of management development exist as real issues and are not likely to disappear with time. Answers and solutions to these problems are being sought from virtually everyone with an opinion on the subject. And suggested solutions are being applied in response to demands for action. This interest and willingness to experiment in the solution of problems of management development is likely to disappear unless it can be demonstrated that conclusive answers and solutions are being obtained. The greatest challenge to management development lies in our ability to utilize this spirit of experimentation for the conducting of the research and study necessary to obtain conclusive answers to the basic questions of management development. Progress in the development of managers will be determined ultimately by our progress in management-development research and evaluation.

The term *research* is frequently misunderstood and applied only to the activities of engineers and scientists. Correctly understood, "research" means careful, critical search and inquiry and is appropriately applied to any problem-solving situation. The research approach is particularly appropriate in management development where there exist many unanswered questions, questions of enough significance to warrant the most rigorous and critical evaluation of answers. The evaluation of management-development activities covers one important aspect of needed management-development research. Answers to other somewhat more basic questions concerning the development of managers are required as well, however, in the design of improved activities for management development.

A need for basic research in management development concerns questions about the nature of the manager's job and responsibilities. The question, "What constitutes effective executive action?" was mentioned above. At present, we are even unsure of the number of possible correct answers to this question. We need to know more about the structuring of the manager's job and how it varies with differences in organizations, subordinates, and incumbents. We should know what, if any, elements of manager performance are common to most management positions, and the patterns and determinants of variation in these elements of performance. And we need to know more about the stability of management job responsibilities and how they are likely to change in the future. Answers to these questions are necessary for a better understanding of the objectives in management development.

Another area for basic research in management development concerns the development and change of manager performance. We should know something about the factors which influence manager performance and the relative contribution of each. Which, for example, exercises a greater influence over manager performance, ability or motivation? It is likely that the relative influence of ability and motivation upon performance will vary considerably among individuals; we should know something about the situations and individuals in which either is likely to be important. We also need to know more about the conditions conducive to change and development of these determinants of manager performance.

A third large area for research concerns the motivation of management personnel. We employ a number of practices intended to provide motivation for development and for performance, and yet we know relatively little about the basic motivations of managers. We vary compensation, status symbols, and opportunities for advancement and recognition to provide motivation on the assumption that they are desired by managers. These reward systems usually are standardized also on the assumption that the majority of managers will react in a common fashion to them. We should know more about the basic motivations of managers, the elements common to most managers and situations, and the patterns of variation in these motivations. Our progress in development of effective programs for motivation could be advanced faster on the basis of such knowledge than in a haphazard trial-and-error approach.

Only a few of the major areas for management development research have been mentioned here. Numerous other problems and questions calling for research have been suggested in previous chapters. Almost every question raised in the design and application of activities for management development is a proper subject for research; few of these questions have been answered conclusively for all situations.

The needs for management-development research are too numerous and too pressing to be left to the universities and other research organizations. Every practitioner of management development should recognize a personal responsibility for research and evaluation as his contribution to the growth and improvement of knowledge within this field. The opportunity for research exists within almost every organization; the ability to perform this research will vary, however, with the size of the organization and the degree of recognition granted to research. As a minimum, those responsible for management development can and should follow published reports of research and reports presented in professional conferences. In this manner, one can keep abreast of research findings in other situations which might be applicable. The organization which is unable to perform its own research also can participate in cooperative projects with other firms through the facilities of university research centers and employers' associations which sponsor research projects. Or, the services of staff members of these research centers and associations may be secured for guidance and assistance in special studies within individual organizations. The possibilities for research, particularly in smaller organizations, frequently are greater than they appear to be. The problem is one of recognizing and defining projects with a scope restricted to a manageable size.[1] Many of the studies referred to in this chapter illustrate the opportunities for management-development research within individual organizations. Results of each of these small studies are a definite contribution, and real progress can be achieved through the addition of the results of numerous such studies.

A coordinate research responsibility concerns the publication and communication of research results. Results of research and evaluation studies must be shared in the development of our knowledge of management development. The literature of management development abounds with descriptions of activities and programs but contains little concerning their evaluation. Many of these activities and programs have been discarded as unprofitable or unworkable, yet this information is rarely published.[2] It is important that unfavorable evaluations be published and communicated as a guide to others in the field. Reports of these unfavorable evaluations are at least as important as reports of successful activities in the improvement of management development.

The era of the huckster and the charlatan in management development is coming to a close with the growing awareness of the nature of management-development problems and the principles of research and evaluation. Patent remedies and solutions to management-development problems have enjoyed a heyday during the last ten years of interest and concern over management development. The success of management development in the future will

---

[1] For guides to management-development research, see Charles A. Drake, "The Place of Personnel Research as a Management Tool," *Personnel*, Vol. 21, No. 1, July 1944, pp. 61-71; A. R. Wiren and C. Heyel, *Practical Management Research* (New York: McGraw-Hill Book Company, 1945); and Dale Yoder, H. G. Heneman, Jr., John G. Turnbull, and C. Harold Stone, *Handbook of Personnel Management and Labor Relations* (New York: McGraw-Hill Book Company, 1958), Chapter 25.

[2] For example, see Brent Baxter, Andrew A. Taaffe, and Joseph F. Hughes, "A Training Evaluation Study," *Personnel Psychology*, Vol. 6, No. 4, 1953, pp. 403-417.

depend less upon the development of attractive gimmicks and more upon the solution of basic problems. The key to this progress lies in management-development research and evaluation.

EVALUATION OF MANAGEMENT DEVELOPMENT

A number of basic questions concerning management development are unanswered today. The increasing research on and study of these questions promise answers which will be helpful in the future improvement of our attempts at management development. In the meantime, however, organizations faced with immediate problems of management development must and will develop tentative approaches to management development and apply them in the solution of these problems. The evaluation of management-development activities is an important and practical application of the research approach to management development. The evaluation and comparison of current practices should contribute to improved activities for management development at the same time that answers are sought to more basic questions.

Many of the needs and opportunities for evaluation in management development are obvious. It may be useful, however, to review the major questions asked concerning management-development activities before considering alternative approaches to evaluation. The first and most general question concerns the worth of management development. Organizations are spending thousands of dollars in attempts to improve the performance of their management teams. We must ask whether this expenditure is justified in terms of the value received. Almost no attempt has been made to measure the absolute worth of management development, despite the obvious relevance of this question. It is true that determination of the value received from management development will be difficult, but we have shown little concern for developing measures of this worth. Instead, we find statements that this value, while actual, cannot be measured, and management-development activities are justified in terms of apparent attractiveness and probable value. Justification on these grounds leads to the acceptance of practices which are obvious in intent and appear reasonable regardless of their actual value. Consequently, we find fads and gimmicks throughout management development. We should attempt to determine the actual worth of these practices through evaluation, to improve the basis for selection of practices and activities for management development. The lack of attempts to measure the over-all value of management development suggests that there will be little to justify the activities and programs for development when the current interest and popularity of management development fade and are replaced by concern for other problems of management.

A somewhat less general and more manageable question concerns the relative effectiveness of alternative approaches to specific problems of management development. Evaluation here compares the results of one approach to management development with results of alternative approaches as an aid in the selection of the most effective approach. A number of alternatives are available for application to any problem of management development, and most of these alternatives are being applied already in one organization or another. Choice among these alternatives is at present based largely upon hunch and reputation rather than upon a critical examination of the results associated with each. Comparison and evaluation of these alternatives are much less difficult than determination of the absolute worth of management development, since we can apply measures of relative value. The evaluation of alternative approaches to problems of management development also has more immediate and practical value than attempts to measure absolute worth. Most of the questions asked about management development concern the relative effectiveness of alternative approaches rather than the absolute worth of management development.

A third area for evaluation concerns the improvement of individual approaches to management development. Evaluation in this sense can be applied to each approach individually, regardless of other activities for management development. Problems and questions for evaluation in this sense tend to be highly specific and, in this respect, can be answered more conclusively than many of the larger questions involved in evaluation. An example of this type of evaluation would be a study to determine those managers most likely to benefit from a specific training program. Benefits obtained by managers participating in the program would be measured and analyzed for relationships with such factors as age, intelligence, job tenure, and level of responsibility in the organization. Factors found predictive of benefits received then could be used in the selection of trainees in the future. Another example would be a study to determine the reactions of managerial candidates to recruiting interviews and their reasons for rejection of recruiting offers. Such evaluations of specific practices can be helpful in the improvement of these practices and in the identification of situations where a practice is of most value. Problems involved in the evaluation of specific practices are much less difficult than the problems involved in the study of more general questions. Although the objectives appear less impressive, the practical contribution of studies concerning limited and specific objectives can be quite significant as a contribution to our knowledge of the value of management-development activities.

Design for Evaluation

Evaluations of management development are intended to provide measures of the benefits and values associated with management-development activities. The simplest approach to evaluation is an informal, after-the-fact search for indications of the benefit of a completed activity. Evidence is sought which logically might have some relationship to the completed activity. This approach, although common, actually should not be termed evaluation. It lacks definiteness and precision, both in the determination of facts and inferences to be sought and in the measurement and interpretation of this evidence. Thus, for example, managers participating in a development program might be polled for their opinions of the value of the program, or the individual responsible for the program might select and cite specific instances of beneficial results known to him. Evidence obtained in this common-sense approach to evaluation is limited to whatever happens to be available and may bear no relationship to the actual value of the program; reasons can be found for excluding critical evidence and selecting only that evidence which is in accord with the bias of the investigator. Furthermore, it is difficult to ascribe these after-the-fact measures solely to the program studied when they may have resulted from other influences operating at the same time. Unfortunately, this informal approach to evaluation of management development is quite common; it probably will continue until those responsible for reviewing management-development activities demand improved evaluations.[3]

The conclusions and inferences which can be drawn from any evaluation depend upon the design of the study. Both the nature and the degree of confidence which can be placed in conclusions are limited by the questions asked in the study, the type of facts and information collected to answer these questions, and the conditions under which this information is collected. An evaluation study is itself judged on the basis of the design and conduct of the study. Effort spent in haphazard and informal evaluation is wasted and, in fact, may be harmful if conclusions and recommendations are based upon the results of this approach. A few well-designed evaluation studies are infinitely more valuable than a host of inconclusive studies.

The evaluation of management development attempts to measure the achievement of objectives of development activities, and it must start with a consideration of objectives. Objectives must be defined and reduced to specific factors which can be measured in evaluation. We can identify various levels of degrees in the definition of objectives of management-development activities, any of which might be relevant for evaluation.[4] The ultimate and most inclusive objectives of management development concern improved performance of the management team. These can be defined more specifically in terms of organization performance measures such as growth of production and sales, costs, rates of return, morale and attitudes of members of the organization, resignations and turnover of personnel, and the availability and adequacy of management replacements. Consideration of changes in these measures in evaluation is relevant only where changes can be attributed to the activity being evaluated, however. For example, they may be relevant in the evaluation of an entire program for management development,

---

[3] For examples of this approach, see Kenneth R. Andrews, "Is Management Training Effective? 1. Evaluation by Managers and Instructors," and "Is Management Training Effective? 2. Measurement, Objectives, and Policy," *Harvard Business Review,* Vol. 35, No. 1, pp. 85-94, and Vol. 35, No. 2, pp. 63-72; Melvin Anshen, "Executive Development: In-Company versus University Programs," *Harvard Business Review,* Vol. 35, No. 5, September-October 1954, pp. 83-91; and Paul C. Buchanan, "Evaluating the Results of Supervisory Training," *Personnel,* Vol. 34, No. 5, March-April 1958, pp. 46-53.

[4] Valuable discussions of this point are found in A. C. MacKinney, "Progressive Levels in the Evaluation of Training Programs," *Personnel,* Vol. 34, No. 3, November-December 1957, pp. 72-77; and Walter R. Mahler, "Evaluation of Management Development Programs," *Personnel,* Vol. 30, No. 2, September 1953, pp. 116-122.

but they rarely are relevant in the evaluation of a single activity. Achievement of these ultimate objectives is determined by a number of factors operating simultaneously, and it becomes almost impossible to identify the change resulting from any single influence. Rather, factors which are more immediately influenced by the activity under evaluation, and which presumably contribute to the achievement of ultimate objectives, are chosen for evaluation. The definition of objectives for evaluation should begin with ultimate objectives, however, as an aid to insuring the relevance of more immediate objectives and measures. Thus, for example, we might begin with the ultimate objective of improved performance of the management team, reduce this to the proper application of principles of work organization by managers in their jobs, and then identify the immediate objective of a training program as the teaching of principles of work organization. Measures of increased knowledge and application of this knowledge would be more relevant in the evaluation of this training program than would uncontrolled measures of organization performance at some future date. The definition of objectives and the selection of factors for evaluation are intimately related. Criterion factors chosen for evaluation become operational definitions of objectives being evaluated; objectives are defined in the evaluation study as improvement in the criterion factors selected. A major weakness of evaluation in terms of immediate objectives lies in the assumed relationship between immediate and ultimate objectives. Relationships which appear logical may not exist in fact. An evaluation of a supervisory training program at International Harvester Company illustrates this problem.[5] The program was found to be effective in changing supervisory attitudes and in teaching concepts and principles of human relations. Follow-up measures of job performance were not related to the change in attitudes or knowledge of human relations concepts, however. Consideration of both immediate and ultimate objectives in management-development evaluation is relevant, in part because we don't know the precise relationship between them, partly because both are meaningful in planning improvements.

---

[5] See Edwin A. Fleishman, Edwin F. Harris, and Harold E. Burtt, *Leadership and Supervision in Industry: An Evaluation of a Supervisor Training Program* (Columbus, Ohio: The Ohio State University, Bureau of Educational Research, 1955), 110 pp.

The management-development audit is distinguished from evaluation since it concerns a specific type of objectives.[6] The objectives evaluated in the audit concern the design and conduct of management-development activities rather than the results of these activities. For example, a management-development audit might consider the organization of responsibility for management development, the training and competence of those in charge, the degree of utilization of available resources, and other standards of operation. The audit serves more as a control over the planning, design, and operation of an activity than as a measure of worth or value. As such, the audit can be quite useful and should not be considered as an alternative to evaluation. Rather, both the audit and the evaluation are important to the success of management-development efforts.

Three basic designs for the collection of evaluative information are found in current practice. The simplest of these, involving the collection of measures after-the-fact, has been mentioned already. Measures obtained in this fashion are of limited value for evaluation regardless of the precision, reliability, or relevance of the measures. Such measures tell us only the degree of goal achievement existing after introduction of management development and cannot indicate the change associated with management development. In the evaluation of management development, we are concerned with change and must have measures obtained prior to the introduction of management-development activities as well as afterward. The second design for evaluation provides for systematic measurement of goal achievement, both before and after the introduction of a particular development activity.[7] Identical methods of measurement obviously must be applied to the same factors before and after the introduction of the activity under eval-

[6] For a suggested audit, see Lester F. Zerfoss, "Progress in Management Development," *The Journal of the American Society of Training Directors,* Vol. 11, No. 6, November-December 1957, pp. 4-17.

[7] For examples of this approach, see R. A. Katzell, "Testing a Training Program in Human Relations," *Personnel Psychology,* Vol. 1, 1948, pp. 319-329; Theodore R. Lindbom, *Supervisory Training and Employee Attitudes* (unpublished Ph.D. dissertation) (Minneapolis, Minnesota: University of Minnesota, 1952); Niles Soik, "Evaluation of a Human Relations Training Program," *The Journal of the American Society of Training Directors,* Vol. 12, No. 3, March 1958, pp. 34-39; Morris S. Viteles, "'Human Relations' and the 'Humanities' in the Education of Business Leaders: Evaluation of a Program of Humanistic Studies for Executives," *Personnel Psychology,* Vol. 12, No. 1, Spring, 1959, pp. 1-28; and "Evaluating a Management-Development Program," *Conference Board Management Record,* Vol. 16, No. 7, July 1954, pp. 264-265.

uation. This means that the design must be formulated prior to initiation of the activity; criteria acceptable as measures of achievement must be developed before the start of the program and in the absence of the biasing influence of impressions gained during the program. This before-after design tends to provide a more objective evaluation. The difficulty with the before-after design lies in the lack of control over influencing factors operating simultaneously with the one being evaluated. For example, before-after measures may indicate a reduction of management turnover associated with the introduction of deferred compensation. It would be hazardous to attribute this achievement to deferred compensation, however, if changes in economic activity, the organization of responsibilities, personalities in the organization, or other factors also occurred. The third basic design for evaluation overcomes this difficulty with the introduction of a control group identical in every respect to an experimental group except for the difference in the factor being evaluated.[8] Thus, deferred compensation might be introduced in one segment of the organization where all other conditions were maintained identical with those in the remainder of the organization. Comparison of the difference between before-after measures in these two groups would then indicate the relative effect of deferred compensation. Of these three basic evaluation designs, the experimental approach is preferred, since it provides for more strict control of non-experimental influences and, thus, more definite conclusions. It should be recognized that the experimental approach contains a built-in biasing influence which should be anticipated and guarded against. This experimental effect arises from the fact that the mere selection and identification of groups of people as experimental and control groups influence their reactions to the experiment. For example, experimental and control groups of managers might be identified in a project to evaluate a particular management-training approach; the experimental group undergoes

[8] For examples, see Brent Baxter, Andrew A. Taaffe, and Joseph F. Hughes, "A Training Evaluation Study," *Personnel Psychology,* Vol. 6, No. 4, 1953, pp. 403-417; R. R. Canter, Jr., "A Human Relations Training Program," *Journal of Applied Psychology,* Vol. 35, No. 1, 1951, pp. 38-45; Edwin Fleishman *et al., op. cit.;* Daniel M. Goodacre, "The Experimental Evaluation of Management Training: Principles and Practice," *Personnel,* Vol. 33, No. 6, May 1957, pp. 534-538; William McGeehee and J. E. Gardner, "Supervisory Training and Attitude Change," *Personnel Psychology,* Winter, 1955, pp. 449-460; and James N. Mosel and Harry J. Tsacnaris, "Evaluating the Supervisor Training Program," *Journal of Personnel Administration and Industrial Relations,* Vol. 1, No. 2, 1954, pp. 99-104.

training and the control group does not. The fact that training opportunities are extended to a select few, that is, the experimental group, may itself influence the reaction of the experimental group to the training and, thus, the results obtained in the training. As a result, training effects obtained in the experimental group may be quite different from what might be expected in an application of the training to all managers. This possible bias can be controlled completely only when there is no knowledge that an experiment is intended and when there is no communication between the experimental and control groups. This control of the experimental approach is difficult but not impossible. The activity to be evaluated might be conducted initially within a single division or department, for example, using other departments as controls. Or, in the case of a training program, all managers might be scheduled for the course and assigned randomly to groups scheduled for training at different times. Evaluation measures might be obtained easily from all managers before and after the training of those scheduled for early participation in the training program. Those scheduled for later training could be considered as a control group without prior identification of experimental and control groups. A number of similar possibilities might be suggested which would limit, if not prevent, the bias resulting from the identification of experimental and control groups. Recognition of the possibility of bias in the interpretation of experimental results also would serve to reduce this particular danger of the experimental approach.

After-the-fact evaluation is the most common approach being applied to the evaluation of management-development activities. The relative popularity of this approach probably is related to both the relative ease of this approach and the failure to recognize a need for evaluation at the time of design and installation of new practices. Both the before-after and the experimental approaches to evaluation require considerable preparation prior to initiation of the activity to be evaluated. The questions for study must be defined, the criteria selected, criterion measures obtained, and provisions made for the control of non-experimental variables before the activity is undertaken. This careful preparation for evaluation is found at present only in organizations where the need for evaluation is recognized and where the limitations and advantages of alternative evaluation approaches are understood. It is encouraging to note that before-after evaluation of training activities is increasing; no corresponding increase in experimental evaluation can be noted, although recognition of the need for experimental approaches appears to be increasing.[9] One practical difficulty in the application of the experimental approach to evaluation lies in a reluctance to establish control groups. Few executives are willing to withhold management-development opportunities from a portion of the management team for control purposes if they are sufficiently convinced of the possible value of these activities to conduct them for an experimental group. They feel that withholding these opportunities might jeopardize the achievement of potential performance by the management team, and they would prefer to make them available to all managers. Furthermore, they would prefer to withhold development opportunities from those least likely to profit from them if the opportunities are not to be made available to all; use of these selected managers as a control group would destroy the value of the experiment. Or, finally, it is argued that withholding opportunities from a control group may jeopardize the careers of these individuals, and that no conceivable experimental results could justify this action. Several control possibilities were noted earlier, however, which merely involve postponement of these training opportunities. The identification of similar control opportunities and the recognition of the importance of conclusive evaluations of management development should facilitate the increased use of the experimental approach. The experimental approach is rather widely recognized and employed in the evaluation of alternative production processes and sources of supply. The need for this experimental approach in the solution of the more critical problems of management development is even greater.

It was stressed early in this book that training activities constitute a single element of management development and that practices in the organization of management responsibilities, recruitment of talent, selection and placement of individual managers, appraisal and coaching of subordinates, and compensation of managers also influence the development of the management team. The greatest advances in the evaluation of alternative practices are being made in the evaluation of training opportunities. Evaluation of practices

[9] See the guide to experimental evaluation, *Evaluation of Training Programs* (Shreveport, Louisiana: American Petroleum Institute, Division of Production, Southern Committee on Supervisory Development, March 1957), 28 pp.

in the remaining areas of management development is equally important.

Criteria of Evaluation

The criteria selected or developed for evaluation are as important as the design of the evaluation study in determining the confidence which can be placed in conclusions. We discussed in Chapter 5 the requirements of criteria for the appraisal of management personnel; the same standards apply in the consideration of criteria for the evaluation of management development. Criteria for the evaluation of management development should provide objective, reliable, and unbiased measures of factors selected as relevant measures of management-development objectives.

The choice of criteria for evaluation of management development can be viewed as two distinct decisions, although it is recognized that these decisions are not distinct and separate in practice. The first of these decisions concerns the determination of factors which are relevant in appraising management development, and it has been discussed already in the definition of objectives for evaluation. Commonly considered criterion factors attempt to measure both immediate and ultimate objectives of management development. Factors relevant in the measurement of immediate gains may include changes in knowledge, attitudes, skills, abilities, and opinions. Factors relevant in the measurement of intermediate gains might include changes in individual performance and changes in the performance and attitudes of subordinates. And factors relevant in assessing ultimate gains might include measures of organization performance such as growth, turnover, rates of costs and returns, and others. Measures of both immediate and ultimate gains may be relevant in any particular evaluation because of ignorance about the relationship between them. Activities which demonstrate immediate gains and little, if any, change in ultimate criteria may require only minor changes to bring about the desired change in ultimate criteria.

The second decision concerns the selection or development of measures of factors selected as relevant for evaluation. This undoubtedly is the more troublesome of the two decisions. Highly relevant factors may be identified for evaluation, but, unless measured adequately, they are of little value in evaluation. Various methods of measurement are discussed under each of the general criterion factors listed below.

Attitudes and opinions. Attitudes and opinions are used widely in the evaluation of management development; they probably are the most common factors included in criteria of management development. Measures of attitudes and opinions are used in a number of different contexts, however, and their value as criteria of management development varies with the context. The most common use of attitudes and opinions is in the measurement of criteria relevant in the evaluation of management-development activities; observers, participants, and others are solicited for their opinions regarding the value of particular courses of development activities or the usefulness of specific aspects of the activity.[10] Used in this context, attitudes and opinions are of little value in evaluation. Only those who have had some connection with the activity are in a position to offer opinions of its value, and these persons can hardly be described as free from bias. Furthermore, when these opinions are sought through interviews, as is common, the interviewer provides another source of bias in his interpretation of comments and opinions. Opinions of observers and participants will be influenced by the criteria they apply in the evaluation of effectiveness, the scope of their observations or experiences, and their personal biases and values. These attitudes and opinions can be used as an indication of the acceptance of management development, but they offer little as measures of other factors of the evaluation.

Measures of attitudes and opinions can provide useful criteria when an objective of management development involves a change of attitudes.[11] Here, however, attitudes are directly relevant as criteria, and not as indirect measures of criteria. The measurement of attitudes through interviews is subject to the same criticisms as above. Techniques of attitude scaling and measurement can be employed here to obtain reliable measures of attitudes and opinions. These techniques can be utilized in the measurement of attitudes

---

[10] See Andrews, *op. cit.;* Anshen, *op. cit.;* Michael G. Blansfield, "Building and Evaluating a University Executive Development Program," *Personnel Administration,* Vol. 21, No. 3, May-June 1958, pp. 35-40; Buchanan, *op. cit.;* and David S. Vogels, Jr., "An Evaluation of a Management Training Course," *The Journal of the American Society of Training Directors,* Vol. 12, No. 1, January 1958, pp. 44-51.

[11] See Lindbom, *op. cit.;* McGeehee and Gardner, *op. cit.;* and "Evaluating a Management Development Program," *op. cit.*

of participants, subordinates, or others as relevant to the evaluation.

Knowledge and skill. Attitudes and opinions unfortunately are solicited too often as measures of knowledge and skill acquired through management development. However, tests of knowledge and skill are being used increasingly for this purpose. Reported evaluations mention the use of tests of knowledge of particular subjects, and tests of skill in making judgments, applying sound reasoning, and using insight. Commercially available psychological tests may be used in the measurement of knowledges and skills, or special tests may be constructed appropriate for the situation. Attempts to construct and interpret tests should be undertaken only by professionals familiar with the principles and techniques of measurement, however. Amateur attempts to build tests as criterion measures are not likely to provide reliable and accurate measuring instruments.[12]

Performance. Techniques for the measurement of performance have already been discussed in some detail.[13] Measures of participant performance and subordinates' performance, as well as measures of organization performance, have been used in evaluations of management development. The measures employed range from unstructured opinions to highly specific performance standards. They also include ratings of performance supplied by individual participants, their subordinates, and their superiors. Probably the most common approach involves the collection of performance ratings or appraisals, where specific aspects of performance are presented for appraisal. An attempt is made in this manner to focus attention upon the specific performance factors most relevant in evaluation. Measures of organization performance would in many instances provide quite objective measures. They are not used commonly, probably because of lack of demonstrated relevance in evaluation of a particular activity. More widespread application of the experimental approach to the evaluation and the control of nonexperimental variables should make possible the use of these organization-performance measures.[14]

---

[12] See Richard P. Barthol and Martin Zeigler, "Evaluation of a Supervisory Training Program," *Journal of Applied Psychology,* Vol. 40, No. 6, 1956, pp. 403-405; Canter, *op. cit.;* Katzell, *op. cit.;* Mosel and Tsacnaris, *op. cit.;* and Soik, *op. cit.*

[13] See Chapter 5.

[14] Examples of performance evaluations include Brent Baxter *et al., op. cit.;* Edwin Fleishman *et al., op. cit.;* and Goodacre, *op. cit.*

SUMMARY

Intense interest and concern for management development have arisen only during the last 10 to 15 years. Organizations concerned with management development have developed and are applying numerous practices and techniques for the improvement of performance of individual managers and the management team. A number of questions concerning management development have been raised in earlier chapters, ranging from "What is the manager's job?" to "How can job performance be predicted?" All of these questions stem from problems encountered in the development of the management team. We also have outlined current practice in the development of managers, research evidence bearing upon the problems of management development, and possible answers and lines of inquiry in the search for solutions to these problems. Organizations faced with immediate problems of management development must and will develop tentative solutions to the problems encountered, and will apply them in the absence of evaluated and proven solutions. Unfortunately, many of these tentative solutions have become accepted through use as final and proven solutions. Individuals responsible for management development often examine the practices of leading companies in the industry or community and select as solutions those practices which appear to fit best the needs and values of their organizations. Then, to assure acceptance and cooperation, these proposed practices may be oversold as final and ultimate solutions to the organization's problems of management development. Such a process tends to perpetuate the spread of fads and gimmicks with an obvious appeal to the uncritical observer. Actually, we know little about the relative effectiveness of alternative solutions to the problems of management development, despite the claims made for certain practices and their popularity among companies attempting management development.[15]

The problems involved in the organization, selection, training, and utilization of management personnel will be with us for some time, although the pressures for improvement may relax. Real progress in the solution of these problems will come only through the study and evaluation of alternative approaches and solutions for these

[15] E. K. Taylor, "Management Development at the Crossroads," *Personnel*, Vol. 36, No. 2, March-April 1959, pp. 8-23.

problems. This research and evaluation should be started now while there is interest in management development. The experimentation and experience with various approaches to management development at the present time should be utilized for the identification and improvement of effective approaches for use in the future. We should begin now to develop and apply criteria other than popularity and usage for the selection of approaches to the solution of problems of management development. Only in this way can we obtain the full value of current experience in management development.

SELECTED BIBLIOGRAPHY

Fleishman, Edwin A., Edwin F. Harris, and Harold E. Burtt, *Leadership and Supervision in Industry: An Evaluation of a Supervisory Training Program* (Columbus, Ohio: The Ohio State University, Bureau of Educational Research, 1955).

Goodacre, Daniel M., "The Experimental Evaluation of Management Training: Principles and Practice," *Personnel,* Vol. 33, No. 6, May 1957, pp. 534-538.

Mahler, Walter R., "Evaluation of Management Development Programs," *Personnel,* Vol. 30, No. 2, September 1953, pp. 116-122.

Taylor, E. K., "Management Development at the Crossroads," *Personnel,* Vol. 36, No. 2, March-April 1959, pp. 8-23.

Index

Index

R